HACK THAT DISH

FANTASTIC FAMOUS FOOD FORGERIES AND SECRET TRICKS YOU CAN USE TO COPY ANY DISH

TODD WILBUR
CREATOR OF
Top Secret Recipes®

Adams Media

New York   Amsterdam/Antwerp   London   Toronto   Sydney/Melbourne   New Delhi

Adams Media
An Imprint of Simon & Schuster, LLC
100 Technology Center Drive
Stoughton, MA 02072

For more than 100 years, Simon & Schuster has championed authors and the stories they create. By respecting the copyright of an author's intellectual property, you enable Simon & Schuster and the author to continue publishing exceptional books for years to come. We thank you for supporting the author's copyright by purchasing an authorized edition of this book.

No amount of this book may be reproduced or stored in any format, nor may it be uploaded to any website, database, language-learning model, or other repository, retrieval, or artificial intelligence system without express permission. All rights reserved. Inquiries may be directed to Simon & Schuster, 1230 Avenue of the Americas, New York, NY 10020 or permissions@simonandschuster.com.

Copyright © 2026 by Todd Wilbur.

All rights reserved, including the right to reproduce this book or portions thereof in any form whatsoever. For information, address Adams Media Subsidiary Rights Department, 1230 Avenue of the Americas, New York, NY 10020.

First Adams Media hardcover edition
April 2026

ADAMS MEDIA and colophon are registered trademarks of Simon & Schuster, LLC.

Simon & Schuster strongly believes in freedom of expression and stands against censorship in all its forms. For more information, visit BooksBelong.com.

For information about special discounts for bulk purchases, please contact Simon & Schuster Special Sales at 1-866-506-1949 or business@simonandschuster.com.

The Simon & Schuster Speakers Bureau can bring authors to your live event. For more information or to book an event, contact the Simon & Schuster Speakers Bureau at 1-866-248-3049 or visit our website at www.simonspeakers.com.

Interior design by Colleen Cunningham
Interior illustrations © 123RF/wawritto, mohsinmajeed7, upiramos
Photographs by Harper Point Photography
Chefs: Kira Friedman, Martine English, Nathan Rega

Manufactured in China

10 9 8 7 6 5 4 3 2 1

Library of Congress Control Number: 2025948016

ISBN 978-1-5072-2550-9
ISBN 978-1-5072-2557-8 (ebook)

Many of the designations used by manufacturers and sellers to distinguish their products are claimed as trademarks. Where those designations appear in this book and Simon & Schuster, LLC, was aware of a trademark claim, the designations have been printed with initial capital letters.

This book is not authorized, approved, licensed, or endorsed by the various restaurants that appear in this book. The recipes in this book were not provided by the included restaurants but are the author's creations based upon his most successful efforts to replicate the various dishes. All rights to the various restaurant and recipe names used in this book, which are either registered or otherwise claimed as trademarks, are fully reserved by the various corporations who own these rights.

Always follow safety and commonsense cooking protocols while using kitchen utensils, operating ovens and stoves, and handling uncooked food. If children are assisting in the preparation of any recipe, they should always be supervised by an adult.

*For curious cooks,
flavor detectives,
gastronomic gumshoes,
and culinary code crackers.*

*And for all the talented chefs who create
the delicious food we spy on.*

Contents

Preface 7
Introduction 9
Recipe Hacking 101 10

Applebee's
Chicken Wonton Tacos 13
Riblets 16
Spinach & Artichoke Dip 18

BJ's Restaurant & Brewhouse
Bacon Jam Wings 20

Bonchon
Chicken Wings 23

Bonefish Grill
Imperial Dip 25

Brach's
Candy Corn 27

California Pizza Kitchen
Butter Cake 29
Carne Asada Pizza 32
Roasted Garlic Chicken Pizza 35

Capital City
Sweet Hot Mambo Sauce 38

Capital Grille
Mushroom and Asparagus Risotto 39

Carl's Jr./Hardee's
Hand-Breaded Chicken & Waffle Sandwich 42

Carrabba's Italian Grill
Cannoli Cake for Two 45
Traditional Cannoli 48

Charms Candy Company
Blow Pops 50

The Cheesecake Factory
Chicken Piccata 53
Shrimp Scampi 56
Spicy Cashew Chicken 58
Steak Diane 60

Chick-fil-A
Banana Pudding Milkshake 62
Spicy Deluxe Chicken Sandwich 65
Spicy Southwest Salad 67
Zesty Apple Cider Vinaigrette Dressing . . 70

Chipotle
Carne Asada 71
Chicken al Pastor 74
Guacamole 76
Smoked Brisket 77
Tomatillo-Red Chili Salsa 80

Church's Texas Chicken
Fried Chicken 83

The Coffee Bean & Tea Leaf
Vanilla Ice Blended Drink 85

Costco (Kirkland)
Almond Poppy Muffins 88

Cracker Barrel
Buttermilk Pie 90
Country Fried Steak 93
Meatloaf 95

Crumbl
Semi-Sweet Chocolate Chunk Cookies ..97

Daelmans
Stroopwafels 100

Del Taco
Tamales............................ 102

Dole Food Company
Dole Whip.......................... 105

Domino's
Chicken Taco Pizza 107
Chocolate Lava Crunch Cake 109
Loaded Tots 112

El Pollo Loco
Shredded Beef Birria 115

Ferrara Candy Company
Butterfinger 118

Five Guys
Cajun Fries........................ 120

Gino's East
Deep Dish Pizza.................... 122

Häagen-Dazs
Vanilla Ice Cream................... 125

IHOP
Classic Eggs Benedict 127
Protein Power Pancakes............. 130
Swedish Crepes 132

Jack Link's
Original Beef Jerky.................. 134

Jason's Deli
Irish Potato Soup.................... 136

Jovy Candy
Fruit Roll 139

Lazy Dog
Bacon Candy 141
Crispy Deviled Eggs 143

Little Caesars
Crazy Puffs........................ 146

Maggiano's Little Italy
Famous Rigatoni "D" 148
Italian Meatballs.................... 151
Mozzarella Marinara 153

Manwich
Original Sloppy Joe Sauce 156

Marie Callender's
Chocolate Satin Pie 158
Fresh Strawberry Pie................ 160

McDonald's
Bacon, Egg & Cheese McGriddles 162
Hotcakes.......................... 166
Strawberry & Crème Pie............. 168

Old El Paso
Taco Seasoning Mix 170

Olive Garden
Chicken Marsala Fettuccine 171
Five Cheese Ziti al Forno............ 174
Lasagna Classico 177

On The Border
Chicken Tortilla Soup 179
Enchiladas 181

The Original Pancake House
49er Flap Jacks 185
Buttermilk Pancakes 187

Outback Steakhouse
Seared Peppered Ahi................ 189
Tasmanian Chili 192
Aussie Twisted Ribs................ 194

P.F. Chang's
Kung Pao Brussels Sprouts 198

Panda Express
Blazing Bourbon Chicken............ 200
Chow Mein 203

Pei Wei
Chicken Pad Thai 204

Pizza Hut
Creamy Italian Dressing............ 206

Popeyes
Ghost Pepper Wings 207

Portillo's
Famous Chocolate Cake............. 209

Qdoba
3-Cheese Queso 212

Red Lobster
Crab Your Way 214
Walt's Favorite Shrimp 217

Shakey's
Mojo Potatoes 218

Smashburger
SmashFries, Smash Tots, and Smash Sauce 220

Southern Comfort
Traditional Egg Nog 223

Starbucks
Almond Croissants 224
Dark Toffee Bundt.................. 228
Pink Drink........................ 230

Subway
Raspberry Cheesecake Cookies 232

Taco Bell
Avocado Verde Salsa................ 234
Cantina Chicken.................... 235
Cinnamon Twists 236
Meximelts 237

Tootsie Roll Industries
Sugar Daddy Pops 240

Totino's
Pizza Rolls 242

Walker's
Shortbread 246

Wonderful
Chili Roasted Pistachios............ 248

Standard US/Metric Measurement Conversions....................... 250

Index............................ 251

Preface

Before pitching a new reality TV show based on my cookbooks for the History channel in 2010, I met with the executive producer at a popular new Los Angeles hamburger chain. The chain, which expanded to twenty-five units in 2017, then mysteriously went out of business, crafted awesome burgers with a secret blend of various cuts of beef, hand ground daily and formed into thick patties. Arriving at Umami Burger early that day, I had a partial view of the kitchen and noticed a worker slicing and grinding steaks, then pressing the ground beef into a burger patty mold. I wondered which cuts he was using to make the "secret" beef blend, so I took out my phone and started recording. I figured that if a butcher could examine the video and identify the cuts of beef the cook was working with, I would have some solid intel on Umami Burger's secret recipe. I captured a few good clips before the cook noticed what I was doing. He shot me the stink eye and moved to block my view of the meat, and that was the end of that.

I had no plans to hack Umami Burger, but the undercover beef-grinding spy video I shot would still be incredibly helpful. At the History pitch meeting, I played the video for the execs as an example of what you might see me do on the show to duplicate a famous brand-name recipe. Apparently, they liked the presentation, because shortly after that meeting I got the green light for a pilot and eventually an eight-episode series called *Top Secret Recipe* that debuted on CMT. It was the first cooking show on CMT and the only food show anywhere that relied heavily on sneaking, spying, disguises, hidden cameras, petty thefts, and dumpster diving.

My mission on *Top Secret Recipe* was to reverse-engineer a famous iconic food, such as KFC chicken, Domino's pizza, or Chili's baby back ribs, in a food truck kitchen in 3 days. I was allowed access to some corporate test kitchens, and I could interview company chefs and sometimes even watch them make the food. I swiped ingredients for analysis, I dug through trash cans, I feigned allergies, I dressed up like a pizza delivery guy—I did whatever sleuthing I could to access the intel I needed to make a great clone of a famous food before my time ran out.

I used clues discovered throughout the show to re-create the famous recipes in my mobile food lab. Then, at the conclusion, I presented my final version to a panel of judges for a blind taste test. Did they know which food was the fake? Whether or not I fooled the judges didn't really matter, because the coolest part was all the stuff in the middle—the culinary spycraft—that made these copycat recipes possible. I revealed a handful of my food hacking tricks on the show, but other than that, I've kept my methods a secret. Until now.

In *Hack That Dish*, I share 101 of my best copycat recipes and reveal insider food hacking techniques that I've never divulged before. The food sleuthing secrets you'll find in this book are the methods I've been using in the field and kitchen for decades as a clandestine one-man culinary cover band, cracking the codes to over 1,500 famous recipes.

Whether you've cloned recipes before or have always wanted to try, you'll find tactics here to help you break down the essential details of a recipe and duplicate its taste and appearance in your home kitchen. And I promise you won't be required to wear disguises or steal ingredients like I did on my TV show. If there's a recipe you want cloned that I haven't hacked yet, you can now use the practical techniques in this book to hack it yourself!

As long as we hunger for new flavor experiences—and we always will—food companies, big and small, will create exciting new products and dishes to capture our taste buds and dollars. And I will be here, with a magnifying glass in one hand and a spatula in the other, ready to share delicious copycat versions of those fabulous, famous foods—and the secrets behind making them.

So, are you hungry yet? Let's get hacking!

—Todd Wilbur, Food Spy

Introduction

Copycat recipes are a culinary phenomenon. From Cracker Barrel Country Fried Steak to Panda Express Chow Mein, there's a special thrill to be found in snooping into the mysterious formulas behind iconic dishes and sharing them with friends and family (or keeping them to yourself!). It's uniquely rewarding to cook something you're not supposed to know how to make, and to re-create your most beloved edible memories.

Hack That Dish is packed with 101 freshly hacked, well-tested copycat recipes that will guide you through duplicating many of America's most popular brand-name eats. From appetizers to entrées, snacks to desserts, and all the tasty bites and sips in between, this book contains easy-to-make versions of famous foods from over sixty brands. You'll have a blast fooling your guests with mouthwatering replicas of many familiar favorites, including:

- Olive Garden Lasagna Classico
- Cheesecake Factory Steak Diane
- Crumbl Semi-Sweet Chocolate Chunk Cookies
- Chick-fil-A Spicy Deluxe Chicken Sandwich
- Häagen-Dazs Vanilla Ice Cream
- Little Caesar's Crazy Puffs
- And many more!

Food hacking isn't just a culinary skill—it's an occasionally absurd adventure filled with trial, error, and moments of triumph that make you feel like a cross between Sherlock Holmes and Julia Child. One day, you're a spy peering into an open kitchen; the next day, you're a lab tech dissecting layers of lasagna or analyzing grill marks. And the day after that, you're a chemist testing the effects of different leaveners in a chocolate chip cookie.

No single approach to reverse-engineering a recipe works for every food. But there are a few general rules and guidelines that may help clarify the process for the food hacking adventures that lie ahead. Turn the page to dig in.

Recipe Hacking 101

This book is filled with hacked copycat recipes for you to cook right away. But if you'd like to crack other secret formulas you will need a good collection of tips and tricks to help you decode the recipes you love most.

Step 1: Research (Away from Home)

To hack a restaurant dish, the first step is to visit the restaurant and order the food. Take photos of the dish to document how it's plated, and then start tasting and examining it. This research phase is when you'll want to ask the server questions about specific ingredients and preparation techniques. This is also when you'll be observing any visual clues that could help later. Small clues most people don't notice can reveal key details you can use to make your recipes great. For example, when I was at Five Guys gathering clues for my hack of the Cajun Fries, I observed that the bags of potatoes stacked around the restaurant had dates printed on them. With that information, I learned that the chain stores its potatoes for a period of time before using them because older potatoes produce crispier French fries.

You might also be able to observe an entire cooking process in restaurants that have a visible kitchen. When I was at Panda Express on a mission to hack the chain's famous chow mein, I noticed they were almost out of the dish, so I ordered two large boxes to go. This prompted them to immediately prepare a fresh batch while I watched the process. I walked away with lots of fresh chow mein that day, along with solid intel on the preparation—which helped me make a killer clone.

Be sure to grab a sample of the food to take home for later analysis and taste tests, and consider ordering an additional serving in a semi-deconstructed state, with the sauces and garnishes packaged separately.

Step 2: Research (at Home)

Before planning your first recipe batch, closely examine the sample you brought home, deconstructing and dissecting it. When workers at Smashburger refused to give me any information about the herbs used on the chain's SmashFries, I made my phone into a powerful magnifying glass by photographing the herbs on the fries and then zooming in on the image to identify which herbs were in the blend, and my copycat version turned out great.

Find similar recipes online or in cookbooks to determine which ingredients and techniques you might need to use for your hack, and look for additional clues about the food you're hacking by exploring the history of the company, the product, or its creator, and by examining publicity materials, including press releases, TV ads, and social media posts. When I duplicated the Mrs. Fields cookie recipe for my first book, *Top Secret Recipes*, I found it helpful to learn more about Debbi Fields. I discovered, from her published interviews, that Mrs. Fields was a young housewife who first baked chocolate chip cookies for her husband's business meetings. I started my hack with a popular chocolate chip cookie formula, as I assumed she did, and baked variations until one version matched hers.

And for my hack of Café du Monde beignets on my *Food Hacker* blog, I discovered that evaporated milk hadn't been invented when the 150-year-old recipe was created. So, unlike other copycat recipes for the beignets, which require evaporated milk, mine calls for whole milk, and the results are a close match.

Step 3: Write a List of Ingredients

After sufficient research, you'll be ready to write a first-batch recipe. Start by listing the ingredients you think you'll use in a column on the left side of a notebook page. Then add your best guess measurement for each ingredient to the right of it. For each new batch you make, create a new column to record your adjusted measurements. The goal is to finalize the recipe before you reach the edge of the paper and run out of room.

Step 4: Make a Batch

While making your first batch, note all crucial preparation details, including measurements, durations, cooking times, temperatures, and how long to mix or knead the ingredients. Be sure to take detailed notes about everything you do—before you get distracted and forget. Too many notes are never a problem, but too few can be.

Step 5: Do Taste Tests

With each new batch, compare the taste and appearance to the original food to determine what changes to implement in your next batch. Try not to make too many measurement adjustments at once—just make incremental changes to a few primary ingredients until they seem right, and then refine the details until your recipe matches the original.

When you believe the recipe is complete, you may even seek second and third opinions to see if there's anything you missed.

Step 6: Finalize It

Is a recipe ever truly done? It can be hard to resist tweaking old recipes as you learn new tricks. Recipes can be micro-adjusted ad infinitum, but you must eventually declare a recipe finished. Once a copycat version of a food provides the same joyful eating experience as the brand-name original, call it complete and move on. New food puzzles are waiting to be solved, and the next mission awaits.

Digging In

The food hacking secrets included in this book serve as a helpful guide, but you don't need to be a copycat recipe chef to enjoy these dishes. In the 101 recipes that follow I've done all the hacking for you.

To be sure things go smoothly as you work through the recipes, here are a few quick tips that can help improve your final product:

- **Read through the entire recipe before starting to avoid any surprises.** You'll want to know if there's a long wait time for a step, such as brining chicken or cold-proofing some dough. You'll also want to check if you need a specific tool, like an ice cream maker or a cake pop mold.
- **When selecting ingredients, choose the best.** The recipes in this book were made with the bestselling, most popular brands, and I suggest you do the same. Using uncommon discount brands just because they are cheaper might lead to undesirable results.
- **Measure ingredients by weight if specified in the recipe.** Weight is a more accurate way to measure some ingredients than using measuring cups, especially when baking. A kitchen scale will help you get consistent results. If you don't already have one, an inexpensive scale is easy to come by online or in most kitchen supply stores.
- **Measure everything very carefully.** When measuring with spoons or cups, always scrape the top with the flat edge of a knife or the handle of another measuring cup so that the ingredients are level with the top edge of the scoop. Or keep clean popsicle sticks in your sugar and flour canisters so you always have a good way to level the ingredients. Scoop, then scrape. And don't compress the ingredients unless specified, as with *packed* brown sugar.
- **Don't increase the yield unless the recipe indicates this can be done.** Unless stated otherwise, many recipes shouldn't be increased to boost yield, since changing the volume could negatively affect your results. If you need to make twice as much, you're better off making the recipe twice.
- **Follow recipes to the letter for the closest clone.** Altering formulas to make recipes uniquely yours is what cooking is all about. However, if you're looking for results that match the original dish, follow these recipes exactly as they are written.
- **Take note of the difficulty level.** I've given each recipe in this book a rating of easy, medium, or hard. Based primarily on how long it will take to make each dish, this rating can help you decide if you only have the time for a quick clone of Chipotle Guacamole, or if you want to take on a bigger challenge, like duping Starbucks Almond Croissants.

Whether you're trying out some of the recipes in this book or crafting your own copycat masterpieces, food hacking is all about having fun in the kitchen and producing great grub. Now that you know many of my secrets for hacking popular dishes, it's time to get cooking! In the pages ahead, 101 original copycat recipes are waiting for you—each one fully decoded so you can skip the spy work and head straight to the kitchen.

Chicken Wonton Tacos

 PREP TIME:
Active: 50 minutes
Inactive: 1 hour

 DIFFICULTY:
Medium

 **SERVES:**
4 as an appetizer
(8 tacos)

The first Applebee's opened in 1980 in Decatur, Georgia, with a drugstore theme, and was called T.J. Applebee's Rx for Edibles & Elixirs. In 1986, the name was shortened to Applebee's Neighborhood Grill + Bar to emphasize a shift toward a more community-focused atmosphere. After the name change, the company grew rapidly, and by 1998 Applebee's had become the first casual chain in America to reach 1,000 units.

The name change isn't the only reason Applebee's became so successful. The restaurant also serves tasty food that middle America wants to eat, including the popular Chicken Wonton Taco. Copying these delicious tacos at home requires cloning four parts, none of which is difficult: grilled chicken, coleslaw, secret dumpling sauce, and the crispy wonton shell that holds all of it.

Crispy wonton taco shells are not usually found in stores, but making your own is easy with wonton wrappers and a skillet of hot oil. It takes less than a minute to fry each wonton taco shell, and take it from me: You'll get better at it as you go. Just be sure to leave plenty of room in the shells for all the delicious fillings.

 Seek shortcuts whenever possible to simplify your build. A coleslaw kit (found in the produce section of most grocery stores) has the perfect blend of pre-shredded cabbage and carrots, which saves lots of prep time. Simply measure out 4 cups of the kit and mix it with the minced cilantro and dressing in this recipe.

FOR COLESLAW:

3 tablespoons mayonnaise
1 tablespoon granulated sugar
1 teaspoon rice vinegar
½ teaspoon lemon juice
1/16 teaspoon salt
4 cups thinly sliced green cabbage
¼ cup shredded carrot
1 tablespoon minced fresh cilantro

FOR DUMPLING SAUCE:

1 teaspoon cornstarch
2 tablespoons water
2 tablespoons soy sauce
1 tablespoon plus 1 teaspoon rice vinegar
¼ cup granulated sugar
¼ teaspoon sesame oil
¼ teaspoon crushed red pepper

FOR CRISPY WONTON SHELLS:

8 (3"–4") wonton wrappers
Oil, for frying

FOR CHICKEN:

2 skinless chicken thigh fillets
2 teaspoons vegetable oil
½ teaspoon paprika
¼ teaspoon salt
¼ cup sweet chili sauce

FOR GARNISH:

1 teaspoon minced fresh cilantro
8 lime wedges

RECIPE STEPS:

1. To make coleslaw: Whisk together mayonnaise, sugar, vinegar, lemon juice, and salt in a large bowl until sugar has mostly dissolved. Add cabbage, carrot, and cilantro; toss well, then cover and chill for at least 1 hour. Allowing it to chill for several hours or overnight is even better.

2. To make dumpling sauce: Stir cornstarch into water in a small saucepan. Add remaining ingredients, and place over medium heat. When sauce starts to bubble, lower heat and let it simmer for 1 minute before turning off heat and covering until needed.

3. Prepare crispy wonton shells by heating 1" of oil in a skillet over medium heat. Once oil is hot, add a wonton wrapper and let it cook until it blisters, which should take only 1–2 seconds.

4. Flip wrapper and cook for another 1–2 seconds. Then use tongs to grab a corner of wrapper and bend it diagonally in half, holding it in that position for 5–10 seconds until side in oil turns golden brown. It can be helpful to use another pair of tongs or another utensil to keep wonton wrapper steady with one hand while you fold it with the other. Flip wrapper to cook other side for an additional 5–10 seconds until it is golden brown, while continuing to hold wonton open with tongs so that there is about 1" of space between sides of shell for filling.

5. To make chicken: Preheat grill to high. Rub chicken thighs with oil and cook for 4–6 minutes per side until they reach an internal temperature of 165°F. Let chicken cool 5 minutes, then dice.

6. When you're ready to build tacos, heat 2 teaspoons of oil in a medium skillet over medium heat. Add diced chicken to pan and season it with paprika and salt. Cook for 1 minute to heat chicken thoroughly, then add sweet chili sauce to pan. Cook for 30 seconds while stirring to coat chicken with sauce, then turn off heat.

7. Spoon diced chicken into wonton shells and top with coleslaw. Drizzle each taco with dumpling sauce, sprinkle minced cilantro over plate, and serve with lime wedges on side.

FIELD NOTES

Holding tacos up while you fill them can be a challenge, especially if you don't have a taco holder. You can make your own taco holder by turning a muffin pan upside down and placing the tacos between the raised muffin cups.

Chicken Wonton Tacos

Riblets

 PREP TIME:
Active: 20 minutes
Inactive: 4 hours

 DIFFICULTY:
Easy

 SERVES:
2

To begin cloning this popular dish from the national chain, I needed an answer to a big question: "What are Riblets?" I soon discovered that "Riblets" is Applebee's branded name for button ribs or rib tips, which are a flat cut trimmed from the back end of pork spareribs.

This particular cut is packed with lots of connective tissue, and that's a good thing because it breaks down after 3–4 hours of braising, producing fork-tender meat that slips off the bone. Of the cooking methods I tried, including steaming, slow-roasting, and smoking, braising resulted in the most tender and flavorful ribs—even before adding the sauce.

For the braising liquid formula, I discovered that chicken broth infused with liquid smoke produces tender ribs that taste like they came out of a smoker. (Liquid smoke is created by condensing the liquid particles in smoke from real burning wood. It's a great secret ingredient for adding smoky flavor to foods when you don't have a smoker.) Finish off the braised ribs on your grill and baste them with this hack for Applebee's honey barbecue sauce or your favorite bottled sauce. Your Riblets, your choice.

 Keep digging until you find the information you need; it's out there somewhere. Riblets are not a standard cut of pork, so I had to identify this unusual cut. Rummaging through online photos, I eventually determined, through visual comparison, that this cut was trimmed from the back end of spareribs. I learned they're called button ribs or rib tips, and I found them at Walmart.

FOR BRAISED RIB TIPS:

2 cups chicken broth
3 tablespoons hickory liquid smoke
2 teaspoons kosher salt
½ teaspoon ground black pepper
2–3 pounds rib tips

FOR HONEY BARBECUE SAUCE:

⅔ cup (1 6-ounce can) tomato paste
1 cup water
⅓ cup molasses
⅓ cup dark brown sugar, packed
3 tablespoons honey
1 tablespoon hickory liquid smoke
1 teaspoon celery salt
¾ teaspoon salt
¼ teaspoon ground black pepper
¼ teaspoon onion powder
¼ teaspoon garlic powder
⅓ cup white wine vinegar

RECIPE STEPS:

1. Preheat your oven to 225°F.

2. Combine broth, liquid smoke, salt, and pepper in a 9" × 13" baking pan. Place rib tips in pan with fattiest side facing up, ensuring they are submerged as much as possible in liquid. Cover pan with foil and bake for 2 hours. Flip rib tips, re-cover, and continue to cook for another 1½–2 hours until meat is tender and has pulled back about ½" from edges of bones. Once rib tips are tender, remove them from oven and keep them covered for 30 minutes while preheating grill to high.

3. While rib tips are cooking, make sauce by combining all ingredients except white wine vinegar in a small saucepan over medium-low heat. When sauce begins to bubble, continue to simmer until sauce thickens, about 20 minutes. Add vinegar and bring sauce up to a simmer again, still over medium-low heat. Simmer for 5 minutes; cool, uncovered, for 10 minutes; then add a cover and let cool until needed.

4. Grill rib tips on first side for 2–4 minutes until grill marks appear. Then flip each one and baste with barbecue sauce. After another 2–4 minutes, once grill marks form on other side, flip rib tips, baste that side with sauce, and arrange them neatly on a serving plate.

FIELD NOTES

Braising is excellent for tenderizing tough cuts of meat that contain a lot of fat and connective tissue. The process can take anywhere from 2–4 hours—occasionally longer, depending on the cut. However, when the meat is fall-apart tender, remove it from the pot immediately. Overcooking can actually dry out the meat, which might seem strange considering it is submerged in liquid, but it happens!

Spinach & Artichoke Dip

 PREP TIME:
Active: 15 minutes
Inactive: 20 minutes

 DIFFICULTY:
Easy

 SERVES:
4–6

When I saw the results of a *Mashed* online poll indicating that most people chose the chain's Spinach & Artichoke Dip as their favorite appetizer from the Applebee's menu, I suddenly realized I hadn't yet cracked the recipe and immediately got to work.

After just one taste of this dip, it was clear why the dish is so popular. Most spinach dips are made with just two cheeses, but this version is made with a delicious blend of several Italian cheeses. Thankfully, many grocery stores sell blends of shredded Italian cheese that work great for this clone.

And there's no need to defrost the frozen spinach ahead of time—that will be taken care of when it steams in your microwave. Serve the hot dip with tortilla chips and salsa on the side.

The menu said the dip contained a blend of Italian cheeses, but it was impossible to determine precisely which cheeses. Fortunately, the pre-shredded blend of Italian cheese sold in many grocery stores is very close to my sample. When I added Asiago to the mix, the flavor was complete, and this solution saved me from having to buy and shred several separate blocks of cheese. Commonly used ingredient blends, like Italian seasoning, pumpkin pie spice, salad kits, and shredded cheese blends, might be worth considering to save time and money when creating your clone recipe.

FOR DIP:

1 (10-ounce) box frozen chopped spinach
1 (8-ounce) package cream cheese
⅓ cup heavy cream
½ cup shredded Italian cheese blend (mozzarella, Parmesan, provolone, etc.)
¼ cup shredded Asiago cheese
¼ cup grated Parmesan cheese
1 (14-ounce) can quartered artichoke hearts in brine
1 teaspoon minced garlic
½ teaspoon salt

FOR TOPPING:

2 tablespoons grated Parmesan cheese

RECIPE STEPS:

1. Place frozen spinach in a microwave-safe bowl and cover it with plastic wrap. Poke a few holes in top of plastic to vent. Microwave on high for 4 minutes, stir, then microwave again on high for 2 more minutes. Keep bowl covered and set it aside.

2. Combine cream cheese, cream, and other cheese in a medium saucepan over medium-low heat. Whisk or stir mixture as it heats until cheese is melted and sauce is smooth, about 5 minutes.

3. While cheese melts, drain artichoke hearts and trim off leafy parts. You want mostly tender hearts for this recipe, and you'll get about 4 ounces of trimmed hearts from one can. Add artichoke hearts, spinach, garlic, and salt to pan. Lower heat to medium-low and let it simmer for 10 minutes until spinach becomes tender and dip thickens. It will continue to thicken as it cools, so turn off heat when dip is still slightly loose.

4. Preheat broiler to high.

5. Spoon dip into an oven-safe dish and sprinkle Parmesan cheese on top. Place dish in a baking pan and broil for 1–2 minutes until Parmesan cheese turns light brown. Serve hot.

FIELD NOTES

This dip freezes great, so you can easily whip up a quick snack for unexpected visitors. To reheat, slowly defrost the frozen dip in your microwave oven or place it in a covered saucepan over the lowest heat and stir often until hot.

BJ'S RESTAURANT & BREWHOUSE

Bacon Jam Wings

 PREP TIME:
Active: 40 minutes
Inactive: 3 hours

DIFFICULTY:
Medium

 SERVES:
4 as an appetizer

The sweet bacon and onion sauce often used to dress up steaks and burgers becomes a fantastic wing topper in this appetizer. I've unlocked the secret bacon jam recipe here, along with a special two-step cooking process to make perfect wings with great flavor.

This copycat version bakes the brined wings with moist heat to simulate the CVap commercial moist ovens BJ's uses to cook ribs and wings. When you're ready to serve the dish, just fry the wings until crispy, toss with bacon jam, and serve with celery and ranch dressing on the side. You should have plenty of bacon jam left over for more wings or to use as a burger spread.

 **TOP SECRET HACK**

Learning what equipment is used in a restaurant's kitchen can provide clues to how the food is prepared. By talking to the server, I found out the kitchen at BJ's uses a CVap commercial moist oven to prepare the wings. By researching the functions of this equipment, I learned that the wings are cooked with moist heat, so I created a technique that simulates the restaurant's process at home. (And while investigating a different hack recipe, I discovered Chili's uses a similar multifunction cooking/smoking appliance from Convotherm in their kitchen to prepare the chain's famous baby back ribs.)

FOR WINGS:

5 cups water
1/3 cup kosher salt
12 chicken wings, drumettes and flats

FOR BACON JAM:

12 ounces uncooked bacon, coarsely chopped
2 cups peeled and diced yellow onion
1 1/3 cups water
1 1/2 teaspoons cornstarch
1/2 cup dark brown sugar, packed
1/2 cup K.C. Masterpiece Barbecue Sauce (or similar peppery BBQ sauce)
2 tablespoons apple cider vinegar
1/4 teaspoon salt
1/4 teaspoon ground cayenne pepper

FOR RUB:

1 tablespoon granulated sugar
2 1/2 teaspoons salt
1 1/2 teaspoons garlic powder
1 1/2 teaspoons coarse ground black pepper
1 teaspoon paprika
1/2 teaspoon onion powder
1/8 teaspoon ground cayenne pepper
1/8 teaspoon citric acid
1 1/2 cups water
Vegetable oil, for frying

FOR GARNISH:

1 teaspoon minced fresh parsley

RECIPE STEPS:

1. To make wings: Combine water and salt in a large bowl or storage container. Add wings and refrigerate for 2 hours, then rinse brine off wings with cold water.

2. To make bacon jam: While wings are brining, add chopped uncooked bacon to a large saucepan over medium heat. Cook until bacon becomes crispy, 15–20 minutes, then strain bacon from fat. Reserve 2 tablespoons of fat.

3. Pour reserved bacon fat back into saucepan over medium heat. Add onion and cook for 6–8 minutes, stirring often, until onion is soft but not browned.

4. Dice bacon into smaller pieces (about the size of onion), then add it to pan.

5. Combine water and cornstarch, then add to pan along with remaining ingredients. Once mixture begins to simmer, cook it for 20 minutes or until it thickens and becomes slightly darker. Cover.

6. Preheat oven to 375°F.

7. To make rub: Combine rub ingredients in a small bowl, then generously sprinkle over wings. Arrange wings on a rack placed in a 9" × 13" baking pan. Add water to bottom of pan, then cover and bake for 30 minutes. Let wings cool, covered, for 10 minutes, then refrigerate them for later or complete frying step.

8. Preheat at least 3" of oil in a large saucepan, Dutch oven, or deep fryer to 350°F. Fry wings in batches for 4–5 minutes until crispy. Then transfer them to a rack or a plate lined with paper towels for a minute to drain off some of oil.

9. Toss wings with bacon jam in a large bowl until well coated. Sprinkle with minced parsley just before serving.

FIELD NOTES

If you've never made a dish before—like bacon jam in this case—examine a variety of recipes and try the one that seems closest to your target. Taste the results side by side with your restaurant sample and decide what needs adjusting. For this hack, I customized an existing bacon jam recipe by adding a popular off-the-shelf barbecue sauce, and it was a great match for the BJ's version.

Chicken Wings

Chicken Wings

 PREP TIME:
Active: 45 minutes
Inactive: None

 DIFFICULTY:
Medium

 SERVES:
2

Korean chicken is famous for its extra-crispy coating, and Bonchon's chicken—especially the wings—is a favorite around the world. The chain's famous formula is why there are now over 473 Bonchon outlets in multiple countries, including over 150 in the US, with plans to open more in the US in the near future.

The biggest challenge when creating this Bonchon Chicken Wings copycat recipe was finding the perfect magical mixture for batter that fries to a golden brown with a light crispiness that stays crunchy long after the wings have been brushed with the flavorful glaze. The wings are par-fried, rested, and then fried again until done, but figuring out just how long to give each stage was also tough to determine—every recipe I found for Korean chicken used different times and temps. Some recipes even changed the temperature between frying steps, but that extra step made the recipe much too tricky to manage when frying multiple batches.

I eventually settled on 350°F, with most of the frying done up front in the par-fry stage. A three-ingredient batter is all that's needed for crispy golden-brown wings, and the soy garlic sauce is an easy hack using your microwave oven. If you like your wings spicy, it's very easy to kick them up by adding 1 tablespoon plus 2 teaspoons Korean red chili paste (gochujang) and 2 teaspoons fine Korean red pepper powder (gochugaru) to the soy garlic recipe.

 Want your fried food extra crispy? Fry it twice. That's the secret to crispy Korean fried chicken. It's also the best way to get crispy French fries. McDonald's fries their potatoes twice, and In-N-Out Burger fries theirs once. If you're familiar with each of those, there's no doubt you've noticed the difference in crispiness between the chains' French fries, and now you know why.

FOR PREHEATING:

Vegetable oil, for frying

FOR SOY GARLIC SAUCE:

1 cup dark brown sugar, packed
2 tablespoons soy sauce
2 tablespoons mirin
2 tablespoons water
1 teaspoon rice vinegar
½ teaspoon garlic powder

FOR WINGS:

1 cup (5 ounces) all-purpose flour, plus 1 more cup for breading
¼ teaspoon plus ⅛ teaspoon baking soda
1⅓ cups water
20 chicken wings (drumettes and flats)

RECIPE STEPS:

1. Preheat 2"–3" of oil (enough to cover wings) in a deep fryer, Dutch oven, or large saucepan to 350°F.

2. To make soy garlic sauce: Combine all ingredients in a medium microwave-safe bowl and cook on high for 1 minute. Stir to dissolve sugar. Cover sauce and set it aside.

3. To make wings: Whisk together 5 ounces of flour and baking soda in a medium bowl, then whisk in water. Measure an additional 1 cup of flour into another medium bowl.

4. Drop several wings into flour, and coat them well with it. Let wings sit in flour for a couple of minutes, then dip each one into wet batter and allow excess batter to drip off. Carefully lower each wing into oil, and cook them in batches for 8 minutes until breading is golden brown. Remove wings from oil and let them sit out for 4 minutes.

5. Fry them a second time for 5–6 minutes until browned. Remove wings from oil and let them sit for 2 minutes, then brush them on both sides with sauce. If you'd like to serve more than a few wings at a time, fry them all and hold unsauced wings in a 250°F oven until they are all fried, then brush them all with sauce just before serving.

FIELD NOTES

Fried chicken wasn't popular in Korea until American soldiers brought it there during the Korean War. Korean chefs put an extra-crunchy spin on the dish, and today Korean-style fried chicken is recognized and enjoyed worldwide.

BONEFISH GRILL

Imperial Dip

 PREP TIME:
Active: 35 minutes
Inactive: None

 DIFFICULTY:
Medium

 SERVES:
4–6

It's creamy and cheesy and doesn't skimp on shrimp and scallops. Bonefish Grill's Imperial Dip might be the best seafood dip at any chain, and after several visits in the early evening to take advantage of the happy hour price, I got even happier when I could construct this delicious clone.

The secret to the dip's great taste is shrimp stock. And that's why this hack starts with an easy way to make your own stock with shells harvested from the shrimp. After sautéing the shelled shrimp and scallops, you'll prepare a sauce with the shrimp stock, cream, and cheese in just minutes. Then you'll combine everything and brown the top in a skillet for a great match to the real thing—except this version will be three times bigger. Serve alongside a big helping of tortilla chips for dipping.

 To extract the most information about a dish, you'll do much better if you're friendly with your server. But don't dive in right away with questions about the food. Start by establishing a rapport with general small talk, and always mention that you're a big fan of the food. Only then should you start with the questions. It's worth mentioning that you'll get more opportunities to interview a server if you sit at the bar. Bartenders usually know as much about the food as they do about mixing the drinks. Grab a seat at the bar when the restaurant opens for lunch, and you'll likely get a good amount of time to chat before the rush begins. Try to find a chair closest to where the server makes the drinks, since that's where they'll hang out most of the time. And don't forget a generous tip before you leave.

- 8 ounces medium or large or shrimp with shells
- 1 tablespoon plus 2 teaspoons vegetable oil, divided
- 1¼ cups water
- ¼ teaspoon plus ⅛ teaspoon salt
- 5 ounces sea scallops
- 2 tablespoons unsalted butter, divided
- 2 teaspoons minced garlic
- 1 tablespoon all-purpose flour
- ½ cup heavy cream
- 4 ounces shredded mozzarella
- 2 ounces cream cheese, softened
- ⅓ cup plus 1 tablespoon grated Parmesan cheese, divided
- ½ teaspoon Worcestershire sauce
- ⅛ teaspoon ground cayenne pepper
- ⅛ teaspoon crushed red pepper
- ½ teaspoon minced fresh parsley

RECIPE STEPS:

1. Remove shells from shrimp and rinse them under cold water. Heat 2 teaspoons of oil in a small sauté pan over medium heat and add shrimp shells. Cook for 3–5 minutes, tossing occasionally, until shells begin to brown.

2. Add water to pan with shells and continue to cook while stirring occasionally for 6–8 minutes until liquid has reduced to $1/2$ cup.

3. Pour shells and liquid into a strainer to extract stock, then toss out shells. Add salt to stock and set it aside.

4. Dice scallops and slice each shrimp into three or four pieces.

5. Heat remaining tablespoon of oil and 1 tablespoon of butter in a medium sauté pan over medium heat, then add shrimp and scallops. Cook for 3–4 minutes, tossing occasionally, until shrimp turns pink. Add garlic and continue cooking for an additional 1–2 minutes until shrimp and scallops start to brown, then remove seafood from heat.

6. Make a roux by melting remaining tablespoon of butter over medium-low heat in a medium saucepan. Stir in flour and cook for 3 minutes, then stir in shrimp stock.

7. Add cream, mozzarella, cream cheese, and $1/3$ cup Parmesan, and cook for 4–5 minutes until cheese is melted and no longer stringy, and sauce is smooth.

8. Add cooked seafood to cheese mixture with Worcestershire sauce, cayenne pepper, and crushed red pepper, and continue heating for 3 more minutes, stirring occasionally.

9. Heat oven to high broil.

10. Pour dip into a heavy 8" or 9" pan, such as cast iron. Sprinkle remaining tablespoon of Parmesan cheese over top of dip. Broil dip for 1–2 minutes until lightly browned on top.

11. As soon as dip comes out of oven, sprinkle parsley over top and serve.

FIELD NOTES

A cast iron skillet holds heat better than other pans, lasts forever, and is affordable. Also, cooking with cast iron increases your intake of iron, an essential nutrient for all the cells in your body.

Candy Corn

 PREP TIME:
Active: 45 minutes
Inactive: 20 minutes

 DIFFICULTY:
Medium

 MAKES:
128–144 candies

It's America's #1 candy corn brand and the winner in many taste tests. But what is it that you're tasting when you munch on this iconic Halloween candy? You're on the right track if you're thinking about popcorn when you eat it: There is a dominant butter flavor and plenty of salt. But there are also notes of vanilla, honey, and the subtle nuttiness of sesame oil. Yes, sesame oil!

This flavor profile allows you to use all-natural ingredients to flavor this candy hack. Real butter and butter extract, vanilla extract, honey, and sesame oil will provide the perfect blend of flavors for a great knockoff. I've also added the pleasant gumminess of gelatin to this recipe to soften the final product. But flavor and texture are only part of the secret. Your fake candy corn also needs to look like real candy corn.

Tap into the childhood days of forming and slicing Play-Doh as you shape tri-colored candy ribbons into flat rings and slice those rings into wedges with a sharp knife. This technique will give you perfect elongated triangles that look legitimate, even when placed right next to the real thing.

 Real candy corn is shaped by pouring sugar syrup into candy corn–shaped cornstarch molds. It's a messy and complex technique that isn't practical for a home copycat, so for recipes like this one, you'll need to devise a simplified process at home. When I laid the real candy corn side by side on a flat surface, they formed a circle. That's when I realized that I could form a ribbon of my homemade candy into a circle and slice it into wedges with a sharp knife to form the candy corn kernels.

1 tablespoon water
½ teaspoon gelatin powder
½ cup granulated sugar
¼ cup corn syrup
1 tablespoon honey
1 tablespoon unsalted butter
¼ teaspoon salt

6 drops sesame oil
½ teaspoon butter extract
¼ teaspoon vanilla extract
1¼ cups (5 ounces) sifted powdered sugar
8 drops yellow food coloring
4 drops red food coloring
8 drops yellow food coloring

RECIPE STEPS:

1. Combine water and gelatin powder in a small bowl and set it aside so thirsty gelatin can hydrate for 2 minutes.

2. Combine sugar, corn syrup, honey, butter, salt, oil, and hydrated gelatin in a medium saucepan over medium-low heat. When butter is melted, add a candy thermometer to pan. When candy reaches 250°F, about 15 minutes in, turn off heat and stir in butter extract and vanilla. Quickly add powdered sugar to pan and stir it into hot syrup.

3. Pour syrup onto a nonstick surface, such as a silicone baking mat, and allow it to cool for 5 minutes.

4. When you can touch candy, split it up by dividing it into a $\frac{1}{2}$-cup portion, a $\frac{1}{3}$-cup portion, and a small leftover portion (about 3 tablespoons). Put bigger portions into two microwave-safe bowls and heat each of them for 15 seconds on high to soften candy.

5. Add 8 drops of yellow coloring and 4 drops of red coloring to largest portion of candy and stir well to combine colors to make a solid orange. Add 8 drops of yellow food coloring to $\frac{1}{3}$-cup portion of candy and stir well until color is a solid yellow.

6. Use your hands to knead candy to make it smooth, then divide each portion of candy in half, including smallest white portion, and roll each piece into a rope that is 12" long. Use a nonstick surface like a silicone mat for rolling.

7. Align three ropes parallel to each other, with yellow on bottom, orange in middle, and white on top: yellow, orange, and white. Press down with your fingers on top of ropes to flatten them together into a ribbon, ensuring candy is flattened at an angle so that yellow part is thicker than white part. Cut ribbon in half. Set one half aside, then stretch other half to a length of 9"–10" and a width of 1". Now slice this ribbon in half and set one half aside. Place an index finger on counter above ribbon, next to white part, approximately in middle, and bend two ends around your finger, joining them on other side to form a flat ring. Repeat with remaining candy, making a total of eight flat rings.

8. Use a clean paring knife to slice each ring—like a pizza—into 16–18 wedges that are $\frac{1}{2}$" wide on outside (yellow part). Arrange them on a sheet pan that has been lightly sprayed with oil. After you spray pan, wipe off excess oil with a paper towel; this will leave just enough oil behind to create a perfect nonstick surface that doesn't make your candy too greasy. If you'd like the candy chewier, leave it out overnight.

FIELD NOTES

Candy corn was invented in the 1880s and was initially called Chicken Feed. Before World War I, corn wasn't generally considered food for human consumption.

CALIFORNIA PIZZA KITCHEN

Butter Cake

 PREP TIME:
Active: 15 minutes
Inactive: 1 hour, 15 minutes

 DIFFICULTY:
Medium

 SERVES:
4

Imagine a giant soft sugar cookie with sweetened cream cheese on top, served warm as if it just came out of the oven, and you have California Pizza Kitchen's Butter Cake. It's a delectable dessert that is easy to prep for service by cooks in the restaurant, since the cakes are made ahead of time and chilled until requested. When an order hits the kitchen, the cake is heated for a minute in the microwave, then topped with a scoop of vanilla ice cream and surrounded by dollops of whipped cream. I've designed this copycat hack the same way, so you can make your cakes in advance and chill them until dessert time. Or, if you prefer, you can serve the cakes right after they come out of the oven.

To make this recipe you'll need four 4" cake pans, ramekins, or any baking dishes that are 4" across. To make the batter, I used a stand mixer with the paddle attachment, but a handheld mixer also does the job.

After about 50 minutes in the oven, you'll have a perfect re-creation of the chain's hit dessert that you're sure to love.

 Recipes such as this one, where you have multiple servings, present a good opportunity to test cooking times and temperatures. Bake only one cake at a time and vary the time and temperature with each one that goes into the oven to discover the optimal settings. Later, when you bake a whole batch, you'll need to add 5–10 minutes to the ideal cooking time you discovered for just one serving.

FOR CAKE:

1 cup unsalted butter, softened
1 cup plus 2 tablespoons granulated sugar
¾ teaspoon salt
3 large egg yolks
1 large egg
1½ teaspoons vanilla extract
1½ cups (7½ ounces) all-purpose flour

FOR CREAM CHEESE TOPPING:

6 ounces cream cheese, softened
¼ cup granulated sugar
½ teaspoon vanilla extract

FOR BAKING:

Softened butter, for greasing pans
Sparkling sugar or Sugar in the Raw

FOR SERVING:

4 scoops vanilla ice cream

2 cups whipped cream

RECIPE STEPS:

1. Preheat oven to 325°F.
2. To make cake: Cream butter, sugar, and salt in a large bowl with an electric mixer on high speed for 3 minutes. If you're using a stand mixer, use paddle attachment.
3. Scrape down sides of bowl, then add egg yolks one at a time while mixing. Add egg and vanilla and mix on high speed for 1 minute. Add flour and mix on low speed until all flour is mixed in.
4. To make cream cheese topping: Combine ingredients in a medium bowl and beat on high speed for 1 minute.
5. Butter insides of four (4") cake pans or ramekins and sprinkle some sparkling sugar or Sugar in the Raw onto bottom of each cake pan.
6. Divide cake batter evenly among cake pans. There should be around 6½ ounces of batter in each pan. Use moistened fingers to smooth out top of batter.
7. Divide cream cheese topping and spoon it over top of batter in each pan (about 3 tablespoons per pan).
8. Bake cakes for 45–55 minutes until edge of cream cheese is light brown.
9. Let cakes cool 30 minutes in pans, then carefully slide a butter knife around inside edges of pans to help release each cake. Turn each cake pan over into your hand to release cakes, then place cakes with cream cheese topping on top in a covered container and refrigerate for up to 4 days until ready to serve.
10. To serve, reheat cakes one at a time in microwave on high for 1 minute; add ice cream and whipped cream on top.

FIELD NOTES

When you order a dish like this to go for study later in your lab (kitchen), request that they not heat the cake because you want to "eat it tomorrow." If they agree to give you a cold cake, you can ask for the heating instructions, and they'll tell you how they prepare it in the restaurant for service, which is insider information that will help with your hack recipe.

Before working on this clone, I sliced the sample cake in half to see the cross section. This visual helped me estimate how much cream cheese to use for the gooey layer. Revealing the cross-section of a dish like this one is a great way to determine ratios and estimate measurements for the layers.

Butter Cake

CALIFORNIA PIZZA KITCHEN

Carne Asada Pizza

 PREP TIME:
Active: 50 minutes
Inactive: Overnight, plus 10 minutes

 **DIFFICULTY:**
Medium

 SERVES:
4–6 (2 pizzas)

One of California Pizza Kitchen's most popular "globally inspired" pizzas is this fabulous pie topped with strips of marinated flank steak, cilantro pesto, and fire-roasted poblano pepper. I broke it down and cloned all the parts for you here—including the excellent salsa verde that goes on top—so you can assemble two beautiful pizzas that look and taste like the real thing.

Deliciousness often requires patience, so plan to make your copycat pizza 1 day in advance to allow the dough to proof properly and the steak to marinate. You can also prep the pesto, salsa verde, and roasted poblano 1 day in advance so that when it comes time to make your pizzas the next day, you'll just need to cook the carne asada, build the pies, and bake. If you've got a pizza stone, use it here to create a crust that's more like the real thing, which is cooked in a stone pizza oven at the restaurant.

 California Pizza Kitchen makes it easy to observe the action (and do some spywork!). You can dine in front of the pizza prep station near the stone pizza oven for front-row access to how this recipe and other favorites are prepped and cooked. Take a seat, watch, and then get to work on your deceptively tasty copycats. Many other chains, such as Auntie Anne's, Panda Express, Crumbl, and In-N-Out Burger, also make it easy to observe the food prep process.

FOR CARNE ASADA:

⅓ cup vegetable oil
3 tablespoons lime juice
2 teaspoons minced garlic
2 teaspoons ground coriander
1 teaspoon ground cumin
1 teaspoon ground black pepper
1 teaspoon salt
¾ teaspoon ground cayenne pepper
½ teaspoon paprika
2 tablespoons chopped fresh cilantro
¾ pound flank steak

FOR DOUGH:

1 tablespoon granulated sugar
1½ teaspoons active dry yeast
¾ cup warm water
2 cups (10 ounces) bread flour
½ teaspoon salt
1 tablespoon extra-virgin olive oil

FOR SALSA VERDE:

1/4 pound tomatillos
1 medium jalapeño
1/4 cup chopped fresh cilantro
3 tablespoons water
1 tablespoon lime juice
1 clove garlic
1 tablespoon peeled and minced onion
1/4 teaspoon garlic powder
1/8 teaspoon salt

FOR CILANTRO PESTO:

1/2 cup extra-virgin olive oil
1/2 cup chopped fresh cilantro
1/4 cup grated Parmesan cheese
2 tablespoons pine nuts
1 clove garlic
1 teaspoon lime juice
1/4 teaspoon salt

FOR TOPPING:

1 medium poblano pepper
1 cup shredded mozzarella cheese
1 cup shredded Monterey jack cheese
1/2 cup peeled and sliced yellow onion
2 tablespoons minced fresh cilantro

RECIPE STEPS:

1. To make carne asada: Combine all ingredients except flank steak in a medium bowl. Pour marinade over steak in a large zip-top bag and refrigerate it overnight.

2. To make dough: Combine sugar and yeast with warm water in a small bowl or spouted measuring cup. Let it sit for 5 minutes until surface of mixture becomes foamy.

3. In a medium bowl, whisk together flour and salt. Make a depression in flour and pour in olive oil and yeast mixture. Use a fork to stir liquid, gradually incorporating more flour as you stir until all ingredients are combined. When you can no longer stir with a fork, use your hands to form dough into a ball.

4. Knead dough with heels of your hands on a lightly floured surface for 5 minutes until texture of dough is smooth. Form dough back into a ball, coat it lightly with oil, and place it in a clean bowl covered with plastic wrap. Keep bowl in a warm place for 1–2 hours until dough doubles in size.

5. Punch down dough, form it back into a ball, and put it back into covered bowl and refrigerate overnight. Take dough from refrigerator 1–2 hours before you build pizza so that dough warms up to room temperature.

6. Prepare salsa verde by heating a grill to high heat. Alternatively, use a grill pan on stovetop over high heat. Remove husks from tomatillos and stem from jalapeño, then place them on grill. Cook for 3–4 minutes, turning tomatillos and jalapeño as they blacken. You want several black spots on tomatillos and jalapeño, but don't let them get fully blackened. Transfer tomatillos and jalapeño into a blender with remaining ingredients and blend on high speed for 5–10 seconds until salsa is smooth with no large chunks. Set aside until ready to make pizzas.

7. To make cilantro pesto: Combine all ingredients in a blender and blend on high speed for 5–10 seconds until smooth. Set aside until ready to build pizzas.

continued on next page

RECIPE STEPS (continued):

8. Prepare poblano pepper by roasting it over a high flame on a gas stovetop until skin is completely blackened, then rinse off blackened skin, remove stem and seeds, and slice. Alternatively, roast pepper in a preheated 450°F oven: Place pepper on a baking sheet and bake for 20–30 minutes, turning twice while baking, until skin is wrinkled and charred.

9. When ready to make pizzas, preheat oven to 500°F. If you have a pizza stone, place it on middle rack to preheat. Also, preheat grill to high.

10. Cook marinated steak on hot grill for 3–4 minutes per side until medium-rare. Alternatively, use a grill pan on stovetop over high heat. Carne asada should be pink in middle, since it will cook again on pizza. Let rest for 5 minutes after it comes off grill, then make thin slices across grain.

11. Divide dough in half, form one half into a ball, then roll it out on a lightly floured surface until it's 10"–11" across. Keep dough as round as possible, and use your fingers to thicken dough around edge. Place dough on a pizza pan or baking sheet.

12. Brush about half of cilantro pesto over dough, but not on raised edge.

13. Combine cheeses in a medium bowl, then sprinkle half (about 1 cup) over pesto. Add half of carne asada on top of cheese. Add onion around carne asada. Top with half of poblano pepper.

14. Bake pizza for 10–12 minutes, on the middle rack or on the preheated pizza stone, turning the pizza halfway through cooking time so it browns evenly. Remove pizza and sprinkle it with about a tablespoon of minced cilantro.

15. Let pizza cool for a couple of minutes, then use a pizza wheel or a big knife to make three cuts through middle for six slices (as CPK does) or four cuts through middle for eight slices. Shape other half of dough, and repeat steps 12 through 15 to build and cook second pizza. Serve with salsa verde on side.

FIELD NOTES

Some people have a genetic mutation that makes cilantro taste like soap. If that's the case with one of your eaters, you can make the pesto with basil, parsley, or arugula instead of cilantro. Pesto is pleasantly flexible, so you can decide what to include. You can also replace the pine nuts with walnuts, almonds, or pecans.

CALIFORNIA PIZZA KITCHEN

Roasted Garlic Chicken Pizza

 PREP TIME:
Active: 60 minutes
Inactive: Overnight, plus 10 minutes

 DIFFICULTY:
Medium

 SERVES:
4–6 (2 pizzas)

You won't miss the pizza sauce on this "white pizza," since the toppings bring bold flavors to the show that you won't want to upstage.

    CPK's wood-fired stone ovens are cranked up to a rocket-hot 800°F, so a pizza bakes in just 3 or 4 minutes. You can bake copycat pizzas in a conventional oven in around 10 minutes. I recommend using a pizza stone, but the recipe works without one. Start your pizzas the day before you plan to eat them so that the dough can rise slowly overnight in your refrigerator. This produces fermentation that will ultimately give your crust a better texture and taste.

The California Pizza Kitchen Cookbook, written by the chain's founders, Larry Flax and Rick Rosenfield, does not include a recipe for this specific pizza. However, I did find their technique for roasting garlic included with another recipe in the book. I have found that restaurant cookbooks don't usually share a chain's most beloved recipes, but you can find helpful preparation techniques and other useful tips hidden throughout the book.

FOR DOUGH:

1 tablespoon granulated sugar
1½ teaspoons active dry yeast
¾ cup warm water
2 cups (10 ounces) bread flour
½ teaspoon salt
1 tablespoon extra-virgin olive oil

FOR ROASTED GARLIC:

⅓ cup coarsely chopped garlic
2 teaspoons extra-virgin olive oil

FOR CARAMELIZED ONION:

2 tablespoons unsalted butter
4 cups peeled and sliced yellow onion
½ teaspoon soy sauce
¼ teaspoon kosher salt

FOR GRILLED CHICKEN:

2 teaspoons coarsely chopped garlic
1 teaspoon soy sauce
½ teaspoon kosher salt
2 tablespoons extra-virgin olive oil
1 (6- to 8-ounce) chicken breast fillet

Roasted Garlic Chicken Pizza

FOR TOPPING:

2 tablespoons extra-virgin olive oil

12 ounces thinly sliced buffalo mozzarella cheese

1/8 teaspoon coarse ground black pepper

1/4 cup grated Parmesan cheese

2 green onions, julienned (white and light green parts only)

RECIPE STEPS:

1. To make dough: Combine sugar and yeast with warm water in a small bowl or spouted measuring cup. Let it sit for 5 minutes until surface of mixture becomes foamy. Whisk together flour and salt in a medium bowl. Make a depression in flour and pour in olive oil and yeast mixture. Use a fork to stir liquid, gradually incorporating more flour as you stir, until all ingredients are combined. When you can no longer stir with a fork, use your hands to form dough into a ball.

2. Knead dough on a lightly floured surface for 5 minutes until texture of dough is smooth. Form dough into a ball, coat lightly with oil, and place in a clean bowl covered with plastic wrap. Keep in a warm place 1–2 hours until dough doubles in size.

3. Punch down dough, form it back into a ball, and put it back into covered bowl and refrigerate overnight. Take dough from refrigerator 1–2 hours before building pizza to warm up to room temperature.

4. To make roasted garlic: Preheat oven to 350°F. Mix garlic with oil in a small oven-safe bowl and cover it with foil. Place in oven for 45 minutes, stirring a couple times as it roasts. It should be soft and lightly browned when it's done. Keep it covered until you need it, and increase oven temperature to 500°F. Add a pizza stone to oven if you have one.

5. To make caramelized onion: Melt butter in a medium saucepan over medium-low heat. Add sliced onion, soy sauce, and salt, and cook slowly, stirring occasionally, for 1 hour until onions are soft and brown.

6. To make grilled chicken: Combine garlic, soy sauce, kosher salt, and olive oil in a medium bowl and add chicken. Coat chicken with marinade and refrigerate 30 minutes. Preheat a grill to high heat while chicken marinates, then grill chicken 4–6 minutes per side until internal temperature reaches 165°F. Slice into bite-sized chunks.

7. To build your pizzas, divide dough in half. Form one half of dough into a ball. Roll it out on a lightly floured surface until it's 10"–11" across. Keep dough as round as possible, and use your fingers to thicken dough around edge. Place dough on a pizza pan or baking sheet, and brush it with olive oil.

8. Arrange half of sliced mozzarella on pizza so that cheese covers all dough except for raised edge. Add half of grilled chicken, then add half of caramelized onion. Spoon half of roasted garlic on next. Sprinkle pizza with a few pinches of ground black pepper. Sprinkle 2 tablespoons of Parmesan cheese over pizza.

9. Bake pizza for 10–12 minutes until crust and cheese are lightly browned. Give pizza a turn halfway through cooking time so that it browns evenly. When you take pizza out of oven, sprinkle it with half of green onions.

10. Let pizza cool for 2 minutes, then use a pizza wheel or a big knife to make three cuts through middle for six slices. Shape second half of dough, brush it with olive oil, and repeat steps 8 and 9 for second pizza.

FIELD NOTES

Roasted garlic tastes nothing like raw garlic. Heat breaks down the sharp, pungent flavors of garlic and transforms the bulb into a sweet and nutty spreadable treat.

CAPITAL CITY

Sweet Hot Mambo Sauce

PREP TIME: Active: 5 minutes Inactive: 15 minutes to cool	**DIFFICULTY:** Easy	**MAKES:** 1 cup

Similar to Chinese sweet-and-sour sauce but spicier and with more tomato in it (like barbecue sauce), mumbo sauce (with a "u") came to fame in the 1950s when it migrated from Chicago to DC-area take-out restaurants for use on practically everything from chicken wings to fried shrimp.

Washington, DC–area entrepreneur Arsha Jones created the most popular version, originally called Capital City Mumbo Sauce. But the name was already taken, and a 2013 trademark decision compelled Arsha to slightly alter her product's name to Mambo Sauce.

Because the sauce is so good on fried chicken, KFC began testing Arsha's sauce in several restaurants in 2021 for a potential chain-wide rollout, and now you can test out some uses for your own home version. This original hack recipe will take you just 5 minutes to make and will give you 1 cup of the iconic sauce to use on fried chicken, wings, shrimp, French fries, Chinese food, or anything that needs a dose of great spicy flavor.

 When wondering where to start with tomatoey red sauces like this, always consider ketchup. It's made with tomato purée and several other ingredients for a sweet-and-sour flavor that works well in many red sauces, including Asian sweet-and-sour sauce.

½ cup ketchup
⅓ cup granulated sugar
3 tablespoons water
1 tablespoon plus 1 teaspoon white wine vinegar
2 teaspoons soy sauce
2 teaspoons cayenne pepper sauce (such as Frank's RedHot or Texas Pete)
¼ teaspoon ground cayenne pepper
¼ teaspoon paprika

RECIPE STEPS:

1. Whisk together all ingredients in a small saucepan or microwave-safe bowl.

2. Warm sauce in saucepan over medium heat just until sugar dissolves, or in microwave for 1 minute on high. Sauce will thicken when it cools. Use as a dip or to baste meats. Cover and chill to store for up to 2 weeks.

 FIELD NOTES

Argia B. Collins Sr. is credited with creating mumbo sauce in the 1950s for his Chicago barbecue restaurant, Argia B's. Today, the sauce that originated in the Windy City is considered a staple of the Capital City.

CAPITAL GRILLE

Mushroom and Asparagus Risotto

 PREP TIME:
Active: 45 minutes
Inactive: None

 DIFFICULTY:
Easy

 SERVES:
4

On lists of the best chain restaurant risottos, Capital Grille's version always seems to appear near the top. Its popular Mushroom and Asparagus Risotto is flavorful but not overly rich, creamy but not gummy, and just fancy enough to accompany entrées that deserve a respectable sidekick yet prefer not to be upstaged. It also has something special. The light green strips in this risotto are not green onions; they're leeks.

Cook the risotto until it's al dente or slightly tough, stirring often to make the rice creamy, and you'll make a dish that tastes like it came from the pro kitchen of an upscale chain.

 For my copycat hack of this side dish, I've called for an ingredient you won't find in most risotto recipes; I found that adding a little whole milk improved the flavor and texture of the finished dish and gave my risotto the bright white appearance of the restaurant version.

2 cups chicken broth
1½ cups water
½ cup whole milk
2 tablespoons unsalted butter, divided
1 cup uncooked Arborio rice
¼ cup minced leek
½ cup dry white wine
1 tablespoon grated Parmesan cheese
½ teaspoon plus ⅛ teaspoon salt, divided
¼ teaspoon ground black pepper
¼ teaspoon minced thyme
½ cup asparagus, chopped on the bias
1 cup thinly sliced brown mushrooms

RECIPE STEPS:

1. Combine broth, water, and milk in a medium spouted saucepan over medium-low heat, and heat just until simmering, then turn heat to low and let sit.

2. Melt 1 tablespoon of butter in a medium saucepan over medium heat, then add rice and cook for 2 minutes. Add leek and cook for 1 more minute until rice becomes opaque but doesn't brown.

3. Add wine to rice and cook until it's absorbed, about 1 minute.

continued on next page

RECIPE STEPS (continued):

4. Ladle enough of hot broth liquid into saucepan to cover rice, and stir often as liquid is absorbed. Repeat process several more times until all broth is used. This should take 30–40 minutes. Stir rice often as it cooks, and your risotto will have a perfectly creamy texture.

5. After adding last of broth, add Parmesan cheese, 1/2 teaspoon salt, pepper, and thyme to rice.

6. Cook asparagus and mushrooms by heating a medium sauté pan over medium heat. Melt remaining tablespoon of butter in pan and add asparagus. Cook for 3 minutes, then add mushrooms and 1/8 teaspoon salt. Cook 3–4 more minutes until asparagus is tender but slightly crisp. Turn off heat.

7. When rice has absorbed all liquid, stir in asparagus and mushrooms and serve.

FIELD NOTES

Risotto gets its creaminess from being stirred as it cooks. When the grains of rice rub together, they release starch that thickens the liquid. If you don't stir enough, your risotto won't be creamy. But be careful not to overdo it. If you stir too much, you'll cool the rice and make it gummy.

Mushroom and Asparagus Risotto

CARL'S JR./HARDEE'S

Hand-Breaded Chicken & Waffle Sandwich

 PREP TIME:
Active: 35 minutes
Inactive: 4 hours 40 minutes

 DIFFICULTY:
Medium

 **MAKES:**
4 sandwiches

In the midst of the fast food chicken sandwich war of 2019–2021 triggered by the debut of Popeye's Chicken Sandwich, Carl's Jr. (and Hardee's) introduced a simple chicken and waffle sandwich that won many fans. Crispy chicken breast is doused with maple butter sauce and sandwiched between two Belgian waffle buns for a sweet-and-savory handful.

To clone the sandwich at home, the chicken in this recipe is brined, breaded, and fried until perfectly golden brown and crispy. The maple butter sauce is a simple hack with just three ingredients and an electric mixer.

 When using chicken breasts for any recipe knockoff, always consider brining them. Chain restaurants often marinate chicken breasts in a salt bath to improve the flavor and moisture of this potentially dry and tasteless cut of chicken, so brining is a crucial step to include when making restaurant-quality chicken dishes at home.

FOR BRINE:

2 cups water
1 tablespoon plus 1 teaspoon kosher salt
1½ teaspoons MSG (monosodium glutamate)
2 (8-ounce) chicken breast fillets

FOR MAPLE BUTTER SAUCE:

⅓ cup maple-flavored pancake syrup
2 tablespoons salted butter, melted
2 teaspoons granulated sugar

FOR BELGIAN WAFFLE BUNS:

2 large eggs
¼ cup granulated sugar
¼ cup salted butter, melted
2 tablespoons vegetable oil

FOR BELGIAN WAFFLE BUNS (continued):

1½ teaspoons vanilla extract
2 cups whole milk
2 cups (10 ounces) all-purpose flour
1 tablespoon baking powder
1 teaspoon salt

FOR CHICKEN BREADING:

1 cup all-purpose flour
2 teaspoons paprika
1½ teaspoons granulated sugar
¾ teaspoon salt
¾ teaspoon MSG
¾ teaspoon baking powder
½ teaspoon ground white pepper
¼ teaspoon onion powder

FOR CHICKEN BREADING (continued):

¼ teaspoon garlic powder
1½ cups buttermilk
Vegetable oil, for frying

RECIPE STEPS:

1. To make brine: Combine water, salt, and MSG in a medium bowl or container and whisk until salt has dissolved.

2. Slice each chicken breast through middle to make four thinner fillets that weigh about 4 ounces each. If necessary, use a kitchen mallet to pound fillets so that they are no more than ½" thick, then add them to brine and refrigerate for 4 hours.

3. To make maple butter sauce: Combine all ingredients in a small bowl and mix thoroughly with an electric mixer on medium speed. Set aside until needed. Sauce will thicken as melted butter cools.

4. To make Belgian waffle buns: Combine eggs with sugar in a medium bowl using an electric mixer on high speed. Mix for 30 seconds, then add butter, oil, and vanilla. Mix for another 30 seconds. Add milk and mix for 1 minute until sugar has dissolved.

5. In another medium bowl, whisk together flour, baking powder, and salt. Pour half of milk blend into dry mixture and combine with electric mixer until all flour is moistened. Add other half of liquid and mix on medium speed until batter is mostly smooth with a few small lumps.

6. Heat up a Belgian waffle iron (or a standard waffle iron) and grease with oil or oil spray.

7. Pour about ¼ cup of batter into bottom of waffle iron. Spread batter to edges of waffle plates, and *do not* close lid. Tear a piece of foil the length of waffle iron, then fold it in half. When batter is less shiny on surface of waffle, after about 3 minutes, coat one side of foil with a spritz of oil spray and lay that side down onto waffle batter.

8. Close lid of waffle iron. Cook for 1 minute until batter has firmed up.

9. Remove foil, close lid, and continue cooking until waffle is lightly browned. Repeat with remaining batter for eight waffle buns. When waffle buns have cooled, store in an airtight container until needed, up to 2 days.

10. To make chicken breading: Combine flour, paprika, sugar, salt, MSG, baking powder, white pepper, onion powder, and garlic powder in a medium bowl. Pour buttermilk into another medium bowl.

11. Working with one chicken fillet at a time, coat with flour blend and shake off excess. Dip chicken in buttermilk, allowing a little to drip off, then return to dry blend. Toss chicken in flour. If coating is not thick enough, repeat breading process. Let chicken sit in flour mixture for 2–3 minutes, then toss to remove excess flour before placing it on a tray or baking sheet while you prepare remaining pieces.

12. Heat at least 3" of oil in a large saucepan, Dutch oven, or deep fryer to 325°F. Fry chicken fillets for 5–6 minutes until browned. Drain on a rack over a baking sheet or a paper towel–lined plate.

13. Build each sandwich by warming two waffle buns for 15 seconds on high in a microwave oven. Position a chicken fillet on flat side of one waffle bun. Pour about 2 teaspoons of maple butter sauce over chicken, then top off sandwich with other warm waffle bun.

🔍 FIELD NOTES

The top-selling brands of pancake syrup in America are not true maple syrups. They're made with corn syrup, maple flavoring, and artificial color. If you want the real stuff for these sandwiches, make sure the label says "pure maple syrup."

Cannoli Cake for Two

CARRABBA'S ITALIAN GRILL

Cannoli Cake for Two

 PREP TIME:
Active: 45 minutes
Inactive: 3 hours

 DIFFICULTY:
Medium

 **MAKES:**
8 (2-person) slices

Cannoli lovers go wild when they taste this three-layer homemade vanilla cake filled with delicious, creamy ricotta cheese cannoli filling. Serve a thick slice on a plate drizzled with chocolate sauce, and sprinkle it with chopped pistachios for the ultimate cannoli/cake mash-up!

The vanilla cake recipe here is an original creation, and it will produce enough batter to fill three (9") pans, which are easiest to bake when prepared simultaneously. If you don't have that many pans, use what you have and bake the cakes in stages, cooling the pan(s) between batches. And if you want thicker cannoli filling, strain the ricotta cheese overnight in a strainer to remove the excess liquid. You can also make lumpy or grainy ricotta cheese smoother by puréeing it on high speed in a blender or food processor before straining it overnight. The smoother your ricotta, the closer your cake will be to the original recipe.

 You may find that you can use a hack recipe for more than one dish from the same restaurant. This dessert is an excellent example of borrowing from a recipe I previously developed (the Carrabba's Traditional Cannoli recipe, which follows) to springboard into another popular recipe from the chain. The cannoli filling for this cake is the same as what's used in the cannoli recipe. You can also use the latter recipe to make an optional garnish for the top of the Cannoli Cake. You will want smaller cannoli to garnish the cake, so if you opt for this step, use mini cannoli tubes to make the shells, or buy pre-made mini cannoli shells.

FOR CAKE:

14 tablespoons unsalted butter, softened
1¾ cups granulated sugar
3 large eggs
2 large egg whites
½ cup buttermilk
½ cup whole milk
½ cup vegetable oil or grapeseed oil
1 tablespoon vanilla extract
3 cups (15 ounces) all-purpose flour
1 tablespoon plus 1 teaspoon baking powder
1¼ teaspoons salt

FOR RICOTTA FILLING:

15 ounces ricotta cheese
⅔ cup (2⅔ ounces) powdered sugar
½ teaspoon lemon juice
½ teaspoon vanilla extract
⅛ teaspoon ground cinnamon
¼ cup mini semi-sweet chocolate chips

FOR BUTTERCREAM FROSTING:

4 cups (16 ounces) powdered sugar
1 cup unsalted butter, softened
2 tablespoons whole milk
2 teaspoons vanilla extract
⅛ teaspoon salt

FOR GARNISH:

¼–⅓ cup chocolate sauce in a squirt bottle
½ cup chopped pistachios
8 mini cannoli (optional)

RECIPE STEPS:

1. Eliminate excess liquid in ricotta by scooping it into a strainer over a bowl. Refrigerate uncovered 2 hours, up to overnight.

2. Preheat convection oven to 325°F. Alternatively, preheat conventional oven to 350°F. If you cook all layers at once (and I recommend it), you'll likely need two racks in your oven to hold all cake pans.

3. To make cake: Mix butter and sugar in a stand mixer with paddle attachment or with a handheld mixer in a large bowl on high speed for 2–3 minutes until it becomes white and fluffy. Scrape down sides of bowl.

4. Add eggs and egg whites one at a time, mixing well after each addition. When final egg white is added, scrape down sides of bowl and mix on high speed for 2 minutes.

5. Whisk together buttermilk, milk, oil, and vanilla in a spouted measuring cup or small bowl. While mixer is on medium-high speed, slowly drizzle liquid mixture into bowl to fully incorporate into batter. It should take 2–3 minutes. When all liquid is in, continue to beat batter for 3 more minutes until it fluffs up and becomes about 50% more voluminous.

6. Whisk together flour, baking powder, and salt in a medium bowl. Slowly add this dry blend to wet ingredients while mixing on medium-low speed. Mix only until flour is completely incorporated into batter.

7. Spray three (9") cake pans (or as many as you have) with nonstick spray and line bottoms with parchment paper. If you have fewer than three pans, bake cakes in batches and cover any leftover batter until you use it. Pour an even amount of batter into all three pans and bake for 30–35 minutes until golden brown on top and firm in middle. Cool for at least 30 minutes and remove cakes from pans.

8. To make ricotta filling: Add ricotta, sugar, lemon juice, vanilla, and cinnamon to a medium bowl. Mix with an electric mixer on high speed for 1 minute until smooth. Roughly chop mini chips to make some smaller pieces in mix, then stir chocolate bits into filling. Place filling in your refrigerator until you are ready to use it.

9. To make buttercream frosting: Combine powdered sugar, butter, milk, vanilla, and salt in a medium bowl with a mixer on high speed. Mix for 1 minute until frosting is smooth and fluffy.

10. Build cake by placing one cake round in center of a cake plate and spreading half of ricotta filling evenly over top. Add another cake layer and spread remaining ricotta filling over top. Place third cake layer on ricotta, then spread buttercream frosting generously over top of cake, with excess frosting hanging over edge of cake. When top of cake is frosted, frost sides of cake by working frosting hanging off sides of cake, and add more frosting as needed.

11. When cake is completely frosted, sprinkle mini chips onto palm of your hand and press them into side of cake all the way around. Chill cake until you're ready to serve it. It will keep for several days.

12. To serve, slice cake four times through middle to make eight large slices. Drizzle chocolate sauce over eight serving plates, then place a slice of cake on chocolate. Sprinkle each slice with 1 tablespoon of chopped pistachios. Optional: Add a mini cannoli garnish on top before serving. Cover and chill any leftovers, which will keep for several days.

FIELD NOTES

How to hack recipes like this: First, take photos of your sample so you remember what your clone should look like. Next, take measurements. Measure the length of the slice, and double it to determine the diameter of the real cake so you know which pans to use. You also want to know how thick the layers are. Dissect the cake and scrape off the filling and frosting to save for comparative samples. Then bake a trial cake to see where you're at. While it's baking, you can work on clones for the filling and frosting, and when the cake is cool, you can assemble the cake to see where you need more or less of something.

CARRABBA'S ITALIAN GRILL

Traditional Cannoli

 PREP TIME:
Active: 35 minutes
Inactive: Overnight, plus 90 minutes

 DIFFICULTY:
Medium

 **MAKES:**
4 servings

For great traditional cannoli, you need not look any further than Carrabba's Italian Grill. These cannoli are precisely what you want cannoli to be: a crunchy shell that isn't soggy or too thick, packed with sweetened ricotta cheese filling that's smooth and not grainy. Along with that classic crunchy/creamy combination comes a hint of cinnamon lingering in the background to complete the traditional taste of Italian cannoli.

To make this copycat Carrabba's cannoli recipe, you'll need eight cannoli tubes to form the shells. You can find them online or in stores that carry baking supplies. This recipe includes easy steps for deep-frying the dough around metal tubes for shells that are perfectly golden brown.

Look for smooth ricotta, and strain it overnight to thicken it before mixing it into the filling. Chopped pistachios around the ends of each shell make for the perfect finishing touch.

 If you can't find ingredients identical to those in a recipe, you may have to customize and use what is available. Carrabba's cannoli is made with a very smooth ricotta, but I found that many brands are too grainy. To smooth it out, run ricotta through a blender or food processor until the lumps are gone, and you'll get a much better clone.

FOR SHELLS:

2 cups (10 ounces) all-purpose flour
3 tablespoons granulated sugar
¼ teaspoon salt
¼ teaspoon ground cinnamon
3 tablespoons unsalted butter, cold
⅓ cup marsala wine
2 large eggs, beaten separately
Vegetable oil, for frying

FOR FILLING:

15 ounces ricotta cheese
⅔ cup (2⅔ ounces) powdered sugar
½ teaspoon lemon juice
½ teaspoon vanilla extract
⅛ teaspoon ground cinnamon
¼ cup heavy cream
¼ cup mini semi-sweet chocolate chips

FOR GARNISH:

⅓ cup chopped pistachios
¼–⅓ cup chocolate fudge sauce, warmed
2 teaspoons powdered sugar

RECIPE STEPS:

1. Eliminate excess liquid in ricotta by spooning it into a strainer in a bowl. Let this sit uncovered for a couple of hours or overnight (best) in your refrigerator.

2. Make dough for shells by whisking together flour, sugar, salt, and cinnamon in a medium bowl. Use your fingers or a pastry knife to work butter into flour until no large chunks remain. Make a well in flour, then add marsala wine and 1 beaten egg. Work dry ingredients into wet ingredients until you can form dough into a ball. Don't overwork flour, or it could become tough. Form dough into a disk and cover it with plastic wrap. Refrigerate dough for 30 minutes while you work on filling.

3. Use a mixer to combine strained ricotta cheese with powdered sugar, lemon juice, vanilla, and cinnamon in a medium bowl.

4. Rapidly whisk heavy cream in a small bowl until stiff peaks form, then fold into sweetened ricotta.

5. Roughly chop mini chips to make some smaller pieces in mix, then stir into filling. Refrigerate filling uncovered for 1 hour to thicken.

6. Preheat 3" of oil in a large saucepan, Dutch oven, or deep fryer to 360°F.

7. Roll dough out on a lightly floured surface until it is $1/8$"–$1/16$" thick.

8. Turn over a bowl or large cocktail glass that is 5" wide onto dough and cut out eight circles using a small sharp knife. A classic margarita glass can be the perfect size for these circles.

9. Place a 5" metal cannoli tube across center of a dough circle, then brush a little beaten egg along edge furthest away from you. Fold dough nearest you over tube, then roll tube and dough up over egg wash and press down to seal. Flare dough out on ends so that oil can get in between dough and tube, and it will be easier to remove tube after cooking. Repeat with all eight dough circles.

10. When oil is hot, fry 2–4 shells at a time for $2\frac{1}{2}$–3 minutes until shells are golden brown. When you take them out of oil, use a towel in each hand to remove hot pastry from tube.

11. When shells have cooled, use a pastry bag with a large round tip to pipe filling into pastry shells. Dip each end of filled cannoli into chopped pistachios. (Only fill cannoli you will be serving immediately, since filled cannoli shells will become soggy if not eaten within a few hours after they're filled.)

12. To serve, drizzle chocolate sauce onto four serving plates. Place two cannoli on each plate, sprinkle each plate with some of remaining chopped pistachios, and dust everything on each plate with powdered sugar.

FIELD NOTES

"Cannoli" means "little tubes" in Italian. While modern recipes use metal tubes to shape the shells of this pastry, in ancient times, the shells were made by wrapping the dough around river reeds.

CHARMS CANDY COMPANY

Blow Pops

 PREP TIME:
Active: 1 hour
Inactive: 30 minutes

 DIFFICULTY:
Medium

 MAKES:
14 pops

The fruity lollipop with gum inside is Charms's bestselling product, but this cool combination candy was actually the brainchild of a different candy company. Thomas T. Tidwell of Triple T Co. invented and patented his method for encasing gum in candy in the 1960s and sold his new lollipop, Triple Treat, for a short time. In 1973, Tidwell sold the product idea to the Charms Candy Company, who renamed it Blow Pop, and for over 50 years, the famous pop has been enjoyed by millions.

While Tidwell's method is kept under wraps, the vertical seam on a real Blow Pop indicates that it's probably made by sealing two halves of the pop together on a stick, one half with gum and one half without. For this copycat, I tried various silicone lollipop molds with little success and decided instead to create a technique using half of a slightly altered cake pop mold with slits cut in the edge to make room for a lollipop stick. To re-create it, you will need fourteen lollipop sticks, a candy thermometer, and a silicone cake pop mold with twenty cups (all found online).

I designed this recipe to call for 1 dram of LorAnn Oils, which you can also find online. This recipe includes instructions for four of the original Blow Pop flavors: cherry, watermelon, sour apple, and grape.

 Adding an invert sugar, such as corn syrup or honey, to a candy syrup prevents the formation of sugar crystals as it heats to your desired temperature. The molecules of the invert sugar are smaller than those of granulated sugar and the size mismatch keeps crystals from forming.

FOR CHERRY:

2 cups plus 2 tablespoons granulated sugar
2/3 cup water
2/3 cup light corn syrup
3/4 teaspoon red food coloring
1 dram LorAnn Oils cherry flavoring
1 1/2 teaspoons citric acid
1 teaspoon hot water
21 (1/4-ounce) pieces Double Bubble bubble gum

FOR WATERMELON:

2 cups plus 2 tablespoons granulated sugar
2/3 cup water
2/3 cup light corn syrup
1/2 teaspoon red food coloring
1 dram LorAnn Oils watermelon flavoring
1 1/2 teaspoons citric acid
1 teaspoon hot water
21 (1/4-ounce) pieces Double Bubble bubble gum

FOR SOUR APPLE:

2 cups plus 2 tablespoons granulated sugar
2/3 cup water
2/3 cup light corn syrup
6 drops green food coloring
1 dram LorAnn Oils apple flavoring
2 1/4 teaspoons citric acid
1 1/2 teaspoons hot water
21 (1/4-ounce) pieces Double Bubble bubble gum

FOR GRAPE:

2 cups plus 2 tablespoons granulated sugar
2/3 cup water
2/3 cup light corn syrup
1 drop purple food coloring
1 dram LorAnn Oils grape flavoring
1 1/2 teaspoons citric acid
1 teaspoon hot water
21 (1/4-ounce) pieces Double Bubble bubble gum

RECIPE STEPS:

1. To make molds for pops, use a twenty-cup silicone cake pop mold. In the half of the mold that doesn't have holes in it, use sharp scissors to make slits in the raised edge—one slit centered on each of the fourteen cups around the outside of the mold, each slit approximately the width of a lollipop stick. (You won't be using the six cups in middle.)

2. Combine sugar, water, and corn syrup in a medium saucepan over medium heat. It's best to use a spouted pan to make it easier to pour candy into molds. Add a candy thermometer to pan when sugar has dissolved and syrup begins bubbling. Cook until candy reaches 300°F or hard-crack stage. This will take 20–30 minutes.

3. While syrup cooks, prepare sticks with gum. Place unwrapped gum pieces on a microwave-safe plate, and heat on high for 20 seconds, then shuffle gum around on plate and heat for another 10–20 seconds until gum is soft but not melting. Slice seven gum pieces in half with a sharp knife, then combine each half piece with a whole piece, forming 14 large gumballs. Pierce each gumball with a lollipop stick, adding some pressure to tighten gum around sticks.

4. When candy syrup reaches 300°F, turn off heat and watch temperature.

5. While you wait for candy to cool, combine citric acid with hot water in a small bowl. Stir until citric acid dissolves, and set it aside.

6. When candy syrup hits 185°F, add food coloring and stir it in with a spoon.

7. When temperature hits 175°F–170°F, stir flavoring into hot candy syrup.

8. When temperature hits 165°F, warm citric acid solution in your microwave for 10 seconds until it begins to bubble. Stir citric acid solution into candy syrup.

9. Pour candy into each of fourteen cups around outside of mold. Fill cups until syrup is about 1/8" from top of each mold.

10. Add a stick with gum to each mold, positioning gum with a bit more candy above gum than below it, since sugar will dissolve from top of pop more quickly than from bottom when consumed. Cover remaining candy syrup in saucepan and leave it off heat. Set a timer for 10 minutes.

continued on next page

RECIPE STEPS (continued):

11. After 10 minutes, remove lid from candy syrup and set heat to medium-low. Stir candy occasionally, and heat it for 7 minutes until it is thin enough to pour. When candy is ready, turn off heat and remove set pops with gum from cups.

12. Pour hot candy syrup into same fourteen cups, this time only filling cups to about $1/4$" from top of mold. (Use any remaining syrup to make a few extra pieces of hard candy by pouring it into remaining six empty cups in center of cake pop mold.)

13. Add gum-filled halves of pops to top of hot candy you just poured. Press down lightly to seal—but not too hard, or candy will squish out of cup.

14. Cool pops for 30 minutes before removing them from mold and storing them in a covered container or wrapping each with a small plastic bag. They will keep for up to 2 months.

FIELD NOTES

You can make cinnamon pops by following this recipe through step 2, then adding $1/2$ teaspoon red food coloring when the candy temperature hits 185°F. Next, add 1 dram of cinnamon oil when the candy reaches 165°F. This flavor requires no citric acid, so you can skip that step. Real Blow Pops don't come in a cinnamon flavor, but after tasting these, you might wish they did.

THE CHEESECAKE FACTORY

Chicken Piccata

 PREP TIME:
Active: 35 minutes
Inactive: 20 minutes

 DIFFICULTY:
Medium

 SERVES:
2

Since the sauce is the key to the great taste of this entrée, I made sure to get a sample on the side for later analysis when I requested my to-go order from the restaurant. While waiting, I asked the server what was in the sauce, and she listed some obvious ingredients—lemon, wine, butter, and cream—and then she mentioned garlic and shallots. When I got home, I rinsed the sauce through a mesh strainer to discover how much garlic and shallot were in the sauce, but there was no evidence of either ingredient left behind in the strainer. I made a batch of the sauce without garlic and shallot, and it tasted flat. So, on the next batch, I added the garlic and shallot back in, then strained out the solid ingredients after they contributed their goodness to the sauce. The result was noticeably better.

After adding mushrooms and capers to the new lemon sauce, I spooned it over sautéed chicken cutlets and was rewarded with a fantastic homemade version of this amazing dish, which you can now copy at home with ease.

 Chilling a sauce, such as the lemon sauce for this Chicken Piccata, in your refrigerator is an effective way to determine its butter content. When the sauce cools, the fat (butter) will rise to the top and solidify. This is how I determined how much butter to include in my Cheesecake Factory dupe.

FOR LEMON SAUCE:

½ cup unsalted butter, divided
2 teaspoons minced garlic
2 teaspoons minced shallot
¼ cup dry white wine
¼ cup chicken broth
⅔ cup heavy cream
3 tablespoons lemon juice
1 teaspoon granulated sugar
¼ teaspoon salt
1 tablespoon unsalted butter
1 cup cremini (baby portabella) mushrooms, sliced
2 tablespoons capers, drained

FOR CHICKEN:

Vegetable oil
2 (10-ounce) chicken breast fillets
Salt, to taste
Ground black pepper, to taste
½ cup (2½ ounces) all-purpose flour

FOR SERVING:

¼ pound uncooked angel hair pasta
1 teaspoon minced fresh parsley
6–8 half-wheel slices of lemon

RECIPE STEPS:

1. To make lemon sauce: Melt 2 tablespoons of butter in a small saucepan over medium heat. Add garlic and shallot to pan and cook for 2 minutes, but don't let garlic brown. Add wine and chicken broth, and cook until volume is reduced by half, 5–6 minutes. Strain sauce to remove garlic and shallot, and add flavorful liquid back to pan over medium-low heat.

2. Add remaining butter to pan, 1 tablespoon at a time, and when all butter has melted, add heavy cream, lemon juice, sugar, and salt. When sauce begins to bubble, reduce heat to low, and cook slowly for 10–12 minutes until it thickens. Turn off heat and cover sauce while following the next steps.

3. To make chicken: Pour about $1/4$" of vegetable oil into a large sauté pan over medium heat. Slice each fillet into three thinner slices, or cutlets, then pound those slices a bit thinner with a kitchen mallet. Sprinkle each cutlet with salt and pepper to taste. Measure flour onto a plate, then press each fillet into flour for a light coating on both sides.

4. Sauté chicken over medium-high heat for $1 1/2$–2 minutes per side until lightly browned around edges.

5. Prepare pasta by bringing 4–6 quarts of lightly salted water to a boil. Cook for 4–5 minutes until pasta is al dente, and drain.

6. Cook mushrooms by melting butter in a sauté pan over medium-high heat. Add sliced mushrooms along with a couple pinches of salt and pepper, and cook just until lightly browned, about 4 minutes. Add mushrooms, along with capers, to sauce, then turn on heat to medium-low to heat it back up.

7. Divide pasta onto two serving plates, using tongs to twirl it into tall piles. Arrange three chicken cutlets on each plate next to pasta. When sauce is hot, spoon it over chicken on each plate.

8. Garnish each dish with parsley, and arrange 3–4 lemon slices on top of chicken on each plate.

FIELD NOTES

Capers are an essential ingredient in chicken piccata, but what exactly are the lemony little nubs? They're flower buds from a bush found in the Mediterranean. They're picked before they bloom, then pickled and used as an acidic component in many dishes from that region.

Chicken Piccata

THE CHEESECAKE FACTORY

Shrimp Scampi

 PREP TIME:
Active: 45 minutes
Inactive: 20 minutes

 DIFFICULTY:
Medium

 SERVES:
2

This top entrée pick from The Cheesecake Factory is a classic dish, but its preparation is far from traditional, and perhaps that's why it's so popular.

The creamy scampi sauce is flavored with a handful of whole roasted garlic cloves, as well as shallot, basil, and tomato. The shrimp are lightly battered and fried until golden, then arranged upright around the plate to keep their crunchy coats from sogging.

Everything you'll need to re-create this top dish is here. In addition to all the secrets for assembling two servings of this copycat recipe, this recipe also includes a technique for easily roasting garlic in just 15–20 minutes. You won't even need to peel the cloves: After your garlic cools, the skins will just slip right off.

 Basil has a unique characteristic that makes it easy to identify in hot mixtures. In either fresh or dry form, basil leaves are very sensitive to heat and will darken to almost black in color when cooked.

FOR GARLIC:

2 tablespoons vegetable oil
14–16 small to medium cloves unpeeled garlic

FOR CREAMY SCAMPI SAUCE:

$1/4$ cup unsalted butter
2 tablespoons extra-virgin olive oil
3 tablespoons minced shallot
$1/2$ cup white wine (Chablis or pinot grigio)
$1/4$ cup chicken broth
$2/3$ cup heavy cream
2 teaspoons lemon juice
$1/3$ cup coarsely chopped fresh basil
$1/4$ cup diced Roma tomato
2 teaspoons minced fresh parsley
$1/4$ teaspoon crushed red pepper

FOR SHRIMP:

Vegetable oil, for frying
$1/2$ cup plus 1 tablespoon all-purpose flour
$1/2$ teaspoon salt
$1/2$ teaspoon coarse ground black pepper
$1/4$ teaspoon garlic powder
$2/3$ cup cold water
12 jumbo shrimp, shelled, with tails on

FOR SERVING:

4 ounces uncooked angel hair pasta

RECIPE STEPS:

1. Heat 2 tablespoons of oil in a small saucepan over medium-low heat. Add unpeeled garlic cloves and cook for 15–20 minutes, until you see some light brown spots on cloves. Garlic should lightly sizzle. If it pops, turn down heat. Turn or toss garlic a few times as it cooks. When garlic is cool, slip skins off each clove and trim off any tough ends.

2. To make creamy scampi sauce: Combine butter and olive oil in a large sauté pan over medium-low heat. When butter is melted, add shallot and cook for 2 minutes. Add wine and chicken broth and simmer for 5 more minutes, then add cream, lemon juice, basil, tomato, parsley, crushed red pepper, and peeled roasted garlic cloves. Bring sauce back to a simmer and cook for 6–8 minutes until it's thicker, then turn off heat.

3. To make shrimp: Heat at least 2" of oil in a Dutch oven, large saucepan, or deep fryer to 350°F.

4. Combine flour, salt, pepper, and garlic powder in a medium bowl. Whisk in cold water.

5. Holding a shrimp by tip of tail, submerge it in batter, let a little batter drip off, then slip it into oil. Cook shrimp, 3–6 at a time, for 5–6 minutes until golden brown, then transfer shrimp to a rack or paper towel–lined plate.

6. Make pasta by bringing 4 quarts of lightly salted water to a boil in a large pot. Add angel hair pasta and cook for 5 minutes until done, then strain.

7. Build each plate by arranging a pile of angel hair pasta on center of plate. Spoon half of scampi sauce around pasta on each plate, then arrange six shrimp in a spoke-like fashion around pasta. Stand shrimp on their sides so that crispy coating doesn't get soggy in sauce.

FIELD NOTES

Although this dish calls for shelled shrimp, some dishes leave the shells on—usually when the shrimp are fried or grilled. Shrimp shells are perfectly safe to eat, but they cannot be digested.

THE CHEESECAKE FACTORY

Spicy Cashew Chicken

 PREP TIME:
Active: 35 minutes
Inactive: 25 minutes

 DIFFICULTY:
Medium

 SERVES:
2

This popular chain wrangles a wide variety of dishes and cooking styles day after day with consistently high quality. From pasta to burgers and tacos, and from salads to pancakes and cheesecakes, there is something for everyone at The Cheesecake Factory.

The diverse menu's Asia-inspired plates include Thai, Korean, and Chinese dishes, but one that consistently stands out is this Mandarin-style spicy chicken entrée, served over your choice of white or brown rice.

The secret of the great flavor is the sauce, which I've hacked for you here. I'll also walk you through the easy process of creating perfect crispy chicken from scratch using juicy chicken tenderloins.

 If you don't feel like breading and frying chicken, you can cook pre-breaded frozen chicken strips and slice them into bite-sized pieces before combining them with the sauce. This way, you can save some time and focus most of your efforts on making the flavorful sauce.

FOR MANDARIN SAUCE:

- 2 teaspoons vegetable oil or peanut oil
- 3 tablespoons minced garlic
- 2 teaspoons minced ginger
- 1/3 cup dark soy sauce (see Field Notes)
- 1/4 cup rice vinegar
- 2 teaspoons cornstarch
- 3/4 cup water
- 1 cup dark brown sugar (not packed)
- 2 tablespoons oyster sauce
- 2 tablespoons black bean sauce
- 1 tablespoon lemon juice
- 1 1/2 teaspoons crushed red pepper

FOR BREADED CHICKEN:

- 1 cup all-purpose flour
- 3/4 teaspoon salt
- 1/2 teaspoon ground black pepper
- 1 large egg, beaten
- 1 cup whole milk
- 1 pound (about 8) chicken tenderloins
- Vegetable oil, for frying
- 1 cup unsalted roasted cashews

FOR SERVING:

- 4 cups cooked white or brown rice, warmed
- 2 tablespoons chopped green onion (green part only)
- 1 teaspoon sesame seeds (white and black or just white)

RECIPE STEPS:

1. To make mandarin sauce: Heat oil in a medium saucepan over medium-low heat. Add garlic and ginger and slowly simmer (sweat) them for 2 minutes, but don't let them brown.

2. Add soy sauce and vinegar to pan, then stir cornstarch into water and add it to pan along with remaining ingredients. Bring sauce to a simmer, and continue to simmer uncovered for 4–5 minutes until slightly thicker. Remove from heat, cover, and cool until needed.

3. To make breaded chicken: Combine flour, salt, and pepper in a medium bowl. Combine beaten egg and milk in another medium bowl.

4. Bread each chicken tender by first coating it with flour, then dipping it in milk mixture. Let some of liquid drip off, then drop chicken back into dry breading and toss until well coated. Arrange breaded chicken on a plate or baking sheet to sit for 10 minutes while you heat oil.

5. Heat at least 2" of oil to 325°F in a wok, Dutch oven, large saucepan, or deep fryer. When oil is hot, fry 2–3 breaded tenderloins at a time for 5–6 minutes until light brown. Drain cooked chicken on a rack over a baking sheet or a paper towel–lined plate.

6. When ready to serve, heat up a large skillet or wok over medium-high heat.

7. While skillet or wok is heating up, cut chicken into bite-sized pieces.

8. When wok or skillet is hot, add cashews to pan and toss for 30 seconds.

9. Add chicken to pan and gently stir for 1 minute to heat chicken. Be careful not to stir too aggressively, or breading may fall off chicken.

10. Add 1–1½ cups of sauce to pan, and stir gently to coat all chicken. Cook until sauce bubbles and thickens, about 2 minutes.

11. Spoon rice onto two plates. Top with chicken and sauce. Garnish each plate with a tablespoon of chopped green onions, followed by about ½ teaspoon of sesame seeds.

FIELD NOTES

You'll want to find dark soy sauce for this recipe. It's fermented longer than regular or light soy sauce; it has a darker caramel color and a richer, less salty, and sweeter flavor. This makes it ideal for dishes that require a rich flavor profile and a darker color, such as braised meats, stews, and noodles.

THE CHEESECAKE FACTORY

Steak Diane

 PREP TIME:
Active: 25 minutes
Inactive: 1 hour

 DIFFICULTY:
Medium

 SERVES:
2

Fans of The Cheesecake Factory's Steak Diane don't seem to mind that the dish isn't a traditional interpretation of the classic recipe. The restaurant chain's version includes mushrooms and medallions of beef tenderloin, similar to the old-school version, but you won't find Dijon mustard, Worcestershire sauce, cognac, or cream—all typically associated with a traditional Steak Diane.

I first hacked the chain's Chicken Madeira many years ago, and I revisited and improved that sauce dupe for this copycat. After some fiddling, I developed a formula that uses less wine and incorporates a longer reduction to intensify the flavors.

When shopping for ingredients to make this recipe, it's okay to pick the least expensive Madeira wine on the shelf. Just know Madeira wines have different characteristics, so your final flavor may vary slightly from the restaurant version. For your tenderloins, begin with thick steaks, as you will be slicing the portions in half through the middle to make them thinner. You will need 7–8 small steak portions sliced in half to yield 14–16 medallions. Serve alongside mashed potatoes to complete the dish.

 Don't assume that a restaurant adheres to the traditional recipe. The Cheesecake Factory avoids ingredients typically found in classic steak Diane sauce, opting instead to use the same Madeira sauce that tops their popular Madeira Chicken dish. To streamline kitchen prep, restaurants often use a favored sauce on multiple dishes.

FOR SAUCE:

2 cups beef stock
1½ cups Madeira wine

FOR STEAK:

18–24 ounces beef tenderloin steaks
¼ teaspoon salt
1–2 teaspoons freshly ground black pepper
3 tablespoons unsalted butter
1 tablespoon diced shallot
2 cups sliced brown or white mushrooms
1 teaspoon minced fresh parsley

RECIPE STEPS:

1. Create a Madeira reduction by combining beef stock and wine in a medium saucepan over medium heat. When mixture begins to boil, reduce heat to a strong simmer and cook for 50–60 minutes until liquid has reduced to around 1/2 cup. Cover and set aside.

2. Slice beef tenderloin steaks into 7–8 chunks, each 2–3 ounces. Slice each portion in half through middle, making two thinner steaks from each portion.

3. Preheat a large sauté pan over medium heat. Salt tenderloin medallions on both sides, and sprinkle a generous amount of black pepper on both sides. Press black pepper into medallions so that it sticks. Cook medallions in sauté pan to your desired doneness, 2–4 minutes per side, then transfer to a plate.

4. Melt butter in same sauté pan, then add shallot and mushrooms. Cook for 2 minutes until mushrooms begin to brown, then pour in Madeira sauce. Cook for 2 more minutes until sauce is bubbling, then add medallions to sauce to reheat them. Flip medallions after 1 minute, cook them on other side for 1 minute, then use tongs to transfer steak to two serving plates.

5. Spoon sauce and mushrooms over top of medallions, and sprinkle dish with parsley before serving.

FIELD NOTES

Steak Diane, named after Diana, the Roman goddess of the hunt, was likely first served in London in the 1930s.

CHICK-FIL-A

Banana Pudding Milkshake

 PREP TIME:
Active: 8 minutes
Inactive: 1 hour

 DIFFICULTY:
Easy

 SERVES:
1

The limited-time-only Banana Pudding Milkshake debuted at Chick-fil-A in 2011 to rave reviews, and then it disappeared for 13 years. In 2024, the chicken chain brought back the specialty milkshake, but once again it was just for a short time, and fans don't know what'll happen with it next. Fortunately, this easy hack can be used any time to make a fantastic clone that looks and tastes just like the real thing, right down to the cherry on top.

For my clone, I wanted to include as much real banana as I could, then add just enough banana pudding mix to round out the flavor. And once ice cream was mixed in, the cornstarch in the pudding became undetectable.

I also discovered a preparation trick that produced a thicker finished product: Place the banana, the blender container, and the serving glass in your refrigerator for about an hour before making the shake. When everything is chilled, the ice cream stays thick while blended. If your shake is too thick and you're having trouble blending it, use the pulse function on your blender to chop up the ice cream. Also, help it out by stirring the shake with a spoon between pulses.

For some of your clones, natural and artificial flavoring and colors may be necessary to supplement whole ingredients to enhance the appearance and taste of the finished product. Just because Chick-fil-A claims this seasonal milkshake is made with real bananas doesn't mean there isn't also some banana flavoring added to enhance the taste. If you were to make this shake with only real bananas, you would need an excessive amount to create the same intense flavor as the real thing. All that banana would affect the consistency and color of the shake, and the flavor would be off.

FOR MILKSHAKE:

1 medium ripe banana
½ cup milk
2 teaspoons banana pudding mix
2 teaspoons granulated sugar
2 cups vanilla ice cream (light ice cream is best)
6 Nilla Wafers cookies

FOR GARNISH:

Canned whipped cream
1 maraschino cherry

RECIPE STEPS:

1. One hour before making shake, place a medium banana (unpeeled), blender container, and 16-ounce glass in refrigerator.

2. When ready to make shake, peel banana and lightly mash it in a medium bowl. A large fork or potato masher works well for this.

3. Add banana, milk, pudding mix, and sugar to blender, and blend on medium speed for 15 seconds to purée banana and dissolve sugar.

4. Add ice cream and blend or pulse just until shake is smooth.

5. Make Nilla Wafers crumbs by placing 6 Nilla Wafers in a zip-top bag and smashing cookies to crumbs with a kitchen mallet or a rolling pin. Remove fine particles and dust by shaking crumbs in a wire mesh strainer. Discard dust and add 3 tablespoons of crumbs to shake.

6. Stir cookie crumbs into shake with a large mixing spoon.

7. Pour shake into chilled 16-ounce glass.

8. Top shake with whipped cream and place a cherry on top. Add a straw and serve.

FIELD NOTES

The window for ripe bananas is short: Bananas are climacteric fruits, which means they will continue to ripen after they're picked. The secret to slowing down that process? Wrap the stems of the bananas with plastic wrap.

Spicy Deluxe Chicken Sandwich

Spicy Deluxe Chicken Sandwich

 PREP TIME:
Active: 35 minutes
Inactive: 4 hours plus 20 minutes

 DIFFICULTY:
Medium

 SERVES:
6

This chain's not-spicy original chicken sandwich, which debuted in 1964, put Chick-fil-A on the map. By diversifying the menu with new products like this kicked-up version of the famous sandwich, the chain grew over the years to become the #1 chicken restaurant in the nation.

One secret to cloning this sandwich lies in the breading for the chicken: The MSG works as a wonderful flavor enhancer. My slicing trick here will make three sandwich-size cutlets from each chicken breast, which are then marinated for 4 hours in a brine before being coated in the breading. It's worth the wait. Your patience will be rewarded with the best Chick-fil-A chicken sandwich dupe—right from your own kitchen!

 Getting all the information you need for the best clone can take some time. I published my original Chick-fil-A chicken sandwich recipe in my first book, *Top Secret Recipes*, in 1993. Despite rumors that pickle juice was used in the brine for the chicken fillet, I didn't include the ingredient in the recipe because I couldn't confirm this rumor. Twenty-eight years later, in 2021, I learned that pickle juice is indeed in the brine, and I've created this updated recipe to reflect that discovery. A mixture of salt and vinegar seasoned with dill pickle juice tenderizes the chicken and helps keep it moist.

FOR BRINE:

2 cups water
2 tablespoons dill pickle juice
1 tablespoon plus 1 teaspoon kosher salt
2 teaspoons granulated sugar
1½ teaspoons MSG (monosodium glutamate)
¼ teaspoon onion powder
¼ teaspoon garlic powder
¼ teaspoon ground white pepper
2 (9-ounce) skinless chicken breast fillets

FOR BREADING:

2 cups (10 ounces) all-purpose flour
3 tablespoons ground cayenne pepper
1 tablespoon powdered sugar
2½ teaspoons salt
2½ teaspoons coarse ground black pepper
2 teaspoons MSG
2 teaspoons baking powder
1 teaspoon paprika
1 teaspoon ground white pepper
½ teaspoon garlic powder
½ teaspoon onion powder
1 large egg, beaten
1 cup whole milk
Peanut oil, for frying

FOR SANDWICHES:

6 tablespoons salted butter, softened
6 plain hamburger buns
18–24 dill pickle slices (hamburger dills)
6 leaves green leaf lettuce
2–3 ripe medium tomatoes, sliced
6 slices pepper jack cheese

RECIPE STEPS:

1. To make brine: Combine all ingredients except chicken in a large bowl or storage container. Stir or whisk until salt and sugar have dissolved.

2. Slice each chicken breast into three equal portions: slice chicken breast in half down through fillet, separating tapered half from thicker half of breast, then turn knife on its side and slice through middle of thicker half of breast, creating two thinner pieces. Cover all chicken pieces with plastic wrap and pound on them with a kitchen mallet until they are between 1/4" and 1/2" thick. Add fillets to brine and let chicken marinate for 4 hours in refrigerator. After 4 hours, rinse fillets under cold water and blot chicken dry.

3. To make breading: Whisk dry breading ingredients together in a large bowl, then combine milk with beaten egg in another large bowl.

4. Working with one piece at a time, dip each fillet in dry mixture and shake off any excess. Dip it in milk/egg and let excess drip off for a couple of seconds, then get it back in dry blend. Toss fillet around in breading for several seconds, then shake it off and get it back into wet stuff. Let excess milk/egg drip off, then give chicken one more coating of breading. Toss fillet around for several more seconds in dry mixture to help build up a nice coating, then let chicken rest for 20 minutes before frying.

5. While chicken rests, preheat at least 2" of oil in a deep fryer, Dutch oven, or large saucepan to 325°F.

6. Fry chicken in small batches for 5–7 minutes until lightly browned, then drain on a rack over a baking sheet or a paper towel–lined plate.

7. While chicken is cooking, spread butter on faces of all buns and toast them in a sauté pan or skillet over medium heat until golden brown.

8. Build each sandwich by placing 3–4 pickle slices on bottom bun, followed by 1 leaf of lettuce and 2 tomato slices. Stack 1 chicken breast on tomatoes, place 1 slice of pepper jack on chicken, then finish off sandwich with top bun. Repeat for remaining sandwiches.

🔎 FIELD NOTES

Because all Chick-fil-A restaurants are closed on Sundays, when *Top Chef* finalist Kevin Gillespie created his hacked version of the chain's signature chicken sandwich for his Gamechanger restaurant in the Mercedes-Benz Stadium in Atlanta, Georgia, he called it the Closed on Sunday chicken sandwich.

Spicy Southwest Salad

 PREP TIME:
Active: 45 minutes
Inactive: 3 hours 15 minutes

 DIFFICULTY:
Medium

 SERVES:
4

If you didn't know this salad came from Chick-fil-A, you could easily be fooled into thinking it was a much more expensive salad from a full-service restaurant. The bed of greens is made with crisp romaine, green leaf, and red leaf lettuce. On top of the lettuce are ingredients you wouldn't typically associate with fast food, such as grilled corn, black beans, roasted peppers, spicy chili lime pepitas, and crunchy tortilla chips. Everything works wonderfully together, and now you can duplicate every bite of it for a perfect home hack.

As with the Chick-fil-A Spicy Deluxe Chicken Sandwich, the chicken for this recipe is easily cloned by marinating chicken fillets in a special spicy brine for a few hours to infuse them with flavor and juiciness. But the star of the salad is the secret recipe that kitchen cloners request the most: the creamy salsa dressing. To create your own version, you'll roast some peppers and combine them with the other ingredients in a blender. When the dressing is smooth, you'll have a bright, spicy salad topper that perfectly replicates the one served on the real Chick-fil-A Spicy Southwest Salad.

 Because a salad is a pile of various ingredients, it isn't easy to accurately gauge the proportions of the components that make it up. The best way to replicate a recipe like this Spicy Southwest Salad is to take the time to separate all ingredients and then measure each one. Put on some good music, then use your fingers—and kitchen tweezers, if you have them—to separate every ingredient into small bowls. It will take some time, but once you're finished, you will have eliminated the guesswork about how much of each ingredient you need for your salad clone.

FOR SPICY GRILLED CHICKEN BREAST:

2 cups water

1 tablespoon salt

2 teaspoons MSG (monosodium glutamate)

2 teaspoons ground chipotle pepper, plus more for sprinkling

1 pound chicken breast fillets (1–2 breasts)

Vegetable oil

1 medium ear of corn

FOR CREAMY SALSA DRESSING:

1 poblano pepper

1 medium red bell pepper

2–3 jalapeños

1 cup mayonnaise

1 tablespoon peeled and minced white or yellow onion

1½ teaspoons white wine vinegar

1 teaspoon lime juice

1 teaspoon ketchup

½ teaspoon ground cumin

¼ teaspoon granulated sugar

¼ teaspoon salt

¼ teaspoon paprika

⅛ teaspoon garlic powder

½ teaspoon minced fresh cilantro

FOR CHILI LIME PEPITAS:

½ teaspoon ground chipotle pepper

¼ teaspoon onion powder

¼ teaspoon garlic powder

¼ teaspoon paprika

¼ teaspoon salt

1 teaspoon lime juice

½ cup roasted pepitas

FOR SALAD:

10 cups chopped romaine lettuce

10 cups chopped green leaf lettuce

4 cups chopped red leaf lettuce

½ cup drained, rinsed canned black beans

1 cup Cheddar/Monterey jack shredded cheese blend

16 grape tomatoes

1 cup fried tortilla strips or crumbled tortilla chips

RECIPE STEPS:

1. To make spicy grilled chicken breast: Combine water, salt, MSG, and chipotle in a container with a lid or a plastic bag. Slice chicken breast(s) through middle to make thinner fillets. Add chicken to brine and let it marinate in refrigerator for 3 hours.

2. When chicken is just about done marinating, preheat grill to high. Blot chicken on paper towels and rub each fillet with some vegetable oil. Rub a little vegetable oil on corn. Cook chicken for 4–6 minutes on each side until done or until temperature in center registers 165°F. Place corn on hot grill with chicken. Turn corn as it cooks so that it doesn't burn. When corn is blackened in spots on all sides, 5–6 minutes, remove it from grill.

3. Let chicken cool for 5 minutes, then sprinkle top with a little more ground chipotle, and refrigerate until cold. Use a sharp knife to thinly slice cold chicken.

4. When corn is cool enough to handle, use a sharp knife to cut corn from cob. Cool corn in your refrigerator for at least 20 minutes, or until cold.

5. To make creamy salsa dressing: Preheat oven to 450°F. Grease a baking sheet with oil.

6. Roast poblano, red bell pepper, and jalapeños on baking sheet 20–30 minutes, turning twice while baking, until skins are wrinkled and charred. (If you have a gas stove you can roast peppers faster by setting them directly over a high flame, turning often until they are completely blackened. Pierce each jalapeño with a skewer to hold them over flame without burning your fingers.)

7. Drop blackened peppers into a covered container for 2 minutes after charring. and skin should easily wash off in cold water. Remove stems and seeds, and dice.

8. Add mayonnaise to a blender. Add 1 teaspoon of diced roasted poblano, 1 teaspoon of diced roasted red pepper, and 1 tablespoon plus 1 teaspoon of diced roasted jalapeño and remaining dressing ingredients to blender and blend on medium speed until peppers and onions are reduced to small bits. Pour dressing into a covered container and chill it until ready to serve salad.

9. To make chili lime pepitas: Preheat oven to 325°F.

10. Combine chipotle pepper, onion powder, garlic powder, paprika, and salt in a small bowl. Pour lime juice into another small bowl, then add pepitas. Stir pepitas in lime juice until they are all moistened, then sprinkle seeds with spice blend.

11. Spread seeds out on an ungreased baking sheet and bake 5 minutes until seeds begin to darken. Set aside.

12. To make salad: Combine chopped lettuce in a large bowl and divide into four serving bowls. Sprinkle 2 tablespoons of black beans on each salad, followed by 2 tablespoons of grilled corn and 1 tablespoon each of diced poblano and diced red bell pepper. Sprinkle 1/4 cup of cheese blend on each salad, followed by 4 grape tomatoes.

13. Place 1/4 of sliced chicken on each salad, then sprinkle each salad with 2 tablespoons of spicy pepitas and top it off with about 1/4 cup of tortilla chips or strips. Serve 3–4 tablespoons of dressing on side for each salad.

 **FIELD NOTES**

You can save on ingredients and chopping time by replacing the romaine, green leaf, and red leaf lettuces with 24 cups (16 ounces) of spring mix.

CHICK-FIL-A

Zesty Apple Cider Vinaigrette Dressing

 PREP TIME:
Active: 15 minutes
Inactive: 34 minutes

DIFFICULTY:
Easy

 MAKES:
1 1/3 cups

The country's largest chicken chain offers some of the best salad dressing options you'll find at any fast-food restaurant. However, you may not have much luck getting a few extra packets for your home salads: Employees are under strict orders to be stingy. Fortunately, you can enjoy this handy hack whenever the craving hits. And rather than corn syrup, which is found in the original recipe, I'm using white sugar to make our copycat taste better.

 One big secret you'll find here is xanthan gum, a natural thickener often used as an emulsifier to prevent salad dressing from separating. You can find xanthan online or at some health food stores, and you won't need much for this recipe.

1/2 cup apple cider vinegar, divided
1/4 cup pineapple juice
1/4 cup granulated sugar
2 tablespoons honey
1/2 teaspoon salt
1/4 teaspoon coarse ground black pepper
1/8 teaspoon dried basil
1/8 teaspoon garlic powder
1/8 teaspoon onion powder
1/8 teaspoon ground cayenne pepper
2 teaspoons lemon juice
1 teaspoon lime juice
1/2 teaspoon xanthan gum
1/3 cup vegetable oil

RECIPE STEPS:

1. Combine 1/4 cup apple cider vinegar, pineapple juice, sugar, honey, salt, pepper, basil, garlic powder, onion powder, and cayenne pepper in a saucepan over medium-low heat.

2. Cook just until it becomes hot and fragrant, stirring often to help sugar dissolve, about 4 minutes.

3. Remove pan from heat, then stir in remaining 1/4 cup apple cider vinegar, along with lemon juice and lime juice. Use a whisk or electric mixer to mix in xanthan gum.

4. Add oil and use mixer to blend until well-combined, then cover and chill for 30 minutes until thick. The dressing will keep in a sealed container in your refrigerator for up to 3 weeks.

 **FIELD NOTES**

Chick-fil-A dressings are in sealed portion packs with the ingredients listed on the label. This helps when creating home clones.

Carne Asada

 PREP TIME:
Active: 20 minutes
Inactive: Up to 2 days to marinate

 DIFFICULTY:
Easy

 SERVES:
4

Chipotle's popular limited offering is a good example of how straightforward and flavorful carne asada can be. It's not overly mysterious, since Chipotle is transparent about the ingredients used for the restaurant's entire menu—fifty-three ingredients in all—but identifying which of those is used here was only the beginning of the process. There was still plenty of sleuthing to do in establishing ratios and settling on an ideal preparation method.

Carne asada is almost always made with flank steak or skirt steak. Flank steak has a better flavor than skirt steak, so it is recommended here. Just be sure not to marinate it for more than 2 days, or the acid in the marinade may toughen your steak.

After you grill it, slice the meat across the grain and use it in burritos, tacos, or bowls, or as a Southwest-style salad topper.

It's always a good idea to ask servers for information about a recipe you're hacking, and they'll usually be quite helpful. But take the information you get from them with a grain of salt. In my experience, not everything they tell you will be correct. At Chipotle, I was told by a server that their carne asada is made with skirt steak. That could be true, but it's more likely they would use flank steak, which is cheaper than skirt steak and is more tender. I tried using skirt steak in my hack but found that flank steak worked much better.

- ½ cup vegetable oil
- 3 tablespoons lime juice
- 2 tablespoons water
- 1 tablespoon minced garlic
- 1 tablespoon plus 1 teaspoon ground coriander
- 2 teaspoons ground cumin
- 2 teaspoons ground black pepper
- 1 teaspoon salt
- 1 teaspoon ground chipotle pepper
- 1 teaspoon dried oregano
- 1 teaspoon dried thyme
- 2 bay leaves
- ½ cup coarsely chopped fresh cilantro
- 1–1½ pound(s) flank steak

RECIPE STEPS:

1. Add all ingredients, except bay leaves, cilantro, and steak, to a medium bowl and whisk well. Stir in bay leaves and cilantro.
2. Pour marinade over steak in a large, resealable plastic bag and refrigerate up to 2 days. Massage meat around in bag a couple of times as it sits to be sure it marinates evenly.
3. When you are ready to cook carne asada, preheat grill to high.
4. Use tongs to place steak on hot grill and cook it for 4–6 minutes per side, or until medium. Remove from grill and let rest for 5 minutes.
5. Slice steak against the grain to serve.

FIELD NOTES

"Carne asada" is a Spanish term that translates to "roasted or grilled meat" in English. The description refers to how the beef is cooked rather than a specific recipe, and the term is versatile. "Carne asada" also describes a social gathering with friends and family where barbecued food is served. Example: "Quick, let's get over to the carne asada before they run out of carne asada!"

Carne Asada

Chicken al Pastor

 PREP TIME:
Active: 30 minutes
Inactive: 4 hours 40 minutes

 DIFFICULTY:
Medium

 SERVES:
3–4

A dish traditionally made with pork was redesigned for chicken in Chipotle's limited-time-only sweet-and-spicy variation. All the key ingredients for good al pastor are here: pineapple, lime, achiote, and chipotle morita peppers—together they make a delicious, bright orange sauce for basting marinated chicken thighs.

The TV commercial for Chipotle's new offering claims the morita peppers are seared and shows wild flames dancing around a pan filled with fresh green and red peppers. That is perhaps not an accurate depiction of the preparation process, considering that morita peppers are made by smoking red jalapeños, not green ones. And smoked jalapeños do not look like fresh jalapeños.

Regardless of how they are or are not prepared in the media, you'll want to find dry morita peppers, then remove the seeds and toast the peppers in your oven before making the secret sauce. Baste the sauce on your chicken just before it's done cooking, then chop the chicken and use it to make delicious tacos, burritos, salads, and bowls.

 Chipotle uses only skinless thigh fillets for its grilled chicken, because they are moister and more flavorful than chicken breasts. Make sure to follow the chain's lead for results at home that mimic the famous restaurant version.

FOR ADOBO MARINADE:

½ cup canned chipotles in adobo sauce
2 cups water
2 tablespoons vegetable oil
2 teaspoons minced garlic
2 teaspoons salt
1 teaspoon ground cumin
½ teaspoon ground black pepper
½ teaspoon dried oregano
1½ pounds skinless chicken thigh fillets

FOR MORITA PEPPER PURÉE:

1 ounce dried morita chipotle peppers, seeds removed
2 cups boiling water

FOR AL PASTOR SAUCE:

1 tablespoon vegetable oil
1 teaspoon minced garlic
2/3 cup pineapple juice
1/3 cup morita pepper purée
2 teaspoons lime juice
1 teaspoon ground achiote (annatto)
1/2 teaspoon salt
1/4 teaspoon onion powder
1/4 teaspoon ground cumin
1/8 teaspoon ground black pepper
1 tablespoon minced fresh cilantro

RECIPE STEPS:

1. To make adobo marinade: Add all ingredients except chicken to a blender, and blend on high speed for 30 seconds until all ingredients are puréed.

2. Combine marinade with chicken in a resealable bag or container with a lid and refrigerate 4–5 hours.

3. To make morita pepper purée: Preheat oven to 350°F. Place moritas on an ungreased baking sheet and roast 3–4 minutes until fragrant.

4. Combine roasted morita peppers with boiling water in a medium bowl. Steep for at least 30 minutes, then combine peppers with 3/4 cup of steeping liquid in a blender. Purée on high speed for 30–60 seconds until no bits of pepper are visible. Add additional water, 1 tablespoon at a time, if purée gets too thick and won't blend well.

5. To make al pastor sauce: Heat oil in a small saucepan over medium heat. Add garlic and sauté it for 1 minute, then add pineapple juice, 1/3 cup of morita purée, and remaining ingredients besides cilantro to pan. When sauce begins to simmer, cook it for 3 minutes, then remove it from heat and cover until needed.

6. When chicken has marinated, remove it from marinade and cook it on a preheated flat grill, skillet, or barbecue grill for 5–6 minutes per side until almost done. Just before taking chicken off heat, baste both sides of each piece of chicken with al pastor sauce, and finish cooking chicken until the internal temperature reaches 165°.

7. Remove chicken to a cutting board to cool for 1 minute, then dice into bite-sized pieces. Toss with cilantro in a large bowl and serve.

FIELD NOTES

Traditional al pastor–style cooking uses a vertical rotisserie that slow-roasts the meat while basting it in its own juices. This shawarma cooking technique was brought to Mexico by Lebanese immigrants in the early 1900s, and it is similar to the meat preparation for Greek gyro sandwiches.

Guacamole

 PREP TIME:
Active: 10 minutes
Inactive: None

 DIFFICULTY:
Easy

 **MAKES:**
1½ cups

In April 2020, restaurant chains in the US closed their dining rooms due to the COVID-19 pandemic but needed to stay connected with customers. Chipotle's solution was to have corporate chef Chad Brauze "reveal" the chain's secret recipe for the guacamole on the corporate Instagram account. Chains have shared versions of secret recipes on news shows in the past, but few of those formulas are the actual restaurant versions. Often, one or more ingredients are eliminated or substituted so that your final product is close but not exact. And that's precisely what Chipotle did. Chef Chad's Instagram video shares a good guacamole recipe, but it's not Chipotle's guacamole recipe. The formula includes most of the ingredients you would need for a perfect hack, but it's missing one: lemon juice. According to Chipotle's website and cooks at the restaurant, Chipotle adds lemon juice in addition to lime juice to its famous guacamole.

With this information, I have tweaked Chef Chad's formula to make this copycat more like the real one. Keep in mind that even with the additional acid (lemon juice) in the mix to preserve the color, this guacamole is best if eaten within several hours of making it.

 Some chains are open about their ingredients, and Chipotle is one of them, which makes hacking the chain's food much more straightforward. It's easy to find the ingredients in Chipotle's food on their website, and it was because of that access that I found an ingredient for the guacamole that I wouldn't have likely tried: lemon juice. Always check for ingredient information on the company website, and you might be surprised at what you find there.

2 large Hass avocados, peeled and pitted
1½ teaspoons lime juice
1 teaspoon lemon juice
½ teaspoon kosher salt
3 tablespoons peeled and diced red onion
2 tablespoons chopped fresh cilantro
1 tablespoon minced jalapeño, seeded

RECIPE STEPS:

1. Add avocados, lime juice, lemon juice, and salt to a medium bowl.

2. Use a potato masher or large fork to mash avocado until just a few small chunks remain for texture.

3. Stir in onion, cilantro, and jalapeño, and serve immediately or press plastic wrap down onto surface and chill up to 8 hours.

 **FIELD NOTES**

Chipotle uses 97,000 pounds of avocados daily, making the chain one of the largest restaurant purchasers of avocados.

Smoked Brisket

 PREP TIME:
Active: 35 minutes
Inactive: 13 hours

 DIFFICULTY:
Medium

 SERVES:
8

In 2021, for a limited time, Chipotle added smoked and sauced brisket to its line of signature meats. The tender brisket is seasoned with a blend of peppers, garlic, cumin, and coriander, then seared and tossed with a smoky barbecue sauce fused with traditional Mexican flavors. It's a significant departure from the chain's signature south-of-the-border protein offerings, and when the dish came back to the menu in 2024, it was a food hacking challenge I could not refuse.

For my copycat hack, I used the flatter end of the brisket, as does the chain, and trimmed away the fat so the seasoning blend came in direct contact with the meat. I let the seasoning sit on the meat for at least 4 hours, then I smoked it and mopped it a couple of times with a vinegar blend to help keep it moist and to wake up the flavor.

Because the process takes 12–14 hours, I find it best to refrigerate the smoked brisket until the next day, when it can be prepped for serving. When everyone's hungry and you're ready to serve the brisket, chop it, sear it, season it, and sauce it with the barbecue sauce in this recipe.

 If you don't have a smoker, you can smoke the brisket using a gas or charcoal grill. Soak several hickory, oak, pecan, or alder wood chips or chunks in water for about an hour and place them in an aluminum foil pan over low direct heat on your grill until the wood begins to smoke. Place the brisket on the grate away from direct heat and cover the grill. Use a thermometer to monitor the temperature inside the grill, and keep it as close to 250°F as possible. If the wood begins to burn, add water to the pan so that the wood continues to smoke.

FOR RUB:

2 tablespoons salt
1 tablespoon plus 1 teaspoon paprika
1 tablespoon onion powder
1 tablespoon garlic powder
1 tablespoon ground black pepper
1½ teaspoons ground chipotle pepper
1½ teaspoons ground cumin
1 teaspoon coriander
1 (4–5 pound) brisket (flat end), fat trimmed

FOR MOP SAUCE:

½ cup apple cider vinegar
2 tablespoons water
1 tablespoon dark brown sugar, packed
1 tablespoon extra-virgin olive oil
1 tablespoon soy sauce
2 teaspoons prepared rub

FOR BARBECUE SAUCE:

½ ounce dried ancho chilies, seeded and de-stemmed
1 large jalapeño or 2 serrano peppers
2 cups boiling water
1⅓ cups ketchup
½ cup dark brown sugar, packed
½ cup peeled and diced white or yellow onion
1 tablespoon plus 1 teaspoon diced canned chipotle pepper
1 tablespoon apple cider vinegar
2 teaspoons minced garlic
1 teaspoon salt
1 teaspoon ground cumin
1 teaspoon liquid hickory smoke

RECIPE STEPS:

1. To make rub: Combine all ingredients minus brisket in a small bowl, then sprinkle a heavy coating on both sides of brisket. Make sure to reserve several teaspoons of rub for use in the mop sauce and for serving. Cover brisket with plastic wrap and chill for at least 4 hours or overnight.

2. Preheat smoker to 250°F. Place brisket in an aluminum foil pan. Add a thermometer to meat and use hickory wood chips or pellets for smoke. You can also use oak, pecan, or alder wood. If possible, add a water bath to your smoker.

3. Smoke brisket until it's 165°F in thickest part, 4–6 hours depending on thickness of brisket.

4. To make mop sauce: While your brisket smokes, combine all mop sauce ingredients in a small bowl.

5. After first 2½ hours of smoking, when brisket has developed a crust, mop it with vinegar blend. Dab to apply liquid. Don't wipe it on or you may remove seasoning from surface of meat. Continue smoking, and after one more hour, apply mop sauce again.

6. When brisket reaches 165°F, cover pan with foil and continue smoking until meat hits 200°F, 3–4 hours.

7. Remove brisket from smoker, wrap it in foil, and place it in a resealable plastic bag. Wrap bag with a heavy towel and let brisket rest in a closed cooler for 2 hours. After it rests, brisket can be prepared for serving immediately, or it can be cooled and chilled to serve the next day.

8. To make barbecue sauce: Preheat oven to 350°F. Place ancho chili on an ungreased baking sheet and roast for 2 minutes until fragrant.

9. Roast jalapeño or serrano peppers by piercing it/them with a skewer and holding/them over a high gas flame until skin blisters, or roasting in oven with ancho pepper. After removing ancho, continue roasting jalapeño in oven for 20 minutes until softened.

10. Place roasted ancho in a medium bowl and pour hot water over it. Add another bowl on top to keep pepper submerged. Soak for 30 minutes.

11. Remove charred skin, stems, and seeds from jalapeño/serrano peppers. Roughly chop roasted peppers. Add ancho and jalapeño/serrano peppers plus 1 cup of soaking liquid to a blender. Blend on high speed for 1 minute until no pepper chunks are visible.

12. Combine puréed pepper with other sauce ingredients in a small saucepan over medium heat. When sauce comes to a boil, reduce heat and simmer for 10 minutes. Remove from heat and cool uncovered for 5 minutes.

13. Pour sauce into a blender and blend on high speed for 30 seconds until smooth and no chunks of anything are visible.

14. Pour sauce back into saucepan over medium heat. When sauce begins to boil, reduce heat and simmer for 10 minutes, then cover and remove from heat until needed.

15. To serve brisket, preheat a large skillet to medium heat. Slice brisket into $1/2$"-thick slices against grain, then chop slices into bite-sized pieces.

16. Transfer brisket to hot skillet and season it with reserved rub. Cook brisket in preheated skillet for 2–3 minutes until seared. Toss brisket as it heats for even browning.

17. Transfer brisket to a bowl and toss it with barbecue sauce. Serve.

FIELD NOTES

Before refrigeration, smoking was used to preserve a variety of meats. Smoking dries meat out, and natural preservatives in woodsmoke help prevent spoilage.

 **CHIPOTLE**

Tomatillo-Red Chili Salsa

 PREP TIME:
Active: 15 minutes
Inactive: 6 minutes

 DIFFICULTY:
Easy

 MAKES:
1 cup

This is my go-to salsa at Chipotle, so it was only a matter of time before I tackled a copycat home hack of the famous secret recipe. And now you can make it at home with just seven ingredients and about 20 minutes of prep. It may just replace store-bought brands in your kitchen.

The process for this Chipotle Tomatillo-Red Chili Salsa copycat recipe is simple: roast tomatillos, red Fresno peppers, and garlic under your broiler for a few minutes, then purée everything in a blender with vinegar and seasoning. Add this great-tasting salsa to anything that needs a hit of heat—tacos, burritos, salads, bowls, and more. It's a hack of Chipotle's spiciest salsa, so be ready for the heat.

 **When making a blended sauce like this one, noting the visible bits in the original recipe will indicate how long you need to blend it. Can you see big or small chunks in the sauce? Are there visible seeds if using fruit, or leaf fragments if using fresh herbs? For this sauce, the tomatillo seeds in the original are visible and whole, so if you blend until the seeds are puréed, you've blended too long.**

8 ounces small tomatillos
4 ounces red Fresno peppers
⅓ cup water
3 cloves garlic, unpeeled
1 teaspoon white wine vinegar
½ teaspoon ground cumin
½ teaspoon salt

RECIPE STEPS:

1. Preheat oven to high broil.

2. Remove husks from tomatillos, then place them on an ungreased baking sheet with unpeeled garlic and peppers. Broil on top rack for 3 minutes, flip everything over, and broil for 3 more minutes until blackened in spots but not charred.

3. Slice stem end from each pepper and cut through one side so that you can open it up. Use edge of a knife to scrape off seeds and membranes, then roughly chop peppers. Add chopped pepper along with ⅓ cup of water to a blender. Blend on medium speed for 20 seconds until most of pepper is puréed and only small chunks about the size of rice grains are visible.

4. Peel roasted garlic cloves, then add them to blender or food processor along with tomatillos, vinegar, cumin, and salt. Pulse to chop until tomatillos are puréed, but don't overblend. You want to see tomatillo seeds in the mix. (This recipe yields just a cup of sauce, so if using a food processor, you may need to double the recipe to increase total volume, depending on size of the food processor.) Cover and refrigerate until ready to use. Will keep for up to 1 week.

FIELD NOTES

Chipotle is a great place to observe the cooking in the visible kitchen behind the counter. But the line needs to keep moving, so you can't just stand and stare. If you want to see a good amount of kitchen activity, visit during the peak of the lunch rush, around 12:15 p.m., when there will be a long line, giving you plenty of time to watch the cooks.

Fried Chicken

CHURCH'S TEXAS CHICKEN

Fried Chicken

 PREP TIME:
Active: 20 minutes
Inactive: 12 hours 50 minutes

 DIFFICULTY:
Medium

 SERVES:
4

On the list of inspirational American food success stories is the small fried chicken restaurant founded by George W. Church Sr., that opened across the street from the Alamo in San Antonio, Texas, in 1952. In the years since, Church's Texas Chicken has exploded into a huge chicken chain with over 1,500 restaurants in 23 countries.

George's special homestyle fried chicken formula was his secret recipe for success, and it seems that nobody has truly hacked it. Until now. The ingredient list for this crispy chicken is shorter than what you might find in "The Colonel's" kitchen. Much of the flavor in this chicken recipe develops during the brining process, which also has the added benefit of keeping the chicken moist and juicy inside. I discovered that Church's marinates their chicken for 12 hours, so I've worked backward and designed a brine that does its job in exactly half a day.

You'll need to plan ahead for this recipe to give your chicken time to marinate. But your patience will be rewarded with the down-home taste of delicious Southern-style fried chicken. And here's some more good news: This hack includes two recipes! I've created a Church's copycat recipe for the original fried chicken, as well as instructions for duplicating the spicy version if you feel like turning up the heat.

 For decades, monosodium glutamate (MSG) had a bad reputation, which was fueled by a letter published in *The New England Journal of Medicine* in 1968 outlining symptoms that have since been debunked. But this flavor enhancer, a natural amino acid with salt attached, is a crucial ingredient in many dishes, and it's hard to make a good copy of many foods without it. Today, after being used in food around the world for over 100 years, it's generally agreed that the ingredient is safe to eat. You will need to use it to re-create the savory umami taste of this famous fried chicken, and many other favorites.

FOR BRINE:

¼ cup plus 2 teaspoons kosher salt
2½ teaspoons MSG (monosodium glutamate)
6 cups water
4 whole chicken thighs
4 chicken drumsticks
Vegetable oil, for frying

FOR ORIGINAL BREADING:

2 cups (10 ounces) all-purpose flour
2 teaspoons baking powder
1¼ teaspoons MSG
1 teaspoon salt
1 teaspoon white pepper
½ teaspoon onion powder
¼ teaspoon garlic powder
2 cups whole milk

RECIPE STEPS:

1. To make brine: Dissolve salt and MSG in water. Add chicken and let it marinate for 12 hours in refrigerator. Remove chicken from brine after 12 hours and rinse it off.

2. Preheat at least 3" of oil in a large saucepan, Dutch oven, or deep fryer. to 275°F. While oil is preheating, remove chicken from refrigerator and let sit.

3. To make original breading: Combine dry ingredients in a medium bowl. Pour milk into another medium bowl.

4. Blot chicken dry, then, working one piece at a time, dip chicken into breading, then knock off excess and dip it into milk. Let excess milk drip off for a moment, then put chicken back into breading. Toss chicken in breading several times, then shake off excess flour and dip it back into milk. Let excess milk drip off again and get chicken back into breading one more time. Toss chicken around thoroughly in breading so that a well-rippled coating of flour forms on chicken. Press down on chicken with your fingers as you toss it to help build up flour on skin of chicken so that large, crispy crumbs will form when it's fried. Allow chicken to rest for 10–15 minutes before cooking to help breading stick.

5. Preheat oven to 250°F and place a sheet pan with a rack on top in oven.

6. Cook a few pieces of chicken at a time in oil for 16–20 minutes until crispy and golden brown. Turn pieces in oil as they cook for even browning. When done, transfer cooked chicken from oil to sheet pan to stay warm. Serve.

FIELD NOTES

To make Church's Spicy Chicken, just add 2 tablespoons of ground cayenne pepper to the original breading mixture before breading the chicken.

THE COFFEE BEAN & TEA LEAF

Vanilla Ice Blended Drink

 PREP TIME:
Active: 5 minutes
Inactive: None

 DIFFICULTY:
Easy

 SERVES:
2

Starbucks's Frappuccino, perhaps the most famous blended coffee drink in the world, is a hacked clone of this blended concoction invented at the California-based chain The Coffee Bean & Tea Leaf. In the mid-1980s, a store manager at the Westwood, California, location mixed diet drink powder with ice, milk, and coffee in a blender and was pleasantly surprised by how delicious it was. The recipe was tweaked to include the chain's chocolate powder instead of the diet powder, and a new hit product was born.

To make the vanilla version of this iconic drink at home, you must first make the secret flavoring powder, which starts with dry coffee creamer. You'll also need vanilla extract powder, which can be found online. And while you're shopping online, I recommend getting superfine sugar (baker's sugar) and superfine salt (popcorn salt) for this recipe as well, because the fine crystals will dissolve better in the cold drink.

Once your secret powder is made, you'll blend it with ice, cold espresso, and milk, and have a delicious re-creation of the original blended coffee drink now served at over 1,100 Coffee Bean & Tea Leaf locations around the globe. This recipe makes two (16-ounce) servings, but you can whip up a smaller portion for one by combining 12 ounces of ice, 3 ounces of espresso, 3 ounces of milk, and $\frac{1}{3}$ cup of the dry mix in a blender until smooth. Just don't forget the whipped cream topping and straw.

Ingredients or kits sold by chains to help customers make clones of their products at home can provide valuable information for a food hacker. Not only do the packages for these products list ingredient information, but you can also see what the mix looks like before it goes into the final product. This coffeehouse chain sells the flavoring powder used in their famous drink as a quick way to make a home version. Tasting the powder on its own made it easy to determine how much vanilla powder to use in my recipe. And I could see that the powder had a fine texture, which led me to use superfine sugar and fine popcorn salt in the recipe.

- 1/3 cup Coffee mate original powdered coffee creamer
- 1/4 cup plus 1 teaspoon superfine sugar (baker's sugar) or granulated sugar
- 2 tablespoons vanilla powder
- 1/8 teaspoon superfine salt (popcorn salt) or table salt
- 3 cups ice
- 6 ounces cold espresso
- 6 ounces nonfat milk
- Canned whipped cream, for garnish

RECIPE STEPS:

1. Combine coffee creamer, sugar, vanilla powder, and salt in a small bowl.
2. Add to a blender with ice, espresso, and milk. Blend on high speed until no more chunks of ice remain. Pour into two 16-ounce glasses, top with whipped cream and straws, and serve.

FIELD NOTES

Superfine sugar (baker's sugar) and superfine salt (popcorn salt) are also great to use in seasoning blends that must stick to foods, such as chips, crackers, and nuts. Their finer grind allows them to adhere better to the food, and they will blend well with the other finely ground ingredients.

Vanilla Ice Blended Drink

COSTCO (KIRKLAND)

Almond Poppy Muffins

 PREP TIME:
Active: 15 minutes
Inactive: 35 minutes

 DIFFICULTY:
Easy

 **MAKES:**
5 large muffins

The real Costco muffins taste great, but they may not be as wholesome as you'd like. The dough has been conditioned with gums to thicken it and ingredients to emulsify it, and to preserve their shelf-life, the muffins contain no butter. The flavors you taste—butter, almond, and vanilla—are artificial.

When I previously hacked Costco's Blueberry Muffins, I tried to stay true to the ingredients by avoiding butter, opting instead for margarine. And since the Costco muffins contain no buttermilk, I also stayed away from that ingredient. This time, though, I've taken a different approach by using more whole egg, real butter, and, yes, buttermilk, to bring great flavor and a better crumb to the finished product. Without the dough conditioners and artificial ingredients found in the original, these cloned muffins have a pleasant homemade charm.

 Don't feel the need to use artificial ingredients just because they're in the original product. Manufacturers usually use those ingredients to save money and/or extend shelf life, but you want the best-tasting results for your home recipes. If you see artificial flavorings in the ingredient list, as on the packaging for these popular muffins, replace them with natural ingredients for an improved final product. Real butter, natural vanilla extract, and natural almond extract will still make your clone taste like the original, but it'll also be a slightly more wholesome version.

½ cup unsalted butter, softened
1 cup granulated sugar
2 large eggs
⅓ cup vegetable oil
2½ teaspoons almond extract
1¼ teaspoons vanilla extract
¾ teaspoon salt

2 cups (10 ounces) all-purpose flour
1 tablespoon baking powder
½ cup buttermilk
¼ cup whole milk
1 tablespoon plus 2 teaspoons poppy seeds

RECIPE STEPS:

1. Preheat oven to 400°F.
2. Blend butter and sugar in a large bowl with an electric mixer on high speed for 1 minute.
3. Add eggs and beat well on high speed for 1 minute until fluffy, then mix in oil.
4. Mix in almond extract, vanilla extract, and salt.
5. Combine flour and baking powder in a medium bowl. Mix half of flour into wet mixture, then add buttermilk and mix. Add remaining flour and milk, and mix just until combined.
6. Mix in poppy seeds.
7. Line a jumbo, or Texas-size, muffin pan with five paper muffin cups, then distribute batter evenly into cups. Fill sixth cup up about halfway with water to add some moisture to your oven. If making smaller, standard-sized muffins, divide batter among ten muffin cups and fill empty cups about halfway with water.
8. Bake large muffins for 10 minutes, then reduce heat to 375°F and cook for another 20–25 minutes until browned on top and a toothpick pushed into center of a muffin comes out clean. If you use a standard-sized muffin pan, bake for 10 minutes at 400°F, then 15–20 minutes at 375°F, until browned on top.

🔍 FIELD NOTES

Commercial dough is often conditioned, improved, and enhanced with enzymes, emulsifiers, and oxidizing agents to create a smoother, more consistent dough with a better crumb structure. If you do want to use conditioner for home baking, you can buy it online. Look for "dough conditioner," "dough improver," or "dough enhancer," and follow the instructions on the package for adding it to your dough.

CRACKER BARREL
Buttermilk Pie

 PREP TIME:
Active: 15 minutes
Inactive: 4 hours

 DIFFICULTY:
Easy

 SERVES:
8

The first buttermilk pie I tasted was at Cracker Barrel, and I was immediately hooked on the sweetened vanilla custard, which has a distinct but not overwhelming tang from buttermilk and lemon juice and is topped with a simple garnish of strawberries and whipped cream. It's a crowd-pleasing dessert that is as well suited for summertime get-togethers as for winter holiday meals (where it has become a longtime Southern tradition).

I've tasted over a dozen versions of this decades-old favorite now on a quest to discover the best way to make Cracker Barrel's popular dessert. Finally, its secrets have been cracked in this recipe. The beauty of this recipe is its simplicity: You'll need just a handful of common ingredients, a whisk, and an unbaked pie shell. You can make a pie shell using your favorite recipe or use a frozen, unbaked crust from the supermarket, such as Marie Callender's. If you have a convection oven, this is a good time to use it to ensure even browning on top when baking the pie. After about an hour in the oven, your pie is done, and when it's chilled, dessert is served.

 You want to copy a custard like the one in this pie, but how do you know how many eggs or egg yolks to use in your clone? Let the color guide you. Use the number of eggs that give your custard the same color as the original you're duplicating. Since 90% of the egg white is water, adding whole eggs to match the color may add too much liquid to your recipe. You'll likely need to use egg yolks or a combination of yolks and whole eggs to achieve the right color and consistency for your custard.

1¼ cups granulated sugar
¼ cup (1¼ ounces) all-purpose flour
¼ teaspoon salt
3 large eggs
1 large egg yolk
6 tablespoons unsalted butter, melted
2 teaspoons lemon juice

1½ teaspoons vanilla extract
1 cup low-fat buttermilk
1 unbaked 9" pie crust
2 cups frozen sliced strawberries in syrup, thawed
2 cups canned whipped cream

RECIPE STEPS:

1. Preheat oven on convection bake to 325°F. If your oven doesn't have a convection setting, preheat to 350°F. Place one rack in bottom position and one in middle.

2. Whisk sugar, flour, and salt in a medium mixing bowl.

3. Combine eggs and egg yolk in a large bowl, then whisk in sugar blend. Mix for 1 minute.

4. Add melted butter and whisk until sugar is dissolved. Mix in lemon juice and vanilla.

5. Warm buttermilk in microwave on high for 30–45 seconds—just make it warm, not hot—then add it to filling. Whisk for 15 seconds or just until everything is incorporated. Don't let mixture become foamy, or top of pie may brown unevenly.

6. Pour filling into unbaked pie shell and bake it on a baking sheet on bottom rack for 20 minutes, then move pie and baking sheet to middle rack and bake it for another 40 minutes until pie is lightly browned on top. If using a conventional oven, rotate pie halfway through baking to ensure even cooking.

7. Remove from oven and let cool completely (1–2 hours), then chill for at least 2 hours and up to overnight before serving. Serve each slice of pie topped with strawberries and whipped cream.

FIELD NOTES

Buttermilk goes bad quickly, and you'll have quite a bit left over when a recipe like this one requires just a small amount. To save the leftovers, measure $\frac{1}{4}$-cup portions into small plastic cups with lids and freeze them. When another recipe requires buttermilk, just defrost what you need.

Country Fried Steak

Country Fried Steak

 PREP TIME:
Active: 50 minutes
Inactive: 1½ hours

 DIFFICULTY:
Medium

 SERVES:
4

I originally hacked this copycat recipe for Cracker Barrel's Country Fried Steak in my book, *Top Secret Recipes Step-by-Step*. Now, after a second look at the dish, I've made a new-and-improved version that works even better—with a tastier gravy formula and a tender breaded steak without any tough bites.

Most chicken-fried steak recipes, including my previous Cracker Barrel copycat recipe, call for cube steak—round steak that's scored in a butcher's tenderizer—which may not be as tender as you like it to be. Connective tissue that remains intact will make some bites chewy, yet if the steak is overtenderized, it will fall apart when cooked. To ensure that every bite of this updated recipe is perfectly tender, you'll avoid cube steak altogether and start with lean ground beef, similar to recipes for Salisbury steak or Hamburg steak, but without an egg binder. Forming the ground beef into steaks and freezing them ensures they hold together, making the breading and cooking process more manageable. And when served, every bite is guaranteed to be fork-tender.

Of course, this iconic clone recipe wouldn't be complete without a spot-on hack for the famous sawmill gravy that gets spooned over the top. The following copycat includes a fresh hack for the gravy that improves on the original formula in my earlier version, and it's super easy to make with just six ingredients.

 To create texture on breaded and fried food such as this steak and Church's Texas Chicken, use a technique called spritzing or misting. Add droplets of water to the dry breading by flicking water into it from your fingers or with a spray bottle. The small clumps of flour formed by the spritzing will create an extra-craggy fried surface on the food that is more visually appealing and will result in a better crunch.

FOR STEAK:

1½ pounds lean ground beef (7%–10% fat)
Salt
Vegetable oil, for frying

FOR BREADING:

1 cup all-purpose flour
¼ cup cornstarch
2 teaspoons granulated sugar
1¼ teaspoons salt
1¼ teaspoons ground black pepper
¾ teaspoon ground white pepper
¾ teaspoon rubbed sage
½ teaspoon baking powder
¼ teaspoon garlic powder
¼ teaspoon onion powder
4 large eggs
½ cup whole milk

FOR SAWMILL GRAVY:

¼ cup unsalted butter
3 tablespoons all-purpose flour
2 cups whole milk
½ teaspoon salt
½ teaspoon coarse ground black pepper
2 tablespoons minced cooked breakfast sausage

RECIPE STEPS:

1. To make steak: Divide ground beef into four (6-ounce) balls. Form balls into four (6") patties on a wax paper–lined baking sheet, and freeze them for 1 hour until solid. (This freezing step will make breading and cooking process easier.)

2. Prepare beef patties for cooking by sprinkling one side with salt and allowing them to sit for 15 minutes. Flip patties over, sprinkle other side with salt, and let them sit for another 15 minutes. Salt will draw moisture out of beef and defrost surface of frozen patties to help dry breading stick.

3. To make breading: Whisk together flour, cornstarch, sugar, salt, peppers, sage, baking powder, garlic powder, and onion powder in a large bowl, pie pan, or baking dish. Whisk together eggs and milk in another large bowl, pie pan, or baking dish.

4. Bread beef by coating a patty with flour blend, letting it rest briefly, then dipping it into milk and egg mixture. Move moistened patty back over to dry mix and coat it well. Repeat process with all patties, then let them rest on a plate or sheet pan for 20 minutes while oil heats.

5. Preheat 1" of oil to 330°F in a large saucepan or sauté pan equipped with a thermometer.

6. To make sawmill gravy: While beef rests and oil heats up, melt butter in a medium saucepan over medium heat. Whisk in flour and continue cooking until it bubbles, then add milk, salt, pepper, and breakfast sausage. Cook until thick, about 2 minutes, then turn off heat and cover gravy to keep it warm.

7. Fry steaks in oil in batches for 6–7 minutes until golden brown and crispy. Flip steaks over halfway through cooking time. Remove steaks from oil and let them rest for 1 minute on a rack or a paper towel–lined plate, then serve your steaks with a generous portion of sawmill gravy spooned on top.

FIELD NOTES

The white gravy, made with milk, flour, and bits of sausage, is called sawmill gravy because it was served to workers in nineteenth-century Southern Appalachian lumber mills. The gravy was commonly served over biscuits for a cheap, high-calorie meal.

CRACKER BARREL

Meatloaf

 PREP TIME:
Active: 20 minutes
Inactive: 1 hour 20 minutes

 DIFFICULTY:
Easy

 SERVES:
8

This Southern-themed chain is famous for its gift shops filled with made-in-America products and delicious homestyle food, including a particularly good meatloaf. This dish ranks high in popularity, alongside the Chicken n' Dumplins and the Hashbrown Casserole, so a good Cracker Barrel Meatloaf clone recipe was an obvious choice for a top secret hacking mission.

Making meatloaf is easy. What's hard is making it taste like the meatloaf at Cracker Barrel, which is tender, juicy, and flavored with onion, green pepper, and tomato. My first attempts were much too dense, but after playing around with the eggs-to-breadcrumbs-to-milk ratios and using gentle hands when combining everything and pressing it into the loaf pan, my final batch was a winner.

Now you can re-create the secret formula in your own kitchen. Keep in mind that it's best to use a meatloaf pan with an insert that lets the fat drip to the bottom, away from the meat. A regular loaf pan will still work, but you'll want to pour off the fat in the pan before slicing the meatloaf.

 You don't need to bake the whole batch to taste your progress when hacking recipes like this. After mixing ingredients into the meat, pinch off a small portion of the beef, make it into a patty, then cook it in a sauté pan on both sides until done. This method cooks just enough so you can taste how things are going, and then you can make incremental additions to the entire blend. Continue to taste test a small portion of the mixture after each addition until you're happy with the recipe, then cook the whole meatloaf as planned.

1 tablespoon vegetable oil
2/3 cup peeled and diced white onion
1/3 cup diced green bell pepper
1 cup plain breadcrumbs
1 3/4 teaspoons salt
3/4 teaspoon ground black pepper
1/2 teaspoon garlic powder
2 pounds 80/20 ground beef
1/3 cup seeded and diced Roma tomato
2 eggs, beaten
2/3 cup whole milk
1/3 cup plus 1/2 cup ketchup, divided

RECIPE STEPS:

1. Preheat oven to 350°F.
2. Heat 1 tablespoon of oil in a medium sauté pan over medium heat. Add onion and green bell pepper and cook for 3–4 minutes until onion begins to brown. Remove vegetables from heat and set them aside to cool during next steps.
3. Combine breadcrumbs, salt, black pepper, and garlic powder in a small bowl.
4. Pour breadcrumbs over ground beef in a large bowl and use your hands to gently mix breadcrumbs into beef. Try not to compress beef as you mix it, or your meatloaf will come out too tough. Use your hands to toss ingredients together while using your fingers to break up any large chunks of beef.
5. When breadcrumbs are mixed into beef, add sautéed vegetables and diced tomato and mix again using same loose technique.
6. Whisk together eggs, milk, and 1/3 cup ketchup in a medium bowl until there are no visible chunks of ketchup remaining.
7. Pour egg mixture over beef and mix it together with your hands just until liquid is incorporated into beef, being careful not to overdo it.
8. Use your hands to place beef in an ungreased 9" × 5" meatloaf pan, and try not to pack it down too much. Make top smooth for ketchup glaze to come later.
9. Bake meatloaf for 30 minutes, then spread remaining 1/2 cup ketchup over top and continue baking for 35–45 minutes, until internal temperature is between 155°F and 160°F.
10. Remove from oven and let cool 15 minutes before cutting it into 1"-thick slices and serving.

FIELD NOTES

Hacking a meatloaf recipe from another favorite restaurant? After you have made your first sample batch, slice the meatloaf so that you can see a cross section. Compare the amount of onion, pepper, or other ingredients you can see in your cross sections to those ingredients in the slices from the restaurant. This will give you a quick visual sign of how much you need to increase or decrease those ingredients.

Semi-Sweet Chocolate Chunk Cookies

 PREP TIME:
Active: 20 minutes
Inactive: 1 hour 20 minutes

 DIFFICULTY:
Easy

 MAKES:
8 large cookies

To ensure success for their new cookie store, cousins Sawyer Hemsley and Jason McGowan knew they had to start with a great cookie recipe. Batch after batch, the partners baked milk chocolate chip cookies and shared them with taste testers for helpful advice on improving the recipe until, finally, they had created the very best cookie. In 2017, the cousins opened their first Crumbl cookie store in Logan, Utah, to sell their new milk chocolate chip cookies. Just 8 years later, Crumbl had grown to over 1,000 stores throughout the US and Canada, and the chain now sells over 1 million cookies every day.

To create this Crumbl Semi-Sweet Chocolate Chunk Cookies copycat recipe, I started with the cookie chain's list of ingredients. I designed a recipe using that information and then systematically tweaked the formula in more than 35 batches. Through that process, I discovered the best ratio of brown sugar to white sugar, and I found that baking the cookies at a higher temperature worked best for crispy edges and chewy middles. I also found that one egg isn't enough, and two eggs are too much, so beating two eggs and measuring ¼ cup after the foam settled was the best method for consistent results.

Crumbl uses a large scoop to portion these cookies, but you can also use your hands to form the dough into mounds with rough tops. Be sure to bake the cookies on parchment paper. I found silicone baking mats too slippery, causing the cookies to spread from the bottom and split. Your cookies are done when they're light brown around the edges and still appear uncooked in the center, so keep at least one eye on them.

For testing purposes, you can add incremental amounts of some dry ingredients to your mixed cookie dough. I wasn't sure how much baking powder, baking soda, and sugar to use in these cookies, so I began with a low measurement for the early batches and baked one small cookie from each batch (before adding the chocolate chips and chunks). I noted the shape, crumb, color, and taste, then repeated the process with small additions until the cookie was perfect. When the recipe looked good, I added the chocolate and made a whole batch with my changes to verify that it worked. Just keep in mind that baking soda will cause your cookies to spread, while baking powder will make them rise. More sugar will also create more spread when it melts.

2½ cups plus 2 tablespoons (13 ounces) all-purpose flour
1½ teaspoons cornstarch
½ teaspoon baking powder
½ teaspoon baking soda
1 cup unsalted butter, softened
1 cup light brown sugar, packed
⅓ cup granulated sugar
1 teaspoon table salt
2 large eggs, beaten
1½ teaspoons vanilla extract
1½ cups semi-sweet chocolate chips
¾ cup semi-sweet chocolate chunks
2 teaspoons sea salt flakes

RECIPE STEPS:

1. Whisk together flour, cornstarch, baking powder, and baking soda in a medium bowl and set it aside.
2. Mix butter, sugars, and salt in a stand mixer with paddle attachment on high speed, or in a large bowl with a hand mixer on high speed for 2 minutes.
3. Scrape down sides of bowl.
4. After beating eggs, wait at least 5 minutes for foam to settle before measuring ¼ cup. Add measured egg and vanilla to bowl and mix on high speed for 30 seconds.
5. Add dry ingredients to wet ingredients and combine with stand mixer on medium speed for 10 seconds or with a large mixing spoon until ingredients are combined.
6. Stir in chocolate chips by hand with a large mixing spoon.
7. Cover dough and let it sit for 30 minutes. Do not refrigerate.
8. Use your hands to scoop out 5–5¼ ounces of dough. Keep dough chunky and ragged on top, shaping bottom round and pressing it onto a parchment-lined baking sheet. Your scoop of dough should be about 1½" tall. Repeat with remaining dough, arranging four portions on one parchment-lined baking sheet and another four portions on a second sheet.
9. Press 10–11 chocolate chunks into top of each dough ball. Sprinkle a couple of pinches of sea salt on each cookie, then let dough sit out for 20 minutes while you preheat oven.
10. Preheat a convection oven to 350°F or a conventional oven to 375°F. Bake cookies, one baking sheet at a time, for 16–18 minutes until light brown around edges. Cookies will appear uncooked in center when ready to remove from oven. Cool for 10 minutes. Cookies will keep in a sealed container for 4 days.

FIELD NOTES

Crumbl's open kitchen allowed me to see how the cookies are portioned and the shape of the dough before it goes into the oven, so I designed the recipe using this intel. While waiting in the long line, I was also able to witness how the cookies rested for quite some time on the baking sheets before going into the ovens. This resting step allows the flour to fully hydrate before baking, giving the cookies better flavor and shape.

Semi-Sweet Chocolate Chunk Cookies

Stroopwafels

 PREP TIME:
Active: 50 minutes
Inactive: 4 hours

 DIFFICULTY:
Easy

 **MAKES:**
16 stroopwafels

Over two centuries ago, a baker in Gouda, South Holland, the Netherlands, created the first stroopwafel, a round waffle cookie split in half and filled with cinnamon-spiced caramel. Stroopwafels, meaning "syrup waffles," gained immense popularity and became a traditional Dutch side nibble. Daelmans, a bakery in the southern Netherlands established in 1904 by Hermanus Daelmans, has become the world's leading producer of stroopwafels. The brand's more recent success in the US is partly due to United Airlines, which has been passing out the stroopwafels to grateful passengers on morning flights since 2016.

Cloning Daelmans's secret recipe starts with a good waffle cookie. To achieve this, you'll need either a waffle cone maker or a pizzelle maker, which can be found inexpensively online. These devices create perfect waffle cookies. Once your waffle cookie is punched out with a 3⅜" biscuit cutter and sliced open, you'll add a simple caramel filling that's made by melting Kraft baking caramels (I like the unwrapped caramel bits) with cinnamon and vanilla. Press the top half of the waffle down onto the caramel and give it a little spin, and you've just cloned a decades-old world-famous food.

When fully closed, a pizzelle maker creates a thin waffle cookie. But by leaving a little breathing room, you can produce thicker waffle cookies that can be easily sliced in half with a butter knife before they cool completely. These will more closely match the cookies used to make Daelmans Stroopwafels.

I was able to determine this by warming up a real stroopwafel in my microwave and pulling the cookie apart. That made it easy to see there was no waffle pattern on the inside surfaces of the cookies, meaning that only one cookie, split in half, was used for each Daelmans Stroopwafel.

FOR COOKIES:

½ cup dark brown sugar, packed
2 large egg whites
3 tablespoons refined coconut oil
3 tablespoons unsalted butter, melted
1½ teaspoons vanilla extract
¼ teaspoon plus ⅛ teaspoon salt
1½ cups (7½ ounces) all-purpose flour
1 teaspoon baking soda

FOR FILLING:

8 ounces Kraft caramel bits (or 32 Kraft caramels)
2 tablespoons water
¼ teaspoon ground cinnamon
¼ teaspoon vanilla extract

RECIPE STEPS:

1. To make cookies: Combine brown sugar, egg whites, coconut oil, butter, vanilla, and salt in a large bowl with an electric mixer on high speed for 1 minute.

2. Whisk flour and baking soda in a medium bowl, then combine with wet ingredients in large bowl. Mix until dough is homogenous, then cover and chill it for 2 hours or overnight.

3. To make filling: Combine caramel, water, and cinnamon in a medium saucepan over medium-low heat. Heat, stirring often, for 10–15 minutes until caramel is smooth. Stir in vanilla, cover pan, and remove it from heat.

4. Preheat a waffle cone maker or pizzelle maker to its hottest setting.

5. Spray waffle cone or pizzelle maker with nonstick oil spray. Measure a heaping tablespoon of dough, roll it into a ball, and press it into middle of hot cooking surface. Lower lid, but don't close it all the way so that you make a small round waffle that is at least 3½" across and ⅛"–3/16" thick. Cook for 1 minute until surface is browned but inside is still soft. Immediately after removing waffle from cooker, use a 3⅜" dough cutting ring to cut waffle into a circle.

6. When waffle is cool enough to handle, about 30 seconds, lay it on a flat surface, then use a butter knife on its side to slice waffle in half. Use one hand to spin waffle around while slicing horizontally through soft middle of waffle with butter knife until two halves come apart.

7. Use a spoon to add approximately 2 teaspoons of warm caramel filling to center of one side of waffle. Place other half on top and spin it while pressing down gently in middle until caramel is pushed to edges of cookie. Repeat cooking and filling process with remaining dough and caramel filling. Let stroopwafels set for 2 hours before eating. Store stroopwafels in a sealed container for up to 1 week.

FIELD NOTES

To sleuth out the flavors of the cookie portion of a cookie sandwich recipe, heat the cookie, then separate the halves and scrape off the filling. This way, you can get a clean bite of just the cookie without the filling affecting what you taste and throwing off your recipe.

Tamales

 PREP TIME:
Active: 55 minutes
Inactive: 5½ hours

 DIFFICULTY:
Medium

 MAKES:
24 tamales

Del Taco celebrates the holidays every year with delicious little $2 corn husk–wrapped pork tamales made from a traditional recipe with an authentic south-of-the-border taste. The only problem is that when the holidays end, so do these tasty tamales. And that's when you'll want to bust out this top secret recipe.

Making authentic tamales is not hard, but it does take time. The pork requires braising for several hours to get it fork-tender, and the wrapped tamales take around 2 hours to steam until they're done. This copycat hack recipe is inspired by traditional tamale recipes, which include a braising sauce for the pork made from rehydrated guajillo peppers. To coax out more flavor, I chose to toast the peppers before adding them to the liquid. And rather than using lard in the dough (a.k.a. masa), I found a combination of vegetable shortening and butter to be a more flavorful alternative.

Steam all 24 tamales until they are fully cooked, and store those you can't eat in your freezer for up to several weeks. Steam the frozen tamales for 20–30 minutes before serving, and they'll taste as good as fresh.

 Vegetable shortening can be used in recipes traditionally made with lard, such as tamales. For better flavor, you may want to blend the shortening with butter or margarine.

FOR FILLING:

2 ounces dried guajillo peppers
1 tablespoon vegetable oil
1 cup peeled and diced yellow onion
1 teaspoon salt, divided
½ teaspoon ground black pepper
4 cups chicken broth
6 cloves garlic
1½ teaspoons ground cumin
1½ teaspoons dried Mexican oregano
2 pounds pork shoulder, cut into large chunks
2 bay leaves
¾ cup water
¼ cup masa harina
⅓ cup Ortega hot taco sauce (or similar sauce)
2 teaspoons lime juice
½ teaspoon ground cayenne pepper

FOR DOUGH (MASA) AND WRAPPERS:

24 dried corn husks
1 cup plus 2 tablespoons vegetable shortening
½ cup plus 2 tablespoons unsalted butter
1 teaspoon baking powder
1¾ teaspoons salt
5 cups masa harina
3¼ cups chicken broth

RECIPE STEPS:

1. Preheat your oven to 350°F.

2. To make filling: Using scissors, cut off stem end of each pepper, then cut up one side so that you can open pepper and dump out seeds. Place seeded peppers on an ungreased baking sheet and bake for 3–4 minutes until fragrant.

3. Heat oil in a large saucepan or Dutch oven over medium heat. Add onion, ½ teaspoon salt, and black pepper, and cook for 5 minutes until onions have softened.

4. Add toasted peppers and chicken broth and bring mixture to a full boil. Cover pan, turn off heat, and let it sit for 30 minutes to soften peppers.

5. Pour entire contents of pan into a blender, add garlic, cumin, and oregano, and blend for 30 seconds until mixture is smooth. Pour this braising sauce over pork and bay leaves in pan on medium-high heat. Reduce heat to a simmer and cover pan. Braise meat for 3–3½ hours until it's easy to flake apart with a fork.

6. While pork braises, pour boiling water over corn husks in a large bowl and let them soak until pliable, about 1 hour.

7. When pork is tender, take it out of pan and put it into a large bowl, then pour liquid out of pan into another bowl. When meat is cool enough to work with, in about 30 minutes, use two forks to flake meat apart into much smaller pieces. Add pork back to pan along with 1¼ cups of reserved braising liquid (remove bay leaves), plus remaining ½ teaspoon of salt, ¾ cup water, ¼ cup masa harina, taco sauce, lime juice, and ground cayenne pepper. Cook over medium heat, stirring often to break up any chunks of pork, until liquid is mostly gone, 10–12 minutes. Cover and cool while making the masa.

8. To make masa: Combine shortening, butter, baking powder, and salt in a large bowl with an electric mixer on high speed for 30 seconds. Add masa harina a little at a time, and mix on medium speed until gravelly. Continue mixing while adding chicken broth until it becomes so thick that you must use your hands. Mix dough until all broth is absorbed, then let rest for 10 minutes.

continued on next page

RECIPE STEPS (continued):

9. Remove corn husks from water and blot them dry. Measure $\frac{1}{4}$ cup of masa and spread it onto corn husk in a rectangle that is approximately $4\frac{1}{2}"\times 3\frac{1}{2}"$. Arrange approximately 1 ounce of pork filling in center of dough, then pull up both sides of corn husk so that dough wraps around filling. Use your fingers to close dough over filling and press on ends to seal up tamale. Fold one side of corn husk over tamale, then continue rolling tamale until it's wrapped snuggly and fold pointed end under. You can use scissors to trim off excess corn husk so that tamales fit better in steamer. Repeat with remaining ingredients until all tamales are wrapped.

10. Prepare a steamer, or a steamer basket over some simmering water in a large saucepan or Dutch oven. If using the latter setup, put a coffee cup in center and arrange tamales with open ends facing up in a spoke-like fashion around cup. Work in batches, refrigerating uncooked tamales until it's time to cook them. Steam each batch $1\frac{1}{2}$–2 hours until masa is fully cooked.

11. Chill or freeze any leftover cooked tamales and re-steam for 20–30 minutes to serve later. They will keep for up to 4 days in your refrigerator and 2 months in your freezer.

🔍 FIELD NOTES

To hack tamale recipes, you'll want to separate the filling from the masa so that you can taste each component separately. Use a sharp knife to slice open the tamale like you're a culinary surgeon, and scrape out the filling with a spoon. Store the filling and masa in separate covered containers and keep them chilled. Heat up small portions in your microwave oven as you need them for taste tests.

DOLE FOOD COMPANY

Dole Whip

 PREP TIME:
Active: 10 minutes
Inactive: 3 hours 20 minutes

 DIFFICULTY:
Easy

 SERVES:
7

Real Dole Whip is a nondairy dessert with artificial flavoring; a small amount of natural pineapple juice; and six different natural gums and gels: cellulose gum, xanthan gum, locust bean gum, guar gum, karaya gum, and pectin. It comes in powdered form, including the pineapple juice, in 4.4-pound bags sold to soft-serve machine operators at fairs, sporting events, and amusement parks. On the back of the bag, instructions explain that you must dissolve the powder in 2 gallons of cold tap water, pour the syrup into a soft-serve machine, and hit the switch.

Until now, almost all recipes that claim to duplicate Dole Whip have used ice cream to mimic the creamy consistency of the real thing. The results from these recipes are tasty, but they don't exactly copy Dole Whip, because Dole Whip is a sorbet, which isn't made with ice cream. Instead, Dole Whip creates its thickness with the assistance of the gums and gels.

For this clone recipe, I used unflavored gelatin and pectin to form a gel similar to what's in the real Dole Whip, resulting in a thick and creamy consistency. But the best part of this recipe is that, unlike the real thing, it contains all-natural ingredients, including real Dole pineapple juice and a little tangerine juice to round out the flavor and enrich the color. This homemade Dole Whip is easy to make with an ice cream maker, and fans of the real thing will love it. Plus, now you can have this DIY Dole Whip whenever you want—no need to wait for your next trip to the amusement park.

 **Another trick to help thicken this sorbet (and other sorbet recipes you decide to hack) is using viscous corn syrup to replace much of the sugar. Corn syrup will give the sorbet body, and in this recipe it also helps tone down the acidic pineapple juice.**

3 cups Dole canned pineapple juice
⅔ cup light corn syrup
¼ cup granulated sugar
¼ cup strained tangerine juice (from 2–3 tangerines, no pulp)
1 tablespoon refined (unflavored) coconut oil
2 teaspoons dry pectin
1¼ teaspoons gelatin powder (I used Knox)

RECIPE STEPS:

1. Combine all ingredients in a medium saucepan over medium heat. Heat until mixture is hot and sugar has dissolved, while stirring occasionally, about 6 minutes. Do not let syrup get hot enough to burn your finger when you touch it, or flavors of juices may change.

2. Once it's hot, remove syrup from heat. Cool it for 20 minutes, then chill it until cold in your refrigerator, about 3 hours.

3. When syrup is cold, churn it in an ice cream maker until thick and nearly doubled in volume, 15–25 minutes. Serve dessert immediately while soft, or freeze until slightly firmer and pipe it through a pastry bag with an extra-large star tip onto a cone or into a cup. If dessert freezes solid, leave it out of freezer for 10 minutes before serving.

FIELD NOTES

According to a 2024 article in *The Sacramento Bee*, a UC Davis Food Science graduate named Kathy Westphal created Dole Whip in 1983 during her first job at Dole when she was just 24 years old. The fruity frozen non-dairy drink mix was designed for soft-serve machines, most notably at Disneyland near the Enchanted Tiki Room (where this dessert debuted in 1984 and quickly gained fame). Today's Dole Whip is made with more artificial ingredients than the original recipe.

DOMINO'S

Chicken Taco Pizza

 PREP TIME:
Active: 45 minutes
Inactive: 1½ hours, plus 2 days for dough

 DIFFICULTY:
Medium

 **MAKES:**
2 (14") large pizzas

If you like both pizza and chicken tacos, you'll love this recipe for Domino's Chicken Taco Pizza. Domino's figured out how to combine grilled chicken, three kinds of cheese, green pepper, onion, and tomato on a hand-tossed crust brushed with a secret seasoning blend so that each bite tastes like a taco.

The taco seasoning brushed on the dough is a big part of the flavor, so you'll find that hack here, along with the cheese blend you'll need and my method for creating a chewy, pizza chain–style crust, including the garlic spread brushed on at the end.

The dough recipe in this hack is based on the Domino's Cheese Pizza copycat I sleuthed out on the TV show *Top Secret Recipe*. For extra bite, it includes high-gluten flour, which you can find online and in specialty chains.

 The high-gluten flour adds elasticity to make a chewy dough like what you'd get at Domino's, but if you can't find it, just increase the bread flour to 5 cups (25 ounces) for delicious pizzas close to the real thing.

FOR DOUGH:

3 tablespoons granulated sugar
1½ teaspoons active dry yeast
2 cups (16 ounces) room-temperature bottled water
2⅔ cups plus 3 tablespoons (13 ounces) bread flour
2¼ cups plus 3 tablespoons (12 ounces) high-gluten flour
2 teaspoons salt
3 tablespoons vegetable oil
½ cup cornmeal

FOR CHICKEN:

1 (8-ounce) skinless chicken breast fillet
3 cups water
2 tablespoons kosher salt
⅓ cup vegetable oil

FOR TACO SEASONING:

2 tablespoons chili powder
1 teaspoon salt
1 teaspoon ground cumin
½ teaspoon granulated sugar
½ teaspoon onion powder
¼ teaspoon ground cayenne pepper
¼ teaspoon garlic powder

FOR GARLIC SPREAD:

½ cup margarine
⅓ cup grated Parmesan cheese
¼ teaspoon dried parsley, crushed
¼ teaspoon garlic powder
⅛ teaspoon salt

FOR OTHER TOPPINGS:

1 cup diced American cheese
1 cup shredded Cheddar cheese
2 cups shredded or petite diced provolone cheese
⅔ cup sliced green bell pepper
⅔ cup peeled and sliced white onion
⅔ cup canned diced tomatoes, rinsed and strained

RECIPE STEPS:

1. To make dough: Combine sugar and yeast with water in a small bowl.
2. Combine flours and salt in a stand mixer using paddle attachment or by hand.
3. When yeast mixture starts to foam, pour it into flour, then add oil. Use a dough hook to mix until all ingredients are combined, or mix by hand. Knead with dough hook or by hand for 5 minutes, then cover and refrigerate for 2 days.
4. To make chicken: Slice chicken breast through middle, making two thinner fillets. Brine chicken 1 hour before building pizzas by dissolving salt in water and adding chicken. Refrigerate for 1 hour.
5. When ready to build pizzas, take dough out of refrigerator to warm up to room temperature while you prepare toppings. Preheat grill to high, or set a grill pan over medium-high heat on stovetop.
6. To make taco seasoning: Combine all dry ingredients in a small bowl. Stir in oil and set aside.
7. To make garlic spread: Melt margarine in a medium bowl in microwave for 30 seconds on high or in a small saucepan over medium-low heat. When margarine is melted, stir in Parmesan, parsley, garlic powder, and salt, and set aside.
8. Remove chicken from brine, blot it dry, and rub it with vegetable oil. Cook chicken for 4–6 minutes per side until it reaches an internal temperature of 165°F. Cool and dice.
9. Preheat a convection oven to 475°F or a conventional oven to 500°F.
10. Divide dough in half. Form half of dough into a ball on a well-floured surface. Sprinkle cornmeal on another clean surface, and on that surface stretch out dough using your hands until you have a round that fits on a 14" pizza pan or pizza screen.
11. Position dough on pizza pan or pizza screen and brush it with half of taco seasoning. Leave a margin of about 1" around edge of dough.
12. Sprinkle half of American cheese (½ cup) over taco seasoning. Add half of chicken. Combine Cheddar and provolone cheeses, and sprinkle half of cheese blend (1½ cups) on pizza.
13. Distribute half of green pepper over cheese, followed by half of onion and half of tomato.
14. Bake pizza 9–12 minutes until cheese begins to brown on top. After removing it from oven, let it cool for 1 minute, then brush crust with garlic spread. Repeat with remaining ingredients for second pizza. Slice pizzas four times through middle making eight slices each. Serve.

FIELD NOTES

The lengthy cold fermentation process is crucial for a professional-style pizza crust. Over 2 days, the yeast breaks down the sugars, developing more complex flavors.

Chocolate Lava Crunch Cake

 PREP TIME:
Active: 25 minutes
Inactive: 1 hour 10 minutes

 DIFFICULTY:
Medium

 MAKES:
12 cakes

A traditional "molten" cake or "lava" cake is baked at a high temperature for a short time so that the outside of the cake is fully cooked but the batter at the center stays unset and gooey. Domino's lava cakes tweak the formula with pure fudge topping hidden in the middle rather than undercooked cake batter. The little dessert is delicious, with a crunchy exterior and two forms of chocolate in every bite. However, the construction presented some challenges during the sleuthing process, such as how to bake soft fudge into the center of a small cake without any visible holes and without the fudge combining with the cake batter.

Since no holes or seams were detected on the real crunch cakes, I concluded that the filling needed to be loaded into the cakes before baking. I thought about freezing the fudge in disk shapes and then concealing those in the middle of a muffin cup of cake batter, but the fudge doesn't freeze solid in a home freezer. Instead, it gets really cold and really sticky.

Returning to the drawing board, I found the clue I needed on the Domino's website: The list of ingredients for the lava cakes includes "cake crumbs" and "cookie crumbs" along with butter, eggs, sugar, flour, vanilla, and cocoa. This suggests that crumbs of pre-baked cake and cookies could be combined with the other ingredients to make firmer cake "dough" rather than a runny cake batter. The soft fudge could then be spooned into the centers of the uncooked mini cakes, topped with more dough, and baked. Using this technique, there is no detectable seam, and the fudge inside gets warm and gooey when you bake it, just like the real thing. Serve these up with a scoop of vanilla ice cream on the side, and watch the fun when everyone takes a bite and warm fudge oozes out.

A food hack saves time and effort when you use a packaged product in a customized way. These cakes contain crunchy bits, so I discovered that I could divide a boxed cake mix and use part of it to make crispy cookies. I crumbled the cookies and used the crumbs in the remaining batter to make small cakes with crunchy cookie bits throughout, just like the product I was cloning. For my copycat recipe of Sonic's Strawberry Cheesecake Shake (available on my website at https://topsecretrecipes.com), I found a Jell-O brand no-bake strawberry cheesecake kit, which includes strawberry syrup, powdered cheesecake mix, and graham cracker crumbs that are the perfect ingredients for hacking the milkshake clone.

Chocolate Lava Crunch Cake

FOR CAKE:

1 (15.25-ounce) box chocolate fudge cake mix
⅔ cups water
4 large eggs, divided
3 tablespoons vegetable oil
¾ cup plus 3 tablespoons unsalted butter, softened
¾ cup plus 2 tablespoons granulated sugar
1 large egg yolk
1¼ teaspoons vanilla extract
2 tablespoons all-purpose flour
1 tablespoon plus 1 teaspoon Dutch-process cocoa (such as Hershey's Special Dark)
1 (12–15-ounce) bottle fudge topping

FOR GARNISH:

1 teaspoon powdered sugar

RECIPE STEPS:

1. Preheat oven to 350°F. Line a 9" cake pan with parchment paper.
2. Place 2 cups cake mix in a large bowl and 1 cup cake mix in a medium bowl.
3. Add water, 2 eggs, and oil to large bowl and mix with an electric mixer on low speed until cake mix is moistened, then mix on high speed for 2 minutes. Pour cake batter into lined cake pan and bake for 30 minutes.
4. While cake is baking make a small batch of cookies by adding 3 tablespoons of butter and 1 egg to remaining 1 cup of cake mix in medium bowl. Mix with mixer on high speed for 1 minute, then put bowl of dough into freezer to firm up until cake is done.
5. When cake is done, remove it from oven and reduce temperature to 325°F.
6. Form cookie dough into six (1¼-ounce) balls and arrange them on a baking sheet lined with parchment paper or a baking mat. Bake for 28 minutes and cool for 30 minutes.
7. When cake and cookies are cool, crumble into fine crumbs. Pound on cookie crumbs with a kitchen mallet or rolling pin or use a food processor. Use your hands for cake. Combine all crumbs into a large bowl.
8. Combine sugar with remaining ¾ cup of butter in a medium bowl with an electric mixer on high speed for 1 minute. Mix in remaining egg, egg yolk, and vanilla until combined, then mix in flour and cocoa.
9. Stir butter mixture into crumbs until all crumbs are moistened, using your hands or a mixing spoon.
10. Preheat oven to 450°F.
11. Lightly spray cups of a Texas-size or jumbo muffin pan with oil cooking spray. Measure ¼ cup of cake dough into a cup and form a well in center of dough. Spoon a heaping tablespoon of fudge topping into well in dough. Form a disk from 2 tablespoons of dough and place on top of filling in muffin cup, pressing down around edges to seal. Repeat with remaining dough and fudge topping. Bake 12 minutes. If pan will not hold all twelve cakes, bake cakes in batches, allowing pan to cool completely in between.
12. When cakes have cooled for 5 minutes, run a knife around edge of each and remove from pan. Serve cakes immediately by inverting each one onto a serving plate and dusting with powdered sugar. Refrigerate leftovers for up to 1 week. To serve later, invert chilled cakes onto a metal baking sheet and bake for 12 minutes at 375°F. Let cool for 3 minutes before serving.

FIELD NOTES

Two chefs claim to have invented the molten lava cake recipe. Jean-Georges Vongerichten says he created it in 1987 when he took a chocolate sponge cake out of the oven too early. Chef Michel Bras says he invented it in 1981 as a tribute to after-ski hot chocolate.

Loaded Tots

	PREP TIME: Active: 15 minutes Inactive: 28 minutes		DIFFICULTY: Easy		SERVES: 2

This oven-baked starter from Domino's, which debuted in early 2023, reveals a great way to transform a boring bag of potato tots into a dish with pizzazz. The pizza chain's Loaded Tots are built with a delicious pile of crispy potato tots topped with cheese, a secret sauce, and other goodies that you will wish you'd been stacking on potato tots years ago.

For this hack, I copied the two best sellers of the three versions offered at Domino's: Philly Cheese Steak and Cheddar Bacon. The Philly Cheese Steak version includes onion, green pepper, steak, and Alfredo sauce, and the Cheddar Bacon is topped with crispy crumbled bacon and garlic Parmesan sauce. You just need to decide which one to make first.

 **TOP SECRET HACK** — If you want a better hack of a dish that uses frozen fried foods such as French fries or potato tots, follow the instructions on the package for frying them, rather than baking. Restaurants will be frying their version, so the best clone will use the same cooking technique.

FOR PHILLY CHEESE STEAK:

2 tablespoons unsalted butter
1 teaspoon minced garlic
½ cup heavy cream
2 tablespoons grated Parmesan cheese
¼ teaspoon salt, divided
24 frozen potato tots
1½ ounces frozen uncooked thin-sliced steak (like Steak-umm)
½ ounce peeled and sliced white onion
½ ounce sliced green bell pepper

FOR CHEDDAR BACON:

½ cup mayonnaise
2 tablespoons grated Parmesan cheese
1 tablespoon half-and-half or heavy cream
1 teaspoon white vinegar
1 teaspoon lemon juice
¼ teaspoon plus ⅛ teaspoon garlic powder
¼ teaspoon dried oregano
¼ teaspoon dried parsley
¼ teaspoon granulated sugar
⅛ teaspoon salt
2 slices cooked bacon, crumbled

FOR POTATO TOTS (BOTH VERSIONS):

24 frozen potato tots
¼ cup shredded mozzarella cheese
¼ cup shredded Cheddar cheese

Loaded Tots

RECIPE STEPS FOR PHILLY CHEESE STEAK:

1. To make Alfredo sauce: Melt butter in a small saucepan over medium-low heat. Add garlic and cook for 1 minute, then add cream, Parmesan cheese, and ⅛ teaspoon salt, and bring to a light simmer.
2. Simmer for 3–4 minutes until sauce is thicker, then remove it from heat to thicken even more as it cools.
3. Cook 24 potato tots as instructed on package. You can bake or fry tots, but frying will yield results that are more like the real thing.
4. When tots are done, increase oven temperature to 475°F.
5. Break up thin frozen steak and cook it in a large sauté pan over medium heat until it's no longer pink. Sprinkle steak with a pinch or two of salt as it cooks.
6. Fold a 12" × 12" square piece of parchment paper in half and place it on a baking sheet. Arrange tots on middle of parchment paper. Make sure they are all touching so toppings can be stacked on top.
7. Arrange onion on tots, followed by green pepper and steak.
8. Drizzle 2 tablespoons of Alfredo sauce over steak, pepper, and onion.
9. Combine two shredded cheeses and sprinkle all of it over top of tots. Bake for 8 minutes until cheese begins to brown, and serve immediately.

RECIPE STEPS FOR CHEDDAR BACON:

1. Make a garlic Parmesan sauce by whisking together mayonnaise, Parmesan cheese, half-and-half or cream, vinegar, lemon juice, garlic powder, oregano, parsley, sugar, and salt in a small bowl. Set aside.
2. Cook 24 potato tots as instructed on package. You can bake or fry tots, but frying will yield results more like the real dish.
3. When tots are done, increase oven temperature to 475°F.
4. Fold a 12" × 12" square piece of parchment paper in half and place it on a baking sheet.
5. Arrange tots on middle of parchment paper. Ensure they're grouped together so toppings can be piled on top.
6. Sprinkle crumbled bacon over top of tots.
7. Combine mozzarella cheese with Cheddar cheese and sprinkle it over top of tots. Bake for 8 minutes until cheese begins to brown.
8. Pour garlic Parmesan sauce into a squirt bottle and drizzle it over top of tots when they come out of oven. Serve.

FIELD NOTES

Tater Tots were created to reduce waste. They were invented in 1953 by the Ore-Ida frozen food company to utilize potato scraps left over from producing frozen French fries.

EL POLLO LOCO

Shredded Beef Birria

 PREP TIME:
Active: 20 minutes
Inactive: 4 1/2 hours

 DIFFICULTY:
Easy

 SERVES:
8

Birria was invented over 400 years ago in Jalisco, Mexico as a cooking method for preparing goat meat. Goat meat can be tough and gamey, so a low-and-slow braising method was developed to make it tender and flavorful. A broth infused with chili peppers and spices was combined with the meat in a covered pot that was then buried in the ground with hot coals. In the morning, the braised birria was ready to eat, which is why the dish became a traditional Mexican breakfast food.

Customers at El Pollo Loco usually have their birria later in the day, and it isn't made with goat meat. Instead, this recipe is made by braising a beef roast in a combination of peppers and spices for 3 hours until the meat is tender enough to shred with a couple of forks.

Use this shredded beef on tacos, burritos, quesadillas, or anything else you crave.

 Braising beef breaks down the collagen, producing fork-tender meat and unctuous broth for dipping. However, the broth may not be as full-bodied as you hoped it would be. To improve it, you can add more of what gives it body by using gelatin. Gelatin is an animal product derived from collagen, and it will contribute a satisfyingly smooth mouthfeel to a sauce such as the one in this recipe. You can improve the body of any broth or consommé by adding increments of 1/4 teaspoon of gelatin soaked in 1 tablespoon of room temperature water for 5 minutes.

FOR BEEF:

2 tablespoons vegetable oil
1 (2- to 3-pound) chuck roast
1 cup peeled and chopped white onion
1 cup peeled and chopped carrots
4 teaspoons chopped garlic
4 cups chicken broth
2 cups water
1/2 cup tomato sauce
1/3 cup chili powder (I used Gebhardt)
1 tablespoon salt

FOR BEEF (continued):

3/4 teaspoon ground black pepper
3/4 teaspoon dried thyme
3/4 teaspoon dried oregano
3/4 teaspoon ground cumin
2 bay leaves
1/2 teaspoon gelatin powder

FOR GARNISH:

1 tablespoon peeled and diced white onion
1 teaspoon chopped fresh cilantro

Shredded Beef Birria

RECIPE STEPS:

1. Heat oil in a large saucepan or Dutch oven over medium-high heat. When oil is hot, add chuck roast and sear for 3–5 minutes on each side until browned. Remove roast to a plate and keep pan on heat.

2. Add onion and carrots to pan and cook for 2 minutes while stirring often. Add garlic and cook for 1 minute.

3. Transfer roast back to pan. Also, add chicken broth, water, tomato sauce, chili powder, salt, pepper, thyme, oregano, cumin, and bay leaves. When liquid begins to boil, reduce heat, then cover and continue to simmer for 3–3$\frac{1}{2}$ hours until meat easily flakes apart.

4. Transfer meat to a platter to cool, then strain solids out of liquid to create a consommé.

5. Transfer strained consommé to a large bowl and chill it for 1 hour until fat solidifies on top. Use a spatula to remove fat from top of liquid.

6. Add 4 cups of strained consommé to a medium saucepan over medium-high heat. Add gelatin. Try to leave behind any solids that have settled to bottom. Cook sauce until bubbling, remove it from heat, and cover.

7. In 30 minutes, when beef is cool enough to handle, shred it into bite-sized pieces. Pour some consommé into a bowl and garnish it with diced onion and chopped cilantro. Serve consommé on side for dipping.

FIELD NOTES

Shredding the meat is easy with two forks. Pierce the meat with the forks, one in each hand, with the tines angled in opposite directions, and pull the meat apart to separate the fibers. Continue until the meat is shredded to your desired consistency.

FERRARA CANDY COMPANY

Butterfinger

 PREP TIME:
Active: 25 minutes
Inactive: 1 hour 20 minutes

 DIFFICULTY:
Medium

 MAKES:
4 (2½-ounce) bars

Break open a milk chocolate–coated Butterfinger candy bar, and you'll see flaky layers of candy inside. It may not seem possible to replicate that mysterious peanuty center at home without some special equipment. However, candy bars as old as this usually began as handmade recipes, so you can certainly craft a Butterfinger clone from scratch in your kitchen.

Ownership of Butterfinger has changed hands a few times since Otto Schnering invented it in 1923 for his Illinois candy company, Curtiss. Standard Brands bought Curtiss in 1964, and Nabisco merged with Standard Brands in 1981. Nestlé purchased Butterfinger from Nabisco in 1990, then later sold it to the Italian candy company Ferrara in 2018, Ferrara claims to have "improved" the formula in 2019 by removing preservatives, adding more cocoa to the chocolate, and using better peanuts, plus a few other tweaks. And this is where the controversy starts. Posts on Butterfinger's social media pages complain that the new Ferrara formula is not as good as the Nestlé version and that it leaves a bad aftertaste.

The new label has fewer ingredients than the old label, but one omission that stands out is the removal of corn flakes. Corn flakes had been used in the Butterfinger recipe since the 1950s, and that's the Butterfinger most fans know and love. For this hack, I chose to rewind to the classic recipe and include corn flakes in this copycat for a treat that's closer to the original.

 Step 5 of this recipe uses an easy microwaving method for melting the chocolate to dip in the bars. However, for chocolate that sets better on the bar, you can instead temper the chocolate by melting ⅔ of the chips (1⅓ cups) in a glass bowl over a saucepan of simmering water. Be sure not to get any water in the chocolate, or it will seize up. Gently stir it occasionally. When the chips are melted and smooth, remove the bowl from the hot water and place it on a bunched-up dish towel. Add the remaining chips and stir vigorously until they are melted. Adding tempered chips to your melted chips will "seed" melted chocolate and temper it. If you are having a tough time getting the chips to melt all the way, you can place the bowl over simmering water again, but just for a couple of seconds, then remove the bowl and stir. When the chocolate is completely smooth, you'll need to work quickly in step 6 before the chocolate gets too thick.

- 3 tablespoons natural creamy peanut butter, unmixed (I used Skippy)
- 2 teaspoons crushed corn flakes
- 1/3 cup light corn syrup
- 3 tablespoons granulated sugar
- 2 tablespoons dark brown sugar, packed
- 2 tablespoons water
- 1 tablespoon unsalted butter, softened
- 1/4 teaspoon salt
- 1 (12-ounce) bag milk chocolate chips

RECIPE STEPS:

1. Measure 3 tablespoons of peanut butter from bottom of jar where it's thickest without stirring it up. Crush corn flakes in a small plastic bag with any heavy object. Combine peanut butter and crushed corn flakes in a small bowl. Set aside.

2. Combine corn syrup, sugars, water, butter, and salt in a medium saucepan over medium heat. Add a candy thermometer to pan and bring candy up to a simmer.

3. When candy reaches 285°F, remove thermometer and immediately pour candy onto a silicone baking mat or a buttered baking sheet. Drizzle candy in a rectangular shape. Spoon peanut butter on top of candy and spread it to edges with a rubber or silicone spatula.

4. Working quickly, fold top and bottom edges over peanut butter, press down with your spatula to flatten it more (you can also use a rolling pin to help flatten it), then fold in left and right sides. Press down with spatula again to flatten out candy, then repeat folding process a few more times until candy becomes too hard to manipulate. Flatten candy to about 1/2" thick with a rolling pin and use a pizza cutter to cut candy into four bars that are about 5" long and 1" wide. Cool at room temperature for 1 hour.

5. Melt milk chocolate chips in a small bowl in microwave for 45 seconds on high. Stir, then continue to heat chips again in increments of 15 seconds until chocolate is melted and smooth.

6. To dip candy, place a center into melted chocolate. Use two forks to lift center out of chocolate, then tap handles of forks on side of bowl to help excess chocolate drip off and to smooth out chocolate coating. Carefully place bars on wax paper to set for 1–2 hours. Store bars in a sealed container for up to 2 weeks.

FIELD NOTES

Butterfinger got its name in a contest held by Curtiss Candy Company in 1923. At that time, "butterfingers" was popular slang for athletes who dropped balls. A contestant who considered himself uncoordinated and clumsy in sports submitted the name "Butterfinger" and won.

Cajun Fries

 PREP TIME:
Active: 30 minutes
Inactive: 2 hours 45 minutes

 DIFFICULTY:
Medium

 SERVES:
4

When Jerry and Janie Murrell founded Five Guys in Arlington, Virginia in 1986, they had four sons and named their new hamburger restaurant after the number of men in the family. Just 2 years later, that number went up when the couple's youngest son Tyler was born. But rather than changing all the signs on his growing burger chain to "Six Guys," Jerry removed himself from the origin of the name and added little Tyler.

While hacking this recipe for the chain's ultra-popular Cajun Fries, I discovered that Five Guys uses a specific variety of Idaho potatoes because they are denser than other russets. I couldn't get those special potatoes, but I found that I could still make crispy, more flavorful fries like Five Guys if I simply let ordinary russet potatoes sit out for a week or so before slicing and frying them.

Just like the restaurant's, the potatoes in my copycat recipe are fried twice and then sprinkled with Cajun seasoning as soon as they come out of the oil. At Five Guys, they salt the fries first and then add Cajun seasoning, but I've included all the salt you'll need in the secret seasoning mix to eliminate that extra salting step. To copy the chain's regular fries, follow all the cooking steps here, but skip the Cajun seasoning and just sprinkle the fries with salt to taste in the last step.

 Always look around for clues. The open kitchens at some chains allow you to see how the food is made, but there may also be other things to note. While waiting for my order, I noticed that Five Guys cooks their French fries twice, so I used that information for my clone. Also, by studying the bags of potatoes stamped with packing dates stacked around the restaurant, I learned that the potatoes should be aged before using them. I discovered that older potatoes are starchier and drier and produce crispier fries. Five Guys knows this, and now you do, too.

1 tablespoon paprika
1½ teaspoons dried oregano
1 teaspoon salt
½ teaspoon garlic powder
½ teaspoon onion powder
½ teaspoon ground black pepper
¼ teaspoon ground cayenne pepper
¼ teaspoon celery salt
Peanut oil, for frying
2 large russet potatoes, washed and unpeeled (1–2 weeks old)

RECIPE STEPS:

1. Mix all ingredients except peanut oil and potatoes together in a small bowl. Transfer seasoning to an empty spice bottle with a shaker top to make it easier to apply, or plan to use your fingers to sprinkle it on the fries in the final step.

2. Slice potatoes into ⅜"-thick sticks using a knife or a French fry cutter with a ⅜" blade. Rinse sliced potatoes in a bowl of cold water, then pour out that water and add more cold water to cover potatoes. Let them soak for 2 hours, then lay sliced potatoes out on a towel to dry for 15 minutes while your oil is heating.

3. Preheat at least 2" of oil in a large saucepan, Dutch oven, or deep fryer to 275°F.

4. Fry sliced potatoes in batches for 3 minutes. Dump par-fried potatoes into a large bowl to sit for 30 minutes and raise oil temperature to 375°F. Fry potatoes again for 4–5 minutes until lightly browned and crispy, then transfer them to a cooling rack over a sheet pan.

5. Let fries sit for 30 seconds, then sprinkle them with about half of Cajun seasoning blend.

FIELD NOTES

The two-stage frying process is crucial if you want crispy fries. The first frying step removes excess moisture from the surface of the fries and begins to soften the middles. The second step gelatinizes the surface starch so that it's absorbed into the potato, making the exterior crispy.

GINO'S EAST

Deep Dish Pizza

 PREP TIME:
Active: 25 minutes
Inactive: 50 minutes, plus 1–2 days

 DIFFICULTY:
Medium

 MAKES:
1 (10") pizza

When three friends—Sam Levine, Fred Bartoli, and George Loverde—opened their pizza joint just off the Magnificent Mile in Chicago, Illinois, in 1966, they hired talented pizza chef Alice Mae Redmond to create the now-famous dough recipe. She added an ingredient that gives the pizza crust its tender texture: cream of tartar.

To make this cloned deep-dish crust at home, start your dough 1–2 days in advance. A slow, chilled rise will improve the quality and taste of your finished crust, bringing it closer to resembling the real thing. I include cream of tartar in this dupe to condition the dough, just like in the original pizza, along with yellow food coloring to achieve the proper tint.

This copycat hack makes a plain cheese pizza, but if you want toppings (sausage, pepperoni, bacon, onions, mushrooms, peppers, etc.), arrange them on top of the cheese before applying the sauce.

 It's rumored that the secret ingredient in the signature crust of Gino's East Deep Dish Pizza is cornmeal, and it's easy to understand why some might think that. The dough's yellow color makes it look like cornbread, and it has a softer quality than most doughs. However, these characteristics come from other not-so-secret ingredients that have nothing to do with corn. Because Gino's ships boxes of frozen pizzas across the country and is required by law to list all the ingredients on the package, I discovered that the "secret" dough additive is cream of tartar, and the dough's yellow tint comes from beta-carotene, a natural source of yellow coloring. When sleuthing recipes for yourself, be sure to check any packaging for insights into "secret" ingredients.

FOR CRUST:

- ⅔ cup room-temperature water
- 1 tablespoon granulated sugar
- ½ teaspoon active dry yeast
- 6 drops yellow food coloring
- 2¼ cups plus 3 tablespoons (13 ounces) all-purpose flour
- ½ teaspoon salt
- ½ teaspoon cream of tartar
- ¼ cup plus 1½ tablespoons corn oil, divided

FOR SAUCE AND TOPPING:

- 6 ounces tomato paste
- 1 cup water
- 1 (14.5-ounce) can diced tomatoes
- ¾ teaspoon salt
- ½ teaspoon granulated sugar
- ½ teaspoon dried basil
- ¼ teaspoon dried oregano
- ¼ teaspoon ground black pepper
- 4 cups shredded mozzarella cheese

Deep Dish Pizza

FOR GARNISH:

2 tablespoons grated Romano cheese
1/8 teaspoon dried oregano

RECIPE STEPS:

1. To make crust: Stir sugar and yeast into water. Stir in coloring, then let it sit for 5 minutes.

2. Whisk together flour, salt, and cream of tartar in a large bowl.

3. Mix yeast mixture and 1/4 cup oil into flour until dough comes together in a ball. Knead dough only as much as necessary to fully incorporate dry ingredients, then form dough into a ball, cover it, and refrigerate 1–2 days.

4. To make sauce: Combine tomato paste, water, and diced tomatoes in a medium saucepan over medium heat. When sauce bubbles, reduce heat and simmer it for 5 minutes to soften diced tomatoes. Use a potato masher to smash tomatoes so that chunks are smaller, then add salt, sugar, basil, oregano, and pepper. Simmer for 12 more minutes, stirring occasionally, then cover and cool. You can make sauce a day ahead and chill it or make it same day as you bake pizza.

5. Before assembling your pizza, make sure that dough, sauce, and cheese are close to room temperature. Preheat oven to 425°F and place a pizza stone, if you've got one, on middle rack.

6. Roll out dough in a circle that is 14" across. Measure 1 1/2 tablespoons of corn oil into a 10" cake pan or deep-dish pizza pan, then fold dough in half and place it in pan. Unfold dough, ensure it's centered, press it down into pan, and form sides 1 1/2" high. If you want dough to have clean look of original, use a paring knife to trim rough edge of dough all the way around so that it's flat and straight on top.

7. Poke a few holes in bottom of dough with a paring knife so it doesn't bubble, then add cheese. Spoon about 2 cups of sauce over cheese and spread it out until it covers cheese and any other toppings—you won't use all sauce. Bake pizza for 30–40 minutes until top edge of crust is nicely browned.

8. While pizza bakes, combine Romano cheese and oregano for garnish and sprinkle it over top of pizza immediately after it comes out of oven. Cool pizza for 5 minutes before cutting it into six or eight slices using a large knife. Serve.

🔍 FIELD NOTES

When added to pizza dough, cream of tartar relaxes the gluten in the flour, making the dough less sticky and easier to handle. It also calms yeast activity, allowing the dough to rise more slowly while developing better flavor.

Vanilla Ice Cream

 PREP TIME:
Active: 20 minutes
Inactive: 4½ hours

 DIFFICULTY:
Medium

 MAKES:
1 quart

If I told you that Häagen-Dazs Vanilla Ice Cream was formulated generations ago on a dairy farm in the rolling hills of Denmark, you might believe me. And that's precisely what Reuben Mattus wanted consumers to think when he created his new ice cream brand in 1960 in the Bronx in New York City.

Reuben used a marketing technique called foreign branding. To set his brand apart from others, he created the impression that his new ice cream was an exotic, special recipe made with hard-to-obtain ingredients. For the name, he considered different made-up words until settling on one that sounded Danish: Häagen-Dazs. The word is meaningless; it's not Danish, and it includes an umlaut, which doesn't exist in the Danish alphabet.

While the name may suggest a fancy and complicated recipe for ice cream, the Häagen-Dazs label is one of the simplest and cleanest you'll find among major ice cream brands. There are just five ordinary ingredients: cream, skim milk, cane sugar, egg yolks, and vanilla extract. To create this clone recipe, I experimented with the ratios of the five ingredients through many batches until I finally zeroed in on the perfect combination for a French vanilla ice cream with the smooth mouthfeel of the original. For this recipe, you'll need an ice cream maker. After 30 minutes of churning, get a spoon ready, because you'll have a generous quart of delicious homemade ice cream that's best when it's soft.

 Be aware that when your taste buds are cold, they become numb and flavors seem less intense, especially in sweet foods like ice cream. To hack very cold or frozen foods, consider warming them up. For this ice cream hack, I let my sample of real Häagen-Dazs melt until it was at room temperature. This allowed me to taste it better for a more accurate comparison to my cloned version before I froze it.

2⅓ cups heavy cream
1 cup fat-free milk
½ cup plus 1 tablespoon granulated sugar
3 large egg yolks, beaten
2 teaspoons vanilla extract

RECIPE STEPS:

1. Combine cream, milk, and sugar in a 2-quart saucepan over medium heat. Stir often while heating until sugar dissolves, about 5 minutes, then remove pan from heat.
2. Temper egg yolks by slowly pouring about ½ cup of warm cream base into beaten egg yolks while stirring. Pour egg yolk mixture into saucepan and place it over medium-low heat.
3. Heat cream base up to 170°F while stirring until it coats back of a spoon. Remove from heat, stir in vanilla, and let cool for 30 minutes. You can cool ice cream base faster by pouring it into a mixing bowl nestled in a larger ice-filled bowl. When base is no longer hot, pour it into a covered storage container and cool it in your refrigerator for 4 hours or overnight.
4. When you are ready to make ice cream, pour mixture through a mesh strainer to remove any solid bits.
5. Pour strained mixture into an ice cream maker and churn it for about 30 minutes until firm. Serve, or spoon ice cream into a covered container and freeze up to several weeks.

FIELD NOTES

Other foreign-branded US companies include **Au Bon Pain bakery café, Frusen Glädjé ice cream, Texas de Brazil, Outback Steakhouse,** and **Ginsu knives.**

Classic Eggs Benedict

 PREP TIME:
Active: 20 minutes
Inactive: None

 DIFFICULTY:
Easy

 SERVES:
2

In 2023, IHOP introduced a variety of new Eggs Benedict dishes that included a great take on the traditional recipe, with perfectly poached eggs, buttery hollandaise sauce, and Black Forest ham. It's the best Eggs Benedict I've had from a national chain, so I set my sights on crafting the perfect copy. And here it is.

For this home clone, I'll show you how to make poached eggs like the pros, how to make hollandaise sauce from scratch in just a few minutes, and how to put it all together on the plate. It's a recipe you may return to time and again, whenever you want an impressive breakfast that doesn't take much work. Serve this dish with crispy hash browns or fruit on the side.

You can prepare parts of this recipe days in advance. The hollandaise sauce and poached eggs will keep for up to 5 days! Cook the sauce as instructed in this recipe, then cool, cover, and refrigerate. When you're ready to build your Benedict, reheat the sauce gently over low heat until hot. Cook the poached eggs as instructed, then immediately plunge them into an ice bath. Store the eggs in a container filled with cold water in your refrigerator. To reheat for the final dish, submerge the poached eggs in simmering water for 30 seconds to 1 minute until hot.

FOR HOLLANDAISE SAUCE:

3 large egg yolks
1 tablespoon lemon juice
1 tablespoon water
$\frac{1}{8}$ teaspoon plus $\frac{1}{16}$ teaspoon salt
$\frac{1}{2}$ cup plus 1 tablespoon unsalted butter, melted

FOR EGGS BENEDICT:

1 tablespoon lemon juice
2 white English muffins, split
8 slices Black Forest ham
4 large eggs

RECIPE STEPS:

1. To make hollandaise sauce: Rapidly whisk egg yolks with lemon juice in a medium metal bowl until volume doubles in size. Whisk in water and salt.

2. Add melted butter in a thin stream to egg yolks while whisking until all butter is added.

3. Heat 1"–2" of water in a medium saucepan over medium heat until water bubbles, then reduce heat to a slow simmer. Place metal bowl on top of saucepan and whisk sauce until it's thick, about 5 minutes. Be sure to stir often and don't let egg yolks get too hot and start cooking. If bowl gets too hot, remove it from pan and continue to stir sauce until thick, then cover with plastic wrap until ready to use.

4. In a large saucepan, bring 3"–4" of water to a boil, then reduce heat so that just a few bubbles are visible on bottom of pan. Add 1 tablespoon of lemon juice to water.

5. Heat English muffin halves in a toaster on second-lowest setting just until very lightly browned around edges.

6. While English muffins are warming, heat ham in a skillet preheated over medium heat for 1 minute until hot. Fold each stack of two slices in half and arrange each folded stack on a face-up English muffin half.

7. Crack an egg into a mesh strainer, let sit 1 minute to remove excess watery liquid, then pour egg into a small bowl and repeat with remaining eggs, each in its own small bowl.

8. Gently tip egg from bowls into hot water and set your timer for 3 minutes.

9. After 3 minutes, check egg you added first for doneness by removing it from water with a slotted spoon and gently pressing on it. If it seems too soft, cook eggs for another 30 seconds until done, then remove each egg from water with slotted spoon. Dab bottom of spoon onto a paper towel or dish towel to remove any excess water, then gently place egg on ham on one of English muffins. Repeat for remaining eggs, then spoon hollandaise sauce over each egg. Serve.

FIELD NOTES

Eggs Benedict inspired the McDonald's Egg McMuffin. The only differences in the famous breakfast sandwich are an additional English muffin half and American cheese instead of hollandaise sauce.

Protein Power Pancakes

 PREP TIME:
Active: 30 minutes
Inactive: None

 DIFFICULTY:
Easy

 SERVES:
4

Protein is powerful. According to a 2024 International Food Information Council survey, 71% of participants are trying to increase their protein intake. That's up from 67% in 2023 and 59% in 2022. Noting the trend, manufacturers have been developing ways to add protein to more products, and restaurants are following suit, as seen with IHOP's protein-packed stack.

For this copycat hack, I carefully measured the ingredients and calculated the protein content so your dupes have just under 10 grams of protein each, like the real ones. A stack of four Protein Power Pancakes in the restaurant (and in this recipe) weighs in at a hefty 37 grams of protein.

As with the restaurant version, most of the protein in this clone is added as unflavored whey protein powder. This recipe also uses the same flours as the chain, including oat flour. Oats can be bought already ground or can be ground into flour using a coffee grinder or small food processor.

Once your batter is mixed, cook the pancakes on a well-buttered flat grill or on two or three nonstick sauté pans to make at least two pancakes at a time. The recipe yields sixteen pancakes, so cooking multiple flapjacks simultaneously will streamline the process. Serve each stack of pancakes with softened butter and maple syrup on the side to mimic the real thing.

You have the option of using either baking powder or baking soda for leavening in pancake recipes such as this one (and in other baked goods). Remember that baking soda needs an acid to activate it and baking powder does not. In this recipe, buttermilk is the activating acid. But you can also use molasses, brown sugar (which contains molasses), lemon juice, vinegar, alcohol, or cream of tartar in your recipes to trigger the chemical reaction that creates the rise. In addition to its leavening properties, baking soda also contributes a yellow to dark brown tint to the finished product, making it well suited for recipes such as this one, which have a pleasant golden-brown color.

2 cups (10 ounces) all-purpose flour
1 cup plus 2 tablespoons (3½ ounces) unflavored whey protein powder
¾ cup (4 ounces) oat flour
⅔ cup granulated sugar
2 tablespoons barley flour
2 tablespoons rye flour
1 tablespoon chia seeds
1 tablespoon baking soda
1½ teaspoons salt
2 cups buttermilk
⅔ cup whole milk
2 large eggs
⅓ cup unsalted butter, melted
2 tablespoons maple extract

FIELD NOTES

What was once considered a waste product of cheesemaking is now a valuable ingredient for protein powder. For centuries, cheesemakers used the curds of aged milk to make cheese, and the liquid whey left behind was discarded. Today, cheesemakers sell their whey, which is dried through a special process that evaporates the water. The dry whey is then ground into powder for use in manufacturing protein shakes and bars.

RECIPE STEPS:

1. In a large mixing bowl, whisk together flours, protein powder, sugar, chia seeds, baking soda, and salt.

2. Mix in buttermilk, milk, eggs, butter, and maple extract until batter is mostly smooth. Batter should contain some tiny lumps of flour. If your batter is too thick, add more milk, 1 tablespoon at a time, to thin it out.

3. Preheat a nonstick pan or griddle to medium-low heat. Add some nonstick oil spray or clarified butter to pan.

4. Add ⅓ cup of batter to hot pan and cook 1–1½ minutes until browned. Then, flip pancake and cook for another minute until browned. Repeat with remaining batter to yield sixteen pancakes. Stack four pancakes each on serving plates.

Swedish Crepes

 PREP TIME:
Active: 40 minutes
Inactive: None

 DIFFICULTY:
Easy

 MAKES:
10 crepes

Good crepes should be soft in the center, crispy around the edges, buttery, custardy, a bit sweet, and slightly salty. While there are many ways to achieve all this, crepes like those served at IHOP have a specific formula.

Over 2 days, I crafted dozens of crepes, making minor adjustments to all seven ingredients, until I finally created the version that best mirrors the look and taste of the delicious IHOP Swedish Crepes. With this hack, you'll get ten tasty crepes using a 10" nonstick skillet.

Top your crepes with the simple formula for lingonberry butter, and your IHOP Swedish Crepe recipe hack will be complete.

 When you get a dish like this to go for analysis later, it's clear that you'll want the butter and syrup on the side, but don't forget to hold the powdered sugar! These chains often dust French toast, waffles, and crepes with powdered sugar. If they add it to your to-go order, it will melt into your warm food, leaving you with food that is sweetened, which will likely throw off your hack.

FOR LINGONBERRY BUTTER:

½ cup unsalted butter, softened
3 tablespoons bottled lingonberries

FOR CREPES:

3 large eggs
⅓ cup plus ¼ cup unsalted butter, melted and divided
5 tablespoons granulated sugar
½ teaspoon vanilla extract
½ teaspoon plus ⅛ teaspoon salt
1 teaspoon baking powder
1 cup (5 ounces) all-purpose flour
1 cup whole milk

FOR GARNISH:

2 tablespoons powdered sugar
½ cup lingonberries (bottled)

RECIPE STEPS:

1. To make lingonberry butter: Combine butter with lingonberries in a small bowl. Set aside.

2. To make crepes: Add eggs, 1/3 cup of melted butter, sugar, vanilla, and salt to a large bowl and mix on high speed with an electric mixer for 30 seconds. Whisk baking powder into flour, then add it to wet ingredients a little at a time, mixing well after each addition. Mix until smooth, then add milk gradually, a little at a time, and continue mixing until smooth.

3. Heat a 10" nonstick skillet over medium heat. Use about 1 teaspoon of remaining butter to grease pan, then pour 1/4 cup of batter into pan and quickly swirl it so that batter mostly covers bottom of pan. Cook for 1–2 minutes until golden brown, then use a spatula to flip and cook for an additional 1–2 minutes, until browned. Fold crepe twice and remove it from pan. Repeat with remaining batter and butter.

4. Serve folded crepes offset-stacked on a plate, with a spoonful of lingonberries and a scoop of lingonberry butter on top. Dust crepes with powdered sugar before serving.

FIELD NOTES

There is a French myth that the first crepe is never successful, so it is given to a pet. People say, "La première crêpe c'est pour le chien," which means "The first crepe is for the dog." I have found this myth to be mostly true. And not only is the first crepe usually the worst one; the first pancake is typically also "for the dog."

Swedish Crepes

JACK LINK'S
Original Beef Jerky

 PREP TIME:
Active: 15 minutes
Inactive: 1 day plus 6–8 hours

 DIFFICULTY:
Easy

 MAKES:
10 ounces

Jack Link created his first kippered beef sticks in Wisconsin in 1985, using his grandfather's sausage and smoked meats recipes, and they quickly became a popular snack throughout the state. Jack then invested in a packaging machine and expanded into other markets. Eventually, with the help of a successful Sasquatch-themed marketing campaign, Jack Link's became the #1 jerky brand in the US.

Beef jerky is usually made in a dehydrator designed to circulate air around the food at a low temperature. The optimal temperature for drying beef jerky in a dehydrator is typically 130°F–140°F, which is a lower temperature than can be maintained by a conventional home oven. But that doesn't mean you can't use your home oven to make a perfectly tasty beef jerky hack like Jack's. And while Jack uses a smoker for his beef jerky, this recipe uses liquid smoke to create smoky beef jerky without fancy equipment.

The pineapple juice in the marinade is a crucial component of the flavor, but its primary contribution is a unique enzyme that helps break down the proteins in the tough cut of meat, thereby tenderizing it. Soy sauce and beef bouillon contribute to the umami savoriness of the jerky.

1 pound flank steak
1 cup pineapple juice
2/3 cup light brown sugar, packed
2 tablespoons liquid hickory smoke
2 tablespoons soy sauce
1 tablespoon salt
2 teaspoons Knorr granulated beef bouillon
1/4 teaspoon onion powder
1/4 teaspoon garlic powder

RECIPE STEPS:

1. Cut flank steak into 1/4"-thick slices against grain. If flank steak is thin, tilt knife blade to a 45-degree angle when slicing for wider slices.

2. Combine remaining ingredients in a large bowl and whisk until sugar is dissolved.

3. Add steak to marinade and refrigerate 24 hours. Stir meat in marinade once or twice while it chills.

4. When ready to make jerky, preheat oven to 175°F.

5. Arrange strips of beef on racks placed over two foil-lined baking sheets.

6. Dry both baking sheets of beef in oven 6–8 hours until strips are dry but not crunchy. Flip strips over after about 4 hours to help them dry evenly. Let jerky cool out of oven for about 30 minutes before storing it at room temperature in a covered container for up to 5 days.

FIELD NOTES

To make this jerky last even longer, store it chilled in a sealed container in your refrigerator for up to 2 weeks.

JASON'S DELI
Irish Potato Soup

 PREP TIME:
Active: 20 minutes
Inactive: 1 hour 10 minutes

 DIFFICULTY:
Easy

 SERVES:
8

Traditional Irish potato soup—a simple formula made with potatoes, onions, stock, and cream—gets an upgrade with the addition of Cheddar cheese, carrots, green onions, and sour cream in Jason's Deli's delicious take. These improvements result in a soup that's not only easy to build but may also be the best-tasting potato soup hack out there.

The secret to this soup clone is that it starts as a Cheddar cheese sauce. You may be skeptical if you've ever made cheese sauce that melted poorly and became grainy. Fortunately, that won't happen here if you use mild or medium Cheddar cheese, as they melt better than sharp varieties. Sharpness indicates the age of the cheese: The sharper the cheese, the older it is, and older cheese contains less water. Cheese with less water will not melt as smoothly as young cheese and is more likely to result in a clumpy or grainy finished product. So, choose your Cheddar wisely.

This recipe yields eight 1-cup bowls of soup, each topped with Cheddar cheese and crumbled bacon, just like the real thing.

 Shred the cheese yourself. Pre-shredded cheese won't melt as smoothly, because it's drier and often dusted with cellulose or starch and possibly other additives to keep the shreds from clumping in the bag. For the best results, I highly recommend that you roll up your sleeves and hunt down your cheese shredder.

FOR SOUP:

- ¼ cup unsalted butter
- ¼ cup (1¼ ounces) all-purpose flour
- 2 cups whole or 2% milk
- 8 ounces shredded mild or medium Cheddar cheese
- 4 cups chicken broth
- 5 cups unpeeled diced russet potatoes
- ½ cup minced carrot
- ¾ cup chopped green onions (white and green parts)

FOR SOUP (continued):

- ½ cup heavy cream
- 2 teaspoons minced fresh parsley
- 1¼ teaspoons salt
- ½ teaspoon hickory liquid smoke
- ¼ cup sour cream

FOR GARNISH:

- 1 cup shredded mild or medium Cheddar cheese
- ¼ cup crumbled cooked bacon

Irish Potato Soup

RECIPE STEPS:

1. Melt butter over medium-low heat in a large 3- to 4-quart saucepan or Dutch oven. Stir in flour and cook for 1 minute, until mixture is bubbling.

2. Whisk in milk as you add it. Continue whisking until no lumps of flour are visible, and turn heat up to medium.

3. Add shredded cheese and whisk gently until cheese is melted and sauce is smooth, about 5 minutes.

4. Gradually whisk in chicken broth and turn heat up to medium-high.

5. Add potatoes and carrot to pan, and when soup begins to boil, reduce heat to a simmer and cook for 30 minutes, uncovered, stirring occasionally.

6. Add green onions, cream, parsley, salt, and liquid smoke, then continue to simmer soup for 40–50 minutes, until potatoes are tender and soup has thickened. Stir soup frequently and use spoon to break up some of diced potatoes, which will help thicken soup.

7. Remove from heat and stir in sour cream.

8. To serve, top each bowl of soup with shredded Cheddar cheese and crumbled bits of cooked bacon.

FIELD NOTES

How to hack recipes like this: Measure $1/2$ cup or more of your soup sample from the restaurant into a mesh strainer and gently rinse it with water. Turn the strainer over onto a plate and spread out the contents. Identify all the ingredients, and you'll know what to shop for. This is also the best way to estimate measurements for those ingredients. When your version of the soup is done, strain the same amount, spread it out on a plate, and compare it to the restaurant sample.

Fruit Roll

 PREP TIME:
Active: 15 minutes
Inactive: 10 hours

 DIFFICULTY:
Easy

 **MAKES:**
9–10 fruit rolls

Fruit leather first emerged in New York City in the 1900s when Syrian immigrants dried apricot paste. Louis Shalhoub, whose grandfather George was one of the first immigrants selling apricot fruit leather in the early days, founded Joray in the 1960s and sold the first commercial fruit rolls in a variety of other flavors. It wasn't long before General Mills came out with their own Fruit Roll-Ups in various kid-friendly forms, including Fruit by the Foot and Gushers. Today, that's the brand that dominates the market.

After checking out the ingredients in the Joray and General Mills chewy fruit products, neither seemed worthy of a clone. Joray rolls are all apricot purée–based fruit rolls, sweetened with corn syrup and sugar, artificially flavored, and diluted with flour to give them a chewy red licorice texture. On the other hand, the taste of the General Mills rolls was terrific, and the products were soft and chewy, as expected. But with so much sugar, these products aren't much different than candy.

As it turns out, food companies with the deepest histories don't always make the best-tasting products. For fruit rolls, the flavor winner is Jovy, a Mexican brand that makes a variety of fruit rolls that taste just like the fruit printed on the label. Founded in 1993, Jovy does this by using real fruit combined with a blend of apples and pears. Apples and pears have a subdued flavor that combines well with other fruits, plus their high pectin content contributes a pleasant texture to the finished product. This Jovy Fruit Roll copycat hack includes three flavors: strawberry, raspberry, and mango, all of which call for frozen fruit or berries, to simplify the process.

 If you have a "time bake" or "cook time" setting on your oven, you can start a batch of fruit rolls in the evening and the oven will turn off automatically when it's done. In the morning your fruit will be cool and ready to roll.

FOR STRAWBERRY FRUIT ROLL:

1 cup plus 2 tablespoons water
2 teaspoons dry pectin
1/4 teaspoon citric acid
2/3 cup granulated sugar
3 cups (14 ounces) frozen sliced strawberries, thawed
3/4 cup (3 ounces) peeled and diced Gala or Honeycrisp apple
3/4 cup (3 ounces) peeled and diced Bartlett pear

FOR RASPBERRY FRUIT ROLL:

1 cup plus 2 tablespoons water
2 teaspoons dry pectin
2/3 cup granulated sugar
3 cups (12 ounces) frozen raspberries, thawed
3/4 cup (3 ounces) peeled and diced Gala or Honeycrisp apple
3/4 cup (3 ounces) peeled and diced Bartlett pear

FOR MANGO FRUIT ROLL:

1 cup plus 2 tablespoons water
2 teaspoons dry pectin
1/2 teaspoon citric acid
2/3 cup granulated sugar
3 cups (14 ounces) frozen mango chunks, thawed
3/4 cup (3 ounces) peeled and diced Gala or Honeycrisp apple
3/4 cup (3 ounces) peeled and diced Bartlett pear

RECIPE STEPS:

1. Preheat your oven to 150°F.
2. To make each flavor: Combine water, pectin, and citric acid (if called for) in a small saucepan over medium heat. Stir often as mixture comes to a boil, then simmer it for 2 minutes. Turn off heat and whisk in sugar until it dissolves.
3. Combine frozen fruit of your choice (strawberries, raspberries, or mango chunks) with apple and pear in a blender or food processor. Pour in warm pectin solution and thoroughly purée fruit blend on high speed until it is smooth, with no visible chunks of fruit remaining, about 1 minute. For raspberry flavor, strain raspberry purée through a sieve or mesh strainer to remove seeds.
4. Measure two 1/3-cup portions of fruit purée onto a silicone mat–lined baking sheet. Drop baking sheet on counter a few times to spread purée into circles measuring 6 1/2"–7" in diameter. If you have more than one silicone mat, use a couple of baking sheets on two oven racks to speed up the process.
5. Bake fruit rolls for 9–12 hours, until they are no longer tacky in middle, then turn off heat and let fruit rolls sit in warm oven for another 30 minutes until pans are cool enough to take out of oven with your hands. The fruit rolls should release cleanly from mat.
6. Peel each fruit roll from silicone mat, place it in center of an 8" × 8" cellophane wrapper, roll it up, and seal it with a small piece of clear tape. Store your fruit rolls in a sealed bag and they'll keep for at least 1 month.

FIELD NOTES

The dry pectin used to thicken jams and jellies, and these fruit rolls, is derived from the soluble fiber naturally present in fruits and vegetables, especially apples, pears, and citrus peels. Pectin gels and thickens when combined with sugar and acid, which explains why the pectin in these recipes is combined with both sugar and, when working with less acidic fruits, citric acid.

LAZY DOG

Bacon Candy

 PREP TIME:
Active: 5 minutes
Inactive: 1 hour 15 minutes

 DIFFICULTY:
Easy

 SERVES:
2–3

The technique of sugaring raw bacon and baking it until crispy is neither complicated nor a secret, but this simple formula has numerous variations. I tried several methods of sugaring bacon to determine what worked best, then customized the recipe to closely match the bacon candy on the appetizer menu at Lazy Dog.

Lazy Dog chefs know that the best bacon candy is more than just sweet and salty, so they sprinkle in some black pepper and crushed red pepper flakes to perk up the party. Thick-cut bacon will be ideal for this clone, and you'll need a rack to allow air to circulate around the slices. You might also want to line your baking sheet with foil for easy cleanup.

When it comes out of the oven, sprinkle your bacon candy clone with fresh parsley and serve it upright in a cup, just like in the restaurant. It's an excellent appetizer or snack, and it also makes a great garnish for my clone of Lazy Dog Crispy Deviled Eggs.

 The best way to preserve some samples for later study is by freezing them. The surface texture of certain foods, like this bacon, will become soggy when stored in an environment where the surface will absorb moisture. Store food with a crispy coating, a crunchy crust, or a glaze in a sealed container in your freezer. If kept at room temperature or refrigerated, moisture in the food will be absorbed into the surface, making glazes melt and turning crispy crusts soft. Freezing food samples will prevent this. To eat, defrost at room temperature until edible.

FOR CANDY:

5 slices uncooked thick-cut bacon
1/3 cup light brown sugar, packed
1/2 teaspoon ground black pepper
1/2 teaspoon crushed red pepper

FOR GARNISH:

1 teaspoon minced fresh parsley

RECIPE STEPS:

1. Preheat oven to 350°F.
2. Line a baking sheet with foil and place a rack on it. Arrange bacon slices side by side on top of rack.
3. Combine brown sugar and peppers in a small bowl.
4. Sprinkle half of sugar mixture on bacon slices and gently pat it down with your fingers. Let it sit for 5 minutes so sugar absorbs moisture and sticks to bacon. Gently flip over each slice of bacon and sprinkle remaining sugar mixture on other side.
5. Bake for 35–50 minutes until bacon is crispy. Thicker bacon will take longer to cook. Allow bacon to cool for 30 minutes, then sprinkle it with minced parsley and serve.

FIELD NOTES

Sugar molecules bond with water molecules, so when the sugar is rubbed onto the bacon, it immediately draws moisture out of the meat and creates a syrup that adheres to the bacon. This allows you to flip the slices of bacon over to coat the other side without the sugar falling off.

LAZY DOG

Crispy Deviled Eggs

 PREP TIME:
Active: 30 minutes
Inactive: 1 hour 15 minutes

DIFFICULTY:
Medium

 SERVES:
2–4

Lazy Dog founder Chris Simms comes from a restaurant family. His father, Tom Simms, founded the West Coast French bistro chain Mimi's, which grew to 150 units in the 1990s. Chris opened the first Lazy Dog in Huntington Beach, California, in 2003 with the intention of providing a relaxed Rocky Mountain–themed environment where customers can dine with their dogs on an outdoor patio. They can even order food for their pets from a menu of dog treats. A popular item on the human menu are these Crispy Deviled Eggs, which are hard-cooked egg whites, breaded and fried until crispy, filled with a creamy yolk mixture, sprinkled with smoked paprika, and topped with the best thing that ever topped a deviled egg: bacon candy! If you want to make extra bacon candy to munch on, check out the previous recipe for Lazy Dog's Bacon Candy appetizer, and you'll get five slices of bacon candy. That's two for this deviled egg copycat recipe and three for you to eat and share.

The commonly used term "hard-boiled eggs" implies that the best way to cook eggs in the shell is to submerge them in boiling water. This recipe includes steps for the standard boiling method. However, if you have a steamer basket, steaming the eggs will produce better-looking results. The yolks will be pure yellow, with no gray surface, and the eggshells will easily slide off. To steam cook the eggs, heat up 1" of water in a saucepan over medium heat. When water is simmering, add a steamer basket and fill it with six eggs, then add a lid. Steam eggs for 14 minutes, then use a slotted spoon or a spider to transfer them to a bowl filled with ice water to halt cooking. After about 30 minutes, eggs will be cold all the way through. Shell each of the eggs, then refrigerate until ready to use.

FOR EGGS:

8 large eggs, divided
2 slices uncooked thick-cut bacon
2 tablespoons light brown sugar, packed
1/4 teaspoon ground black pepper
1/4 teaspoon crushed red pepper
2 tablespoons mayonnaise
2 teaspoons Dijon mustard
1/2 teaspoon apple cider vinegar
1/8 teaspoon granulated sugar

FOR EGGS (continued):

1/8 teaspoon salt
1/8 teaspoon ground black pepper
Vegetable oil, for frying
1 tablespoon water
1/2 cup all-purpose flour
1/2 cup panko breadcrumbs

FOR GARNISH:

1/4 teaspoon smoked paprika

Crispy Deviled Eggs

RECIPE STEPS:

1. Cook 6 of the eggs by placing them in a medium saucepan and filling it with cold water until it's 1" above eggs. Place pan over high heat, and when water comes to a rolling boil, wait 30 seconds, then turn off heat, cover pan, and set your timer for 14 minutes. After 14 minutes, remove eggs from pan with a slotted spoon or a spider and transfer them to a bowl of ice water. Leave eggs in ice water for 30 minutes, then peel them and refrigerate until ready to use.

2. Preheat oven to 350°F.

3. Line a baking sheet with foil and place a rack in pan. Arrange bacon slices side by side on top of rack.

4. Combine brown sugar and peppers in a small bowl.

5. Use your fingers to sprinkle brown sugar on top of bacon and gently pat it down with your fingers. Let it sit for 5 minutes until sugar absorbs moisture from bacon and sticks to it. Gently flip each slice of bacon over and sprinkle remaining sugar on other side.

6. Bake for 35–50 minutes until bacon is crispy, then let it cool. Thicker bacon will take longer to cook.

7. While bacon cooks, preheat 2"–3" of oil in a large saucepan or Dutch oven with a thermometer attached over medium heat to 325°F.

8. Peel hard-cooked eggs, slice them in half lengthwise, and remove yolks. Set aside 4 egg white halves. You'll use 8 of them for this recipe, so you can use the 4 leftover whites for another recipe or eat them. Use a fork to crush yolks and mix them with mayonnaise, mustard, vinegar, sugar, salt, and pepper in a medium bowl until smooth.

9. Beat the 2 uncooked eggs in a medium bowl with 1 tablespoon of water. Measure flour into another medium bowl and breadcrumbs into a third medium bowl.

10. Toss egg whites in flour until lightly coated. Shake off excess flour, dip egg whites into beaten egg until thoroughly moistened (allowing excess to drip off), then toss them in breadcrumbs until completely coated. Arrange breaded egg whites on a plate until all are breaded.

11. Fry breaded egg whites in hot oil for 2–3 minutes until golden brown. Remove them to a rack or paper towel–lined plate.

12. Spoon 2 teaspoons of yolk mixture into each crispy egg white. Sprinkle top of each egg with a dash of smoked paprika.

13. Cut each slice of bacon candy into four pieces, then stick edge or corner of a piece of bacon into each yolk and serve.

FIELD NOTES

"Deviled" is a culinary term that refers to something that has been heavily seasoned, especially with spicy ingredients such as paprika, mustard, and pepper.

LITTLE CAESARS

Crazy Puffs

 PREP TIME:
Active: 1 hour
Inactive: 2 days, plus 1 hour 5 minutes

 DIFFICULTY:
Medium

 MAKES:
21 puffs

One of Little Caesars's most successful recent products is these mini deep-dish pizzas. Baked until browned and bubbly, brushed with buttery garlic spread, and sprinkled with herbs and cheese, they come with pepperoni and cheese or just cheese and are too good to resist.

This Little Caesars Crazy Puffs copycat recipe includes dough made from scratch, which is a big improvement over online versions that use pre-made dough. Cold-proofing the dough for 48 hours will create a nicely fermented, chewy finished product that matches Little Caesars's in texture and flavor.

Using this original secret recipe, you can make 21 Crazy Puffs clones (both pepperoni and cheese and only cheese) in two batches using a twelve-cup muffin pan.

 Find insider information, and your hack just got easier. After a worker revealed that Little Caesars Crazy Sauce is the same recipe as their marinara pizza sauce, I redesigned the sauce hack from my 1994 cookbook, *More Top Secret Recipes*. This time, I made the sauce without cooking it. At Little Caesars, the pizza sauce only gets cooked when it goes into the oven on the pizza. Meanwhile, in the kitchen, some of that sauce is packaged into to-go cups and chilled until it's served to customers as Crazy Sauce for dipping.

FOR DOUGH:

1 cup room-temperature water
1 teaspoon active dry yeast
1 tablespoon plus 2 teaspoons granulated sugar, divided
2½ cups (12½ ounces) bread flour
1¼ teaspoons kosher salt
3 teaspoons extra-virgin olive oil, divided
Butter-flavored oil spray (such as Pam)

FOR SAUCE:

1 (6-ounce) can tomato paste
¾ cup water
1 teaspoon lemon juice
1 teaspoon dried oregano
¾ teaspoon dried basil
½ teaspoon granulated sugar
¼ teaspoon salt
¼ teaspoon coarse ground black pepper
¼ teaspoon crushed red pepper
¼ teaspoon garlic powder
⅛ teaspoon onion powder
⅛ teaspoon dried crushed rosemary

FOR CHEESE BLEND:

2½ cups shredded mozzarella cheese

1¼ cups shredded Muenster cheese

FOR PEPPERONI PUFFS:

63 pepperoni slices

FOR GARLIC SPREAD:

¼ cup margarine or butter, melted

¼ teaspoon garlic powder

¼ teaspoon salt

FOR CHEESE AND HERB BLEND:

½ teaspoon dried parsley

¼ teaspoon dried oregano

¼ teaspoon dried basil

2 teaspoons grated Parmesan cheese

RECIPE STEPS:

1. To make dough: Combine water, yeast, and 1 teaspoon of sugar in a large bowl (if using a handheld mixer) or bowl of a stand mixer. Let it sit for 5 minutes until surface turns foamy.

2. Combine flour and salt in a medium bowl, then add to mixing bowl with 2 teaspoons oil and remaining sugar. If using a stand mixer, mix with a kneading hook until dough comes together, and then continue to knead for 4 minutes. If using a handheld mixer, mix until dough comes together, then knead by hand for 4 minutes.

3. Form dough into a ball and coat it with remaining teaspoon of oil. Place dough in a covered container and refrigerate it for 48 hours.

4. To make sauce: Mix all ingredients in a medium bowl. Cover and chill for at least 2 hours, up to overnight, before using.

5. When you're ready to make puffs, remove dough from refrigerator and uncover it. Let it sit out for 1 hour.

6. Preheat a conventional oven to 500°F or a convection oven to 475°F. Spray cups of a muffin pan with butter-flavored oil spray.

7. Combine shredded cheeses in a medium bowl.

8. Assemble each puff by rolling 1 ounce of dough into a ball, then use a rolling pin to flatten ball into a disk on a lightly floured surface. Press disk of dough into a cup and make a well in center of dough.

9. For pepperoni puffs: Place one slice of pepperoni in well. Add a big pinch of shredded cheese on pepperoni. Spoon about 1 teaspoon of sauce on cheese. Add two overlapping pepperoni slices on top of sauce. Add enough cheese to cover pepperoni and repeat for remaining puffs. Bake for 10–12 minutes until cheese has browned on top.

10. For cheese and herb puffs: Place a big pinch of shredded cheese in dough well. Spoon about 1 teaspoon of sauce onto cheese. Add enough cheese to cover sauce and repeat for remaining puffs. Bake for 10–12 minutes until cheese has browned on top.

11. While puffs are baking, mix ingredients for garlic spread in a small bowl.

12. Make cheese and herb blend by combining herbs in a small bowl and crumbling between fingers. Mix in Parmesan cheese.

13. Brush all puffs with garlic spread and sprinkle each with a couple of pinches of herb and cheese blend.

FIELD NOTES

The Little Caesars "Pizza! Pizza!" slogan was created in 1979 when the company began offering two pizzas for the price of one. That offer appears to have ended sometime in the late 1990s; however, the tagline is still used today.

MAGGIANO'S LITTLE ITALY

Famous Rigatoni "D"

 PREP TIME:
Active: 2 hours
Inactive: 5 hours

 DIFFICULTY:
Medium

 SERVES:
4

"D" was chef David DiGregorio's nickname at the first Maggiano's, which opened in Chicago, Illinois, in 1991, and he's the one who created the best-selling pasta dish on the menu.

After many trials and several errors, I finally replicated David's fantastic creamy marsala sauce for my Maggiano's Famous Rigatoni "D" hack by reducing two bottles of inexpensive marsala wine to just half a cup of intensely flavored liquid. Mushrooms contributed a savory umami goodness, and after about an hour and a half I had the perfect flavoring solution for the cream sauce.

Besides those in the sauce, the rest of the mushrooms in the dish are served unsliced, so make sure they're small enough to eat in one bite. For this recipe, you can use either white (button) or brown (cremini) mushrooms. They are the same mushroom species, with only minor differences (white mushrooms are a cultivated mutation of the brown ones), so either will work. If you want a slightly deeper flavor, go with creminis.

 A great way to use marsala wine for a sauce is to make an extreme reduction, in which the wine is reduced to about one-tenth of its original volume. This process eliminates all the alcohol in the wine and creates a thick, sweet syrup that bursts with flavor.

FOR CHICKEN:

2 cups chicken broth
¼ cup extra-virgin olive oil
1 tablespoon plus 1 teaspoon kosher salt
1 tablespoon Italian seasoning blend (oregano, marjoram, rosemary, basil, etc.)
½ teaspoon ground black pepper
24 ounces (3 medium) skinless chicken breast fillets

FOR MARSALA CREAM SAUCE:

1 head garlic
1 tablespoon extra-virgin olive oil
2 (750ml) bottles marsala wine
8 ounces white (button) or baby portobella (cremini) mushrooms, sliced
6 tablespoons unsalted butter
2 tablespoons minced or pressed garlic
½ cup pinot grigio wine
4 cups heavy cream
1¼ teaspoons salt

FOR CARAMELIZED ONION:

2 tablespoons unsalted butter

2 teaspoons extra-virgin olive oil

2 cups peeled and diced yellow onion

FOR MUSHROOMS:

6 tablespoons unsalted butter, divided

40 (12 ounces) bite-sized white or brown mushrooms, divided

1/4 teaspoon salt, divided

1/4 teaspoon ground black pepper, divided

1/4 teaspoon dried oregano, divided

2 tablespoons balsamic vinegar, divided

FOR SERVING:

1 pound uncooked rigatoni pasta

1 teaspoon minced fresh parsley

2 tablespoons grated Parmesan or Romano cheese

RECIPE STEPS:

1. To make chicken: Combine broth, oil, salt, seasoning blend, and pepper in a large storage container or resealable bag, then add chicken breasts. Marinate chicken for 4 hours in refrigerator.

2. Preheat oven to 400°F.

3. To make marsala cream sauce, start by roasting a whole head of garlic. Remove all but last layer of papery skin, then slice 1/2" off top and place head cut-side up in an oven-safe baking dish. Drizzle olive oil over garlic and bake it uncovered for 40–45 minutes until browned on top. When garlic cools, squeeze head of garlic like a tube of toothpaste to extract roasted garlic. Alternatively, you can roast garlic by peeling all cloves and drizzling olive oil over them in a small oven-safe baking dish. Cover garlic with foil and bake for 25–30 minutes until cloves are soft and slightly browned. Mash cloves before using.

4. Combine marsala wine, sliced mushrooms, and roasted garlic (about 2 tablespoons) in a 2-quart saucepan over medium heat. Simmer for 1 1/2–1 3/4 hours until liquid has been substantially reduced to just 1/2 cup. Strain out mushrooms and garlic and set reduced sauce aside.

5. Clean out pan, place it over medium-low heat, and add 6 tablespoons of unsalted butter. When butter has melted, add garlic and sweat it for 5 minutes, but don't let it get brown.

6. Add pino grigio and turn heat up to medium. Cook for 5 minutes to reduce wine, then add cream and salt and reduced marsala wine and simmer for 20 minutes, stirring often. Reduce heat if necessary so cream sauce is at a gentle simmer and not a rapid boil. After 20 minutes, sauce will have reduced slightly to just over 4 cups. Set it aside uncovered.

7. To make caramelized onion: Heat butter and oil in a medium sauté pan over medium-low heat. Add onion and cook for 45 minutes to 1 hour, stirring occasionally until it's dark brown. The 2 cups of diced onion will reduce to a little over 1/4 cup of caramelized onion. Set aside.

8. Preheat oven to 450°F.

9. Remove chicken breasts from marinade and place them on baking sheets without rinsing them off. They should be coated with some oil, which will help prevent sticking. Bake for 18–24 minutes until lightly browned and 165°F in center. Cool chicken for 15 minutes and shred it into bite-sized chunks. Set aside.

10. Prepare pasta by adding it to 4 quarts of boiling water over medium-high heat. Cook for 12 minutes until al dente or slightly tough. Drain.

continued on next page

RECIPE STEPS (continued):

11. Melt 3 tablespoons of butter in a sauté pan over medium heat. Put half of mushrooms into pan, followed by half of salt, pepper, and oregano. Cook mushrooms for 3 minutes, tossing occasionally, then add 1 tablespoon of balsamic vinegar and cook for 1 more minute.

12. Add half of chicken to pan and cook for 2 minutes.

13. Add half of caramelized onions to pan, stir, then add half of cream sauce into pan.

14. Bring dish to a simmer, then add half of pasta to pan. Cook for 3–5 more minutes until pasta is soft and starch has helped to thicken sauce. Repeat steps 11–14 with remaining ingredients.

15. Split pasta and sauce onto four serving plates, then sprinkle each dish with minced parsley and serve with grated Parmesan or Romano cheese on side for topping.

FIELD NOTES

Marsala wine is used more for cooking than for drinking. It's fortified during fermentation with additional alcohol, usually brandy, that gives the wine a more complex flavor profile, which makes it excellent for sauces.

MAGGIANO'S LITTLE ITALY

Italian Meatballs

 PREP TIME:
Active: 35 minutes
Inactive: 1 hour 15 minutes

 DIFFICULTY:
Medium

 **MAKES:**
8 large meatballs

Several years ago, I duplicated Maggiano's signature Tenderloin Medallions, and recently I returned to copy the chain's Italian Meatballs. The manager recognized me as the food sleuth who re-created their tenderloins and shared valuable intel about the famous meatballs recipe. He told me that Maggiano's makes their meatballs with just ground chuck and not with other meats such as pork and veal, which are often used in traditional formulas. I also met the location's executive chef, who told me about the recipe's braising process and the importance of forming the meatballs loosely in your hands and not packing the meat. He explained that you should be able to "cut the meatballs with a plastic spoon."

Now, with these helpful insider tips, you can hack the chain's mouthwatering meatballs and marinara sauce for restaurant-quality results in your home kitchen.

 You can make your own breadcrumbs from scratch for a personal touch to this recipe. Tear a small loaf of Italian or other white bread into pieces and dry it on a baking sheet in an oven at 250°F for 30–45 minutes until dry. Use a food processor or blender and pulse the dry bread to create coarse crumbs.

FOR MARINARA SAUCE:

- 1/4 cup extra-virgin olive oil
- 1/4 cup peeled and minced white onion
- 1 tablespoon plus 1 teaspoon minced garlic
- 1 (28-ounce) can crushed tomatoes
- 2/3 cup water
- 1 1/2 teaspoons granulated sugar
- 1/2 teaspoon salt
- 1/2 teaspoon dried oregano
- 1/2 teaspoon dried basil
- 1/4 teaspoon dried thyme

FOR MEATBALLS:

- 2 pounds ground chuck
- 1 1/4 cups breadcrumbs
- 2/3 cup grated Parmesan cheese
- 3 tablespoons chopped fresh flat-leaf (Italian) parsley
- 2 1/2 teaspoons garlic powder
- 1 1/4 teaspoons salt
- 1/4 teaspoon crushed red pepper
- 2 large eggs, beaten
- 2/3 cup whole milk

FOR GARNISH:

1 tablespoon grated Parmesan cheese
1 teaspoon minced fresh flat-leaf (Italian) parsley
8 crostini (see Field Notes)

RECIPE STEPS:

1. To make marinara sauce: Heat olive oil over medium-low heat. When oil is hot, add onion and garlic. Cook for 3 minutes, and don't let garlic brown. Add crushed tomatoes, water, sugar, salt, oregano, basil, and thyme. Bring sauce to a slow simmer and cook for 15 minutes, stirring occasionally. Remove pan from heat, cover it, and set it aside while you make meatballs.
2. Preheat oven to 425°F.
3. Use your hands to combine ground chuck with breadcrumbs in a large bowl, but keep beef loose and don't compact it.
4. Add Parmesan, parsley, garlic, salt, and red pepper to meat and mix well with your hands. Again, use light hands to keep beef crumbly and not packed together.
5. Combine beaten egg with milk and add it to beef. Use your hands to mix it in.
6. Use both hands to form eight meatballs, weighing approximately 6 ounces each. Form meatballs loosely and do not compress them. Arrange all meatballs in a 9" × 13" baking pan that has been lightly sprayed or rubbed with oil. Meatballs should not touch each other.
7. Bake meatballs for 25–30 minutes until lightly browned on top. Remove them from oven and reduce heat to 325°F.
8. Add 1 cup of marinara sauce and 1½ cups of water to baking pan. Cover pan with aluminum foil.
9. Bake covered meatballs for 50–60 minutes until tender.
10. To serve meatballs, heat remaining marinara sauce and spoon it over each meatball, followed by a sprinkle of grated Parmesan cheese and some minced parsley.

FIELD NOTES

Make an easy crostini side for this dish by slicing a loaf of Italian bread and cutting slices diagonally through middle to make pointed halves. Brush bread with olive oil, sprinkle with a bit of salt, and bake at 400°F for 8–10 minutes until lightly browned.

MAGGIANO'S LITTLE ITALY

Mozzarella Marinara

 PREP TIME:
Active: 35 minutes
Inactive: 45 minutes

 DIFFICULTY:
Medium

 SERVES:
2–3 as an appetizer

Maggiano's elevates a typically mundane finger food appetizer, turning it into a stunning starter of thickly breaded mozzarella slices, generously topped with melted mozzarella and a delectable marinara sauce.

To create a dish at home that resembles the original in appearance and flavor, begin with a large 2-pound block of mozzarella. After breading the cheese using the method here, allow the cheese to rest while you prepare the marinara; this helps the breading adhere better when frying the cheese pieces. This copycat recipe produces three crispy cheese slices. If you prefer a larger serving, you'll have ample breading and marinara to double the recipe for six breaded cheese slices.

 If you don't always want to hack a sauce from scratch, keep an assortment of popular sauces in your refrigerator to compare to restaurant sauces for the closest match. I have 5 different bottled marinara sauces and 7 different brands of barbecue sauce in my fridge right now that I can use for a test taste when necessary.

FOR BREADED MOZZARELLA:

1 cup all-purpose flour
1½ teaspoons salt
1½ teaspoons freshly ground black pepper
½ cup plain breadcrumbs (such as Progresso)
3 tablespoons grated Parmesan cheese
2 large eggs, beaten
3 tablespoons water
3 (⅜"-thick) slices mozzarella cheese
1½ thin deli-style slices mozzarella cheese
Vegetable oil, for frying

FOR MARINARA SAUCE:

2 tablespoons extra-virgin olive oil
2 tablespoons peeled and minced white onion
2 teaspoons minced garlic
1 (15-ounce) can crushed tomatoes
⅓ cup water
¾ teaspoon granulated sugar
¼ teaspoon salt
¼ teaspoon dried oregano
¼ teaspoon dried basil
⅛ teaspoon dried thyme

FOR GARNISH:

1 teaspoon minced fresh basil

RECIPE STEPS:

1. To make breaded mozzarella: Combine flour, salt, and pepper in a shallow bowl or tray. Combine breadcrumbs and grated Parmesan in another shallow bowl or tray. Combine beaten eggs and water in a medium bowl.

2. Coat 1 slice mozzarella with seasoned flour, then dip cheese into egg, covering both sides. Return cheese to seasoned flour and ensure it's fully coated. Let sit in flour for 5 minutes so that it adheres properly. Then, dip slice back into egg and into breadcrumbs until well coated. Repeat with remaining mozzarella slices. Place slices on a tray or plate and refrigerate 1 hour.

3. To make marinara sauce: Heat extra-virgin olive oil over medium-low heat. When oil is hot, add onion and garlic. Cook for 3 minutes, and don't let garlic brown. Add crushed tomatoes, water, sugar, salt, oregano, basil, and thyme. Bring sauce to a slow simmer and cook for 15 minutes, stirring occasionally. Remove pan from heat, cover it, and set it aside while you cook mozzarella.

4. When mozzarella has chilled, preheat at least 2" of oil in a large saucepan, Dutch oven, or deep fryer to 350°F. Preheat oven to 425°F.

5. Fry slices in oil for 1–1½ minutes until golden brown. When you see any cheese beginning to ooze out of breading, your mozzarella is done. Use a spatula to remove breaded cheese from oil and place slices on a baking sheet. Cut thin mozzarella slices from corner to corner, then place ½ slice on each fried mozzarella chunk. Place cheese in preheated oven and bake 2–3 minutes until sliced cheese on top is melted.

6. Build dish by spooning some marinara sauce onto a serving plate. Place fried mozzarella slices in a row on marinara sauce, then spoon some more marinara just over upper part of mozzarella. Sprinkle dish with minced basil and serve.

FIELD NOTES

The marinara sauce at Maggiano's is made with tomatoes grown in California exclusively for the restaurant chain.

Mozzarella Marinara

Original Sloppy Joe Sauce

 PREP TIME:
Active: 20 minutes
Inactive: 30 minutes

 DIFFICULTY:
Easy

 SERVES:
4

Loose meat sandwiches originated in Iowa in 1926, when Maid-Rite began selling burgers made with ground beef that wasn't shaped into patties. These sandwiches became a Midwest sensation and were often served with a spoon to scoop up the pieces that would inevitably fall out. The dry and crumbly nature of a loose meat sandwich might explain why, in 1930, a chef named Joe, as legend has it, created a tomato-based sauce, possibly with ketchup, which he mixed into the ground beef. Joe's new sandwich had more flavor than its loose meat predecessor, and the meat now stayed in the bun.

Sloppy Joes became a popular choice on restaurant and diner menus, with sandwiches selling for as little as ten cents each in the 1930s and 1940s. In 1969, Hunt's brought sloppy Joes from restaurants to homes by introducing the first canned sloppy Joe sauce. Combining a can of flavorful sauce with 1 pound of browned ground beef created enough sloppy Joes to serve a family of four. It was simple, affordable, and loved by both kids and adults.

When this cloned sauce is added to 1 pound of ground beef, as with the original version, you'll have an excellent re-creation of the iconic dish. Like the real thing, this version is easy, cheap, and delicious.

 Food manufacturers commonly use corn syrup as a sweetener because it is cheaper than sugar. However, you do not necessarily need to do the same unless a recipe requires corn syrup for a particular reason, such as preventing the formation of sugar crystals in a syrup. Using granulated sugar to replace any corn syrup listed in the ingredients is often preferable for your copycat hacks.

FOR SAUCE:

1½ cups water
2 teaspoons petite diced red bell pepper
2 teaspoons petite diced green bell pepper
2 teaspoons petite diced Fresno pepper, seeded
6 ounces tomato paste
1¼ cups water
2 tablespoons plus 1 teaspoon granulated sugar
1 tablespoon plus 1½ teaspoons white wine vinegar
2½ teaspoons chili powder
¾ teaspoon salt
¼ teaspoon plus ⅛ teaspoon garlic powder

FOR SANDWICHES:

1 pound ground beef
4 hamburger buns

RECIPE STEPS:

1. To make sauce: Bring 1½ cups of water to a boil in a small saucepan over high heat. Add diced peppers and reduce heat to a simmer. Cook for 10 minutes until peppers soften, then strain.

2. Combine remaining ingredients with cooked peppers in a small saucepan. Bring sauce to a boil over medium heat, then reduce heat to low and let it simmer for 4 minutes. Turn off heat, cover, and allow it to cool for at least 30 minutes.

3. To make sloppy Joes: Cook 1 pound of ground beef in a large skillet until no pink remains, about 5 minutes. Tilt pan and spoon out excess fat.

4. Pour all sloppy Joe sauce into pan and cook over medium heat for 5–7 minutes until thick. Pile sloppy Joe beef onto hamburger buns and serve.

FIELD NOTES

In different regions of the US, sloppy Joes go by other names, including "Dynamites," "Barbecues," "Sloppy Janes," "Wimpies," "Slushburgers," "Steamers," and "Yum Yums."

MARIE CALLENDER'S
Chocolate Satin Pie

 PREP TIME:
Active: 40 minutes
Inactive: 2 hours 55 minutes

 DIFFICULTY:
Medium

 SERVES:
8

Marie Callender's Chocolate Satin Pie features a creamy chocolate mousse in an Oreo cookie crust and is one of the most requested pies on the restaurant chain's menu. This pie is so popular that a frozen version is available in most supermarkets. (This copycat replicates the fresh variety.)

To prepare the chocolate cookie crust for your clone, you'll use Oreo cookies crushed or ground into fine crumbs. Once the crust is baked and cooled, you'll fill it with rich chocolate mousse made from real dark chocolate, cream, and eggs, just like the original.

Once the filling has set in your refrigerator, simply top your taste-alike pie with homemade whipped cream (that recipe is here, too) and chocolate sprinkles, and no one will ever suspect it's not the real deal.

 When searching for clues, remember that supermarket versions of restaurant dishes are typically prepared differently. Manufacturers modify or substitute ingredients to stabilize store versions or to reduce costs. For example, the frozen Marie Callender's Chocolate Satin Pie available in grocery stores has a crust that is less flavorful than the dark chocolate cookie crust of the restaurant version. The store pie is smaller and topped with chocolate chips instead of the sprinkles that are found on the fresh restaurant pie. While the ingredients listed on the packaging may provide insights for creating your hack, obtaining the original item fresh from the restaurant is advisable for the best reference.

FOR CRUST:

24 Oreo cookies
6 tablespoons unsalted butter, melted

FOR FILLING:

3 tablespoons unsalted butter
¼ teaspoon plus ⅛ teaspoon salt
1¼ cups (8 ounces) dark chocolate (chips or bar)
3 large eggs
6 tablespoons granulated sugar
1½ teaspoons vanilla extract
1 teaspoon gelatin powder
1 tablespoon water
¾ cup heavy cream

FOR TOPPING:

1 cup heavy whipping cream
2 tablespoons granulated sugar
½ teaspoon vanilla extract
¼ teaspoon cream of tartar
1 tablespoon chocolate sprinkles

RECIPE STEPS:

1. Preheat oven to 350°F.
2. Scrape off and discard filling from Oreo cookies, leaving 48 chocolate cookie wafers. Grind cookies into fine crumbs in a food processor. Alternatively, place cookies in a resealable plastic bag and use a rolling pin to crush them.
3. In a large bowl, combine cookie crumbs and butter until crumbs are thoroughly moistened. Press crumbs firmly into a 9" pie dish. Use a flat-bottomed drinking glass to compact bottom of crust so it is flat and firm. Pack the crust tightly against bottom and sides of pie plate to prevent it from slipping down. Use fingers to press crust onto side of pie dish and make top edge of crust align evenly with top rim of pie plate. Bake for 10 minutes, then cool completely (about 20 minutes).
4. Make filling by adding 2" of water to a pan and setting it over medium-low heat. Add butter and salt to a large bowl and place it over pan of water.
5. When butter in bowl has melted, add chocolate chips and stir gently with a spoon to help melt chips.
6. As chocolate melts, combine eggs, sugar, and vanilla in a medium bowl with a mixer on high speed. Mix for 30 seconds.
7. Combine gelatin and water in a small bowl. Heat for 15 seconds on high in microwave until it becomes foamy.
8. Allow gelatin to cool for 2 minutes, then mix it into eggs using a mixer on high speed.
9. When chocolate is melted and smooth, remove bowl from heat and stir in egg mixture. Return bowl to pan for 3 minutes, stirring occasionally until warm and smooth. Place bowl in freezer to cool filling 30–45 minutes, until no longer warm.
10. When chocolate filling is cool, use an electric mixer on high speed to whip for about 30 seconds until it has increased in volume and is a lighter color.
11. In a medium bowl, whip heavy cream with an electric mixer on high speed until fluffy with stiff peaks, about 1 minute. Fold whipped cream into chocolate filling using a spatula. Be gentle so you don't deflate fluffy whipped cream as you combine it.
12. When filling is homogenous, with no more visible streaks of white, pour it into pie shell, spread it flat, and place it in your refrigerator to set, about 2 hours.
13. Just before serving, prepare whipped cream topping by adding cream, sugar, vanilla, and cream of tartar to a large bowl. Use a mixer on high speed to beat mixture until it becomes fluffy. Then, use a pastry bag fitted with a decorative tip to create swirls of whipped cream on top of pie.
14. Add chocolate sprinkles on top of whipped cream, then slice pie into eight servings. Leftovers should be chilled for up to a week, or frozen for 1 month.

🔍 FIELD NOTES

How to hack recipes like this: Measure the dimensions of the pie, then disassemble it. Separate whipped cream from any toppings to obtain a clean sample of the toppings. Prepare a filling recipe and determine what adjustments can be made to match the original version. Next, do the same with the crust. Once those parts are correct, assemble the pie and make final tweaks to the recipe, such as adjusting the filling volume.

MARIE CALLENDER'S
Fresh Strawberry Pie

 PREP TIME:
Active: 40 minutes
Inactive: 3 hours 40 minutes

 DIFFICULTY:
Medium

 SERVES:
6–8

Since Marie Callender sold the family car to raise money for her growing pie business in the 1940s, she had to deliver her pies to local restaurants on her son's bicycle. Her sacrifice paid off. Marie Callender's wholesale pie business was so successful that in the early 1960s, the family opened the first of many casual restaurants, serving a variety of home-style meals. And, of course, fresh pies.

From March to November, Marie Callender's sells fresh, made-to-order strawberry pies made with the chain's signature flaky crust, piled high with whole strawberries in a sweet glaze, and topped with whipped cream.

To hack this fantastic pie, I created the glaze to use frozen strawberries, so it's quick and easy, and devised simple steps for homemade whipped cream and pie crust. You can buy each of these pie components pre-made to speed up your build, but taking a little time to make the whipped cream and/or crust from scratch will be worth the extra effort.

 The original glaze mixed with the berries in the restaurant pie tastes like the common product found in grocery store produce sections, usually made with corn syrup and other artificial ingredients, without any natural fruit. For this clone recipe, I set out to improve the glaze by using real strawberry purée to create a more flavorful finished product. The new glaze is vibrant and fruity; it turns into a lovely gel that doesn't upstage the strawberries in the filling.

FOR GLAZED STRAWBERRIES:

8 ounces frozen whole strawberries, thawed
2/3 cup water
6 tablespoons granulated sugar
2 1/2 teaspoons cornstarch
2 pinches salt
6 drops red food coloring (optional)
32 ounces fresh strawberries, stem ends removed

FOR PIE CRUST:

1 1/4 cups (6 1/4 ounces) all-purpose flour
1 teaspoon granulated sugar
1/4 teaspoon plus 1/8 teaspoon salt
1/4 cup vegetable shortening, cold
1/4 cup unsalted butter, cold
2 1/2 tablespoons ice water

FOR WHIPPED CREAM TOPPING:

1 cup heavy whipping cream
1 teaspoon vanilla extract
¼ cup (1 ounce) powdered sugar
1 tablespoon water
¾ teaspoon gelatin powder

RECIPE STEPS:

1. To make strawberry glaze: Add thawed strawberries and water to a blender and blend on high speed until no visible chunks of strawberry remain, but don't overmix. Strain purée using a wire mesh strainer.

2. Combine strained strawberry purée with sugar, cornstarch, and salt in a small saucepan over medium heat. When sauce bubbles, lower heat and simmer, stirring often, for 15 minutes until it becomes a deeper red and less cloudy. Cool uncovered for 20 minutes, then stir, cover, and chill for 3 hours until glaze is cold and thick.

3. To make pie crust: Whisk sugar and salt into flour in a medium bowl.

4. Using a pastry knife or large fork, cut chilled shortening and butter into flour until it reaches a crumbly, sand-like texture. Mix ice water into dough with a mixing spoon, then shape dough into a disk with your hands. Be careful not to overwork dough, or it may lose its flakiness. Wrap dough disk in plastic wrap and refrigerate 45 minutes.

5. When dough is ready, preheat oven to 400°F.

6. Roll dough out on a well-floured surface until it forms a large circle. To estimate size, place a 9" pie dish or pan upside down onto dough. The dough should extend about 1" beyond edge of pie dish. When dough is right size, fold it in half and lift it into pie dish, then unfold it.

7. Mold crust with your fingers to create a lip over top edge of pie dish, then slice off any excess dough using a sharp paring knife.

8. Use a skewer or toothpick to create several holes in crust, spacing them about ½" apart. These holes will help prevent crust from bubbling.

9. Bake 18–22 minutes until crust puffs up and begins to brown around top edge. Make sure there are no areas that appear uncooked. Cool for 30 minutes.

10. To make whipped cream topping: Combine cream with vanilla in a large mixing bowl. Add powdered sugar and beat it at high speed until soft peaks form when you pull out beaters.

11. In a small bowl, stir gelatin into water, then heat it on high for 10 seconds in microwave until it is hot and gelatin dissolves. Drizzle gelatin solution into whipped cream while mixing and continue to mix on high speed until whipped cream is smooth and forms stiff peaks. Avoid overmixing, or cream could get lumpy.

12. When ready to assemble pie, gently toss strawberries with glaze in a large bowl, then carefully pour into baked pie shell. Form strawberries into a mound.

13. Fill a piping bag fitted with a large star-tipped nozzle with whipped cream, then create large swirls on strawberries just inside crust rim. Keep center of pie free of whipped cream to showcase beautiful strawberries in middle. Cut into 6 or 8 slices to serve. Will keep in your refrigerator (uncovered) for up to 2 days.

🔍 FIELD NOTES

Strawberries are the only fruit with seeds on the outside. We strain them out of the sauce in this recipe for better flavor and brighter color.

MCDONALD'S

Bacon, Egg & Cheese McGriddles

 PREP TIME:
Active: 45 minutes
Inactive: 45 minutes

 DIFFICULTY:
Medium

 SERVES:
4

The creator of Jif Peanut Butter, Smashburger, and Pizza Hut's Stuffed Crust Pizza had the idea to cook bits of maple syrup into griddle cake buns for a new sweet-and-savory breakfast sandwich from the world's #1 fast food chain. Tom Ryan, a food mad scientist, invented McGriddles in 2003 for the popular McDonald's breakfast menu, and the sandwich remains a top seller.

Be sure to use maple flavoring rather than maple extract for the maple bits in this recipe. Maple flavoring has a more intense flavor than the extract, and its dark brown caramel coloring will make your maple bits look like pancake syrup. You'll also need one or two 3½" rings to make griddle cakes that are the perfect size for your clones.

This McGriddles hack recipe duplicates the bacon and egg version of the sandwich, but you can replace the bacon with a patty made from breakfast sausage (for the sausage and egg version), or just use egg and cheese.

 Many online copycat recipes are not even close to the real deal. Other recipes I found for these McGriddles instruct you to make hard candy from maple syrup, but the shattered shards of hard candy do not fully melt when the griddle cakes are cooked, resulting in a distinct crunch not present in the real McDonald's product. Additionally, breaking the hard maple candy into small, uniform bits is challenging and messy. My solution was to create a flavorful maple gummy puck that could be neatly diced into tiny cubes and sprinkled into the batter as it cooks. The soft gummy bits melt perfectly in the pancake buns, making them look and taste like the original—without a mess.

FOR MAPLE BITS:

3 tablespoons water
¼ cup granulated sugar
2½ teaspoons gelatin powder
½ teaspoon maple flavoring (I used Mapleine)

FOR GRIDDLE CAKE BUNS:

1 large egg
2 tablespoons granulated sugar
¼ plus ⅛ teaspoon salt
1 cup buttermilk
¼ cup whole milk
1¼ cups (6¼ ounces) all-purpose flour
1¼ teaspoons baking soda
2 tablespoons unsalted butter, melted

FOR MCGRIDDLES:

4 large eggs, beaten
2 tablespoons whole milk
$1/8$ teaspoon salt
1 tablespoon unsalted butter
4 slices American cheese
4 slices cooked bacon

RECIPE STEPS:

1. To make maple bits: Dissolve sugar and gelatin in water in a small bowl. Microwave on high for 1 minute until solution bubbles. Stir in maple flavoring, then refrigerate 45 minutes until gelatin is firm and can be sliced.

2. When maple gelatin is cold, remove it from bowl and slice it into strips that are $1/8"$–$1/4"$ thick, then slice across those strips to create small maple gummy cubes. You will need around 200 of these small maple bits to add 20–25 of them to each of eight griddle cake buns.

3. To make griddle cake buns: Combine egg, sugar, and salt in a medium bowl. Mix in buttermilk and milk.

4. Whisk together flour and baking soda in another medium bowl. Add flour to bowl with wet ingredients and mix well with a mixer on high speed for about 30 seconds until batter is mostly smooth. Add melted butter and mix until it's fully incorporated.

5. Preheat a large nonstick skillet with 1–2 ring molds in it over medium-low heat. When pan is hot, grease insides of rings with oil spray. Spoon 3 tablespoons of batter into each ring. Add 20–25 maple bits to top of batter in each ring, then use a teaspoon or tip of a knife to submerge maple bits in batter so they are not visible. Try to keep maple bits away from edge of batter so that they don't touch ring mold. When all maple bits are pushed into batter, place a lid over pan to help cook tops of griddle cakes.

6. Cook 3 minutes until edges of griddle cakes look dry. Use tongs to lift molds, then gently flip each pancake over. They should be nicely browned. Cook another 3–4 minutes until other side has browned. Transfer griddle cakes to a plate and trim off any excess batter so each griddle cake is perfectly round. Repeat process with remaining batter so that you have a total of eight griddle cakes.

7. When griddle cakes are done, make eggs by preheating a 12" nonstick skillet over medium heat. Beat 2 eggs in a medium bowl with 1 tablespoon of milk and a pinch of salt. Add $1/2$ tablespoon of butter to hot pan, then pour eggs into it. Swirl pan so that eggs coat entire bottom of pan and cook evenly.

8. When eggs are mostly cooked, about 2 minutes, use a spatula to fold over about $1/2"$ of top and bottom of eggs, then fold over approximately 1" on sides. You now have an egg rectangle. Use a butter knife to slice down middle of eggs, making two long strips. Use a spatula to flip over each strip, then turn off heat.

continued on next page

Bacon, Egg & Cheese McGriddles

RECIPE STEPS (continued):

9. Allow eggs to sit in pan 1 minute, then slide them onto a plate and fold them into thirds, like a letter, to form a square. Repeat this for remaining 2 eggs so you have a total of 4 folded eggs.

10. Build each sandwich by placing a slice of American cheese on one griddle cake, followed by a slice of bacon, broken in half. Place an egg on bacon and top off sandwich with another griddle cake. Before serving, heat each sandwich in microwave on high for 20 seconds to warm griddle cakes and soften cheese.

FIELD NOTES

If you want cooked bacon with lots of ripples and curls, cook it in a hot pan. If you want bacon that finishes flat, start it in a cold pan.

Hotcakes

 PREP TIME:
Active: 30 minutes
Inactive: None

 DIFFICULTY:
Easy

 **MAKES:**
16 hotcakes

With the invention of the Egg McMuffin in 1971, McDonald's became the first fast-food restaurant to serve breakfast. The morning sandwich was so successful that by 1977, the chain had expanded nationally with a complete breakfast menu rollout, featuring scrambled eggs, hash browns, sausage, bacon, and these popular golden-brown hotcakes.

Many pancake recipes require buttermilk for lift, but since the McDonald's original recipe doesn't use it, you won't need it for this clone. And you won't miss it: This McDonald's Hotcakes copycat recipe makes fluffy pancakes with self-activating baking powder for a satisfying rise and beautiful browning. It's a handy pancake recipe when you don't have any buttermilk.

This recipe makes sixteen hotcakes, and you can freeze the leftovers, then easily reheat a stack for just 1 minute in your microwave whenever you need a quick breakfast or snack. Serve with softened butter and maple syrup on the side.

 To hack a recipe like these hotcakes, estimate low amounts for ingredients like salt, sugar, and leavening in the batter. Cook small test batches, then make incremental additions of those ingredients to enhance flavor, color, and lift, and continue cooking small samples until they match the original. Often, you won't know which measurement for an ingredient is the perfect amount until you've gone too far.

2 large eggs
¼ cup granulated sugar
¼ cup unsalted butter, melted
¾ teaspoon salt
½ teaspoon vanilla extract
1 tablespoon vegetable oil
2 cups whole or 2% milk
2½ cups (12½ ounces) all-purpose flour
2¾ teaspoons baking powder

RECIPE STEPS:

1. Add eggs and sugar to a large bowl and mix with an electric mixer on medium speed for 30 seconds. Add butter, salt, vanilla, and oil and mix for 15 seconds. Mix in milk.

2. In a separate medium bowl, combine flour and baking powder. Add this mixture to wet ingredients and mix thoroughly with mixer set to medium speed for 30 seconds until only tiny lumps of flour remain visible.

3. Preheat a large nonstick pan over medium-low heat. When pan is hot, lightly grease with oil spray, then add ¼ cup of batter to center of pan. Cook hotcake for 1–1½ minutes until several bubbles emerge on surface and edges appear dry. Flip hotcake and cook for another 1–1½ minutes, until golden brown. Repeat with remaining batter; if you have a good nonstick pan, you likely won't need to add more oil between hotcakes. Serve.

FIELD NOTES

In 1889, entrepreneurs Chris Rutt and Charles Underwood revolutionized the food industry by creating Aunt Jemima pancake mix, a dry blend that only required the addition of water to make pancake batter. It was the world's first ready-mix food.

MCDONALD'S
Strawberry & Crème Pie

 PREP TIME:
Active: 45 minutes
Inactive: 1½ hours

 DIFFICULTY:
Medium

 MAKES:
10 pies

Tiny apple pies have been a signature dessert on the McDonald's menu for decades, but the chain upped its pie game with a tasty new treat featuring a duo of fillings encased in a flaky, lightly iced crust.

To re-create these personal McDonald's Strawberry & Crème Pies at home, I've developed a new crust formula and filled it with thickened, puréed frozen strawberries alongside a sweetened cream cheese filling. You'll find everything you need to duplicate these mouthwatering pies in your own kitchen.

Simply squeeze the fillings onto the dough, seal the pies, brush them with light icing, and pop them in the oven. This recipe makes ten pies, which is a good thing because everyone will want one.

 If you don't have a piping bag, you can make one with a zip-top storage bag. Fill the bag with the ingredients to be piped, squeeze out the air, and seal the bag. Then, snip off a corner and squeeze to distribute the filling or icing as needed.

FOR PASTRY DOUGH:

- 2 cups (10 ounces) all-purpose flour
- 3 tablespoons granulated sugar
- 1 teaspoon salt
- ½ cup shortening
- 6 tablespoons unsalted butter, softened
- ⅓ cup water

FOR STRAWBERRY FILLING:

- 1 cup frozen strawberries in syrup or sugar, thawed, with liquid
- 1 tablespoon granulated sugar
- 1 tablespoon water
- 1 tablespoon cornstarch

FOR CREAM CHEESE FILLING:

- 4 ounces cream cheese, softened
- ½ teaspoon vanilla extract
- ⅛ teaspoon lemon juice
- ⅓ cup (1⅓ ounces) powdered sugar
- ¹⁄₁₆ teaspoon salt
- 1 large egg, beaten

FOR GLAZE:

- ⅓ cup (1⅓ ounces) powdered sugar
- 1 tablespoon water

RECIPE STEPS:

1. To make pastry dough: Mix flour, sugar, and salt in a medium bowl. Incorporate shortening, butter, and water, and mix until ingredients can form a ball. Next, shape dough into a thick square or rectangle, then cover and chill for 1–2 hours, until surface is cold. Forming dough into a straight-sided shape before chilling will make it easier to roll out a rectangular portion later.

2. To make strawberry filling: Pulse strawberries with their liquid in a blender until no strawberry pieces are larger than a dime. Combine strawberries and sugar in a small saucepan over medium-low heat. Combine cornstarch with water in a small bowl and add slurry to strawberries. Cook for 5–8 minutes until thickened, then remove filling from heat, cover it, and allow it to cool to room temperature, 30–45 minutes. Filling will thicken as it cools.

3. To make cream cheese filling: Blend cream cheese with vanilla and lemon juice in a medium bowl using a mixer on high speed until mixture is smooth and creamy. Add powdered sugar and salt, mixing again at low speed before increasing to high speed once ingredients are combined. Continue mixing on high speed for 30 seconds until filling is perfectly smooth. Cover until needed.

4. When dough has rested, preheat convection oven to 375°F or preheat conventional oven to 400°F.

5. Split dough in half and roll out one half on a clean, floured surface until it measures 12 1/2" long by 10" wide and is between 1/16" and 1/8" thick. Use a sharp knife or a pizza slicer to cut dough into ten rectangles, each measuring 5" long by 2 1/2" wide. Arrange these ten dough slices on a sheet pan lined with a baking mat. Repeat process with remaining half of dough, and after you have cut rest into 5" × 2 1/2" portions, use a sharp knife to make a 3" slit in center of each portion.

6. Spoon strawberry filling and cream cheese mixture into two piping bags.

7. To build each pie, brush beaten egg around edge of a piece of dough on sheet pan. Then, squeeze a strip of 1–1 1/2 tablespoons of cream cheese down one side of dough (leaving a margin), followed by 1 1/2 to 2 tablespoons of strawberry filling on other side of dough. Carefully place one of top portions of dough over filling and use your fingers to press firmly around edges to seal it. Repeat process to build remaining pies.

8. To make glaze: Mix powdered sugar and water in a small bowl. Use a brush to apply glaze to top of each pie, then bake for 18–22 minutes until pies are lightly browned around edges and just slightly browned on top. Serve. Store leftovers in a sealed container at room temperature for 2 days or freeze for 4 weeks.

FIELD NOTES

McDonald's Apple Pie, introduced in 1968, was the first dessert added to the chain's menu. Originally, the pies were fried, but in 1992, the company began baking the pies to address customers' health concerns. Not every McDonald's switched to baked pies, though. In Hawaii, there are still a few McDonald's restaurants selling the fried version.

OLD EL PASO

Taco Seasoning Mix

 PREP TIME:
Active: 5 minutes
Inactive: None

 DIFFICULTY:
Easy

 MAKES:
¼ cup (enough for about 12 tacos)

The Old El Paso brand originated in 1917 as The Mountain Pass Canning Company, but its name changed when the company was sold to a new owner in El Paso, Texas. Initially, the company specialized in canned tomatoes and pinto beans, but it expanded its product line over the years. In 1969, Old El Paso became the first American company to offer a national line of Mexican meals in supermarkets and the first to advertise Mexican cuisine. This growing market for Mexican food is why US stores created Mexican food sections in the 1970s.

Many of those who grew up with "family taco night" may be familiar with the Old El Paso packet of spices added to browned ground beef for a quick and easy taco filling. When the seasoned beef is added to crispy or soft taco shells with your favorite combination of cheese, lettuce, tomato, avocado, and other ingredients, any day can be Taco Tuesday. This Old El Paso Taco Seasoning Mix knockoff includes all the spices you'll need for a perfect match to the real thing, along with just the right amount of cornstarch to thicken it up. Plus, it's easy to make. Once you've mixed these ingredients, just add the blend to 1 pound of cooked ground beef with water, cook until thick, and fill your tacos.

As in this taco mix, it is common to use garlic powder (granulated garlic) and onion powder (granulated onion) together in seasoning blends. This dynamic duo is often found in dry blends, sauces, dressings, and breadings. So, if you're adding one of these to your recipe hack, always consider adding the other. When examining a food sample you're cloning, onion granules appear as tiny white specks, while garlic granules are light yellow.

- 1 tablespoon plus 1 teaspoon cornstarch
- 1 tablespoon plus ¾ teaspoon chili powder
- ½ teaspoon paprika
- ½ teaspoon powdered sugar
- ½ teaspoon plus ⅛ teaspoon salt
- ½ teaspoon ground cumin
- ¼ teaspoon onion powder
- ⅛ teaspoon garlic powder
- ⅛ teaspoon ground black pepper

Combine all ingredients in a small bowl. Can be stored in a sealed container for several months.

 FIELD NOTES

To make tacos, cook 1 pound of ground beef in a 10" skillet over medium-high heat for 6–8 minutes, then drain fat. Stir in seasoning mix along with ¾ cup of water. Heat until bubbling, then reduce heat and simmer for 3–4 minutes, stirring until thickened. Spoon filling into shells. Top with favorite toppings.

OLIVE GARDEN

Chicken Marsala Fettuccine

 PREP TIME:
Active: 50 minutes
Inactive: 2 hours

 DIFFICULTY:
Medium

 SERVES:
2

This menu replacement for the chain's Stuffed Chicken Marsala offers a tasty variation on the popular theme. It features breaded chicken tenderloins arranged on fettuccine pasta with wilted spinach and sautéed mushrooms and doused with plenty of delicious creamy marsala sauce.

For many dishes, most of the flavor comes from the sauce, so an accurate hack of the sauce is the key to creating a great culinary clone. That's why I spent most of my time working on a perfect hack of the great mushroom marsala sauce in this dish. The sauce contains mushrooms, and you'll also need more to sauté later. I found that an 8-ounce tub of mushrooms is the perfect amount for the whole recipe.

Give yourself an hour to brine the chicken for flavor and juiciness, and 30 minutes for the coated chicken to sit in the refrigerator so that the breading stays put when you cook the chicken. This recipe makes two restaurant-sized servings but can easily be split into four smaller portions.

 To save time, you might be able to use elements from previously hacked recipes for new recipes developed by the same chain. Olive Garden replaced its Stuffed Chicken Marsala with this new dish, using the same marsala sauce. I was able to quickly hack this recipe by referring to my old marsala sauce formula and then modifying it to duplicate this new dish.

FOR CHICKEN BRINE:

3 cups water
2 tablespoons kosher salt
10 chicken tenderloins

FOR MARSALA SAUCE:

1 tablespoon unsalted butter
1 cup sliced white mushrooms
2 teaspoons minced garlic
2 cups marsala wine
1 teaspoon minced fresh parsley

FOR MARSALA SAUCE: (continued)

1 teaspoon dried Italian seasoning blend (oregano, marjoram, rosemary, basil, etc.)
$3/4$ teaspoon plus $1/8$ teaspoon salt, divided
$1/4$ teaspoon ground black pepper
$1/4$ teaspoon crushed red pepper
2 cups heavy cream

FOR PASTA:

8 ounces uncooked fettuccine
4–6 quarts water

FOR CHICKEN BREADING:

1 cup all-purpose flour
¾ teaspoon plus ⅛ teaspoon salt, divided
¼ teaspoon dried Italian seasoning blend (oregano, marjoram, rosemary, basil, etc.)
¼ teaspoon ground black pepper
¼ teaspoon crushed red pepper
¼ teaspoon MSG (monosodium glutamate)
¼ cup whole or 2% milk
2 eggs, beaten

TO COMPLETE DISH:

½–¾ cup plus 2 tablespoons extra-virgin olive oil
2½ cups sliced white mushrooms
3 cups fresh spinach
1 teaspoon minced fresh parsley

RECIPE STEPS:

1. To make chicken brine: Dissolve salt in water. Cover tenderloins with plastic wrap and pound them to a thickness of about ½" using a kitchen mallet. Immerse them in brine and refrigerate for 1 hour.

2. To make marsala sauce: Melt butter in a medium saucepan over medium heat. Add mushrooms to pan and cook for 4 minutes until they begin to brown. Add garlic and cook for an additional minute.

3. Add wine to pan, along with parsley, Italian seasoning, salt, pepper, and crushed red pepper. When sauce returns to a simmer, cook it for 6 minutes to reduce it by about a third.

4. Add cream to pan. When it bubbles, reduce heat to medium-low and simmer gently for 25–30 minutes until it thickens. Once sauce is done, turn off heat and cover it.

5. Bring water to a boil in a pot. Add pasta, cook for 14 minutes until done, and strain.

6. Remove chicken from brine, then rinse all tenderloins and blot them dry.

7. To make chicken breading: Combine flour, ¾ teaspoon salt, herbs, black pepper, red pepper, and MSG in a shallow bowl. Combine milk with eggs in another shallow bowl.

8. Toss chicken tenderloins in breading. Dip each floured tenderloin in milk and egg, then back into flour for a final coat. Arrange breaded chicken on a tray and refrigerate uncovered for 30 minutes.

9. Heat ¼" of olive oil in a large sauté pan over medium-low heat. Cook breaded tenderloins in olive oil for 3–4 minutes per side until golden brown. Transfer cooked chicken to a paper towel–lined plate.

10. Heat another large sauté pan over medium heat and add 2 tablespoons of olive oil. When oil is hot and shimmering, add sliced mushrooms along with remaining salt, and cook for 3–4 minutes, until mushrooms begin to brown.

11. Add cooked chicken to pan with mushrooms. Heat chicken for 2 minutes, then flip pieces to warm other side and add spinach to pan.

12. When spinach has started to wilt, about 1 minute, add marsala sauce to pan. Continue heating for 1–2 minutes until sauce is hot.

13. To serve, split pasta onto two plates. Divide chicken, mushrooms, spinach, and sauce over pasta. Sprinkle with parsley.

FIELD NOTES

Chain restaurants will rotate their dishes to keep the menu from getting stale. This Chicken Marsala Fettuccine replaced the Stuffed Chicken Marsala at Olive Garden, but as I was researching this book, the chain switched back and replaced the Chicken Marsala Fettuccine with the Stuffed Chicken Marsala.

Chicken Marsala Fettuccine

OLIVE GARDEN

Five Cheese Ziti al Forno

 PREP TIME:
Active: 30 minutes
Inactive: 10 minutes

 DIFFICULTY:
Medium

 SERVES:
4

Creating a copycat version of Olive Garden's famous baked ziti wouldn't be possible without a perfect replica of the chain's popular five-cheese marinara sauce. Luckily, I had previously replicated Olive Garden's regular marinara for their chicken parmigiana, so I adjusted that recipe to suit this hack by adding five types of Italian cheese and heavy cream.

After the sauce is added to the pasta, it's topped with more cheese, along with breadcrumbs, known as "ziti topping." Then, it's browned in a salamander at the restaurant or under a broiler at home. The result is a beautiful dish with excellent sauce and a cheesy topping that satisfies even the pickiest baked ziti fans.

 It's hard to know precisely which five Italian cheeses are used in this dish, so I asked the server, who asked the chef, and I got the answer I needed. But not all would have been lost if I hadn't been so fortunate to have gotten a cooperative server and chef. For a recipe such as this, you can guess which Italian cheeses are used by referencing the most popular cheeses in Italian cooking. With that information, your guess should be close. For this recipe, if you guess that the cheese blend is made with mozzarella, Parmesan, Romano, Asiago, and ricotta, you are right.

FOR SAUCE:

- ¼ cup extra-virgin olive oil
- ⅓ cup peeled and diced white onion
- 2 teaspoons minced garlic
- 1 (28-ounce) can crushed tomatoes
- ½ cup water
- 2 teaspoons granulated sugar
- 1 teaspoon lemon juice
- 1 teaspoon salt
- ½ teaspoon dried Italian seasoning blend (oregano, marjoram, rosemary, basil, etc.)
- ½ teaspoon ground black pepper
- ⅛ teaspoon crushed red pepper
- ⅓ cup grated Parmesan cheese

FOR SAUCE (continued):

- ¼ cup ricotta cheese
- 2 tablespoons shredded mozzarella cheese
- 2 tablespoons shredded Asiago cheese
- 2 tablespoons grated Romano cheese
- ¾ cup heavy cream

FOR ZITI AND TOPPING:

- 1½ cups shredded mozzarella cheese
- 1 cup panko breadcrumbs
- 2 tablespoons grated Parmesan cheese
- 1 tablespoon minced fresh parsley
- 1 pound uncooked ziti (or penne) pasta

RECIPE STEPS:

1. To make five-cheese marinara sauce: Heat olive oil in a medium saucepan over medium heat. Once oil is shimmering, add onion and garlic and cook for 1–2 minutes until garlic starts to brown. Add crushed tomatoes to pan, along with water, sugar, lemon juice, salt, Italian seasoning, black pepper, and crushed red pepper. When mixture bubbles, reduce heat to a simmer and cook sauce uncovered for 20 minutes, stirring occasionally.

2. Stir all five cheeses into sauce and continue to simmer it for 5 more minutes. Stir in heavy cream, and let sauce gently simmer (not boil) for another 5 minutes, then turn off heat and cover pan.

3. To make ziti topping: While sauce is cooking, combine all ingredients in a medium bowl.

4. Cook ziti (or penne) pasta in a large pot of boiling water for 10–12 minutes until slightly tough. Strain.

5. Preheat broiler to high.

6. Assemble each dish by spooning a quarter of pasta into an oven-safe, shallow bowl. Pour a quarter of sauce (1 cup) over pasta, then sprinkle $1/2$–$3/4$ cup of ziti topping over sauce. Place dish on a sheet pan and slide it under hot broiler on top rack for 1–2 minutes until topping is browned. Repeat this process for remaining three servings.

FIELD NOTES

"Ziti" is the Italian word for "bride," which may be why this dish is traditionally served at Italian wedding parties.

Lasagna Classico

OLIVE GARDEN

Lasagna Classico

 PREP TIME:
Active: 45 minutes
Inactive: 1 hour 50 minutes

 DIFFICULTY:
Medium

 SERVES:
8

Crafting Olive Garden's signature Lasagna Classico recipe presented the perfect opportunity to create a beautiful, multilayered lasagna hack recipe that uses an entire box of lasagna noodles and fills the baking pan all the way to the top. This top secret recipe produces a lasagna that tips the scales at nearly 10 pounds and can feed hungry mouths for days, with every delicious layer directly copied from the carefully dissected Olive Garden original.

I found some credible intel in a video featuring an Olive Garden chef demonstrating what he claimed was the real formula for this lasagna on a midday news show. However, the recipe was abbreviated for TV, and the chef omitted numerous crucial details. One ingredient he notably left out of the recipe was the secret layer of Cheddar cheese near the middle of the stack.

This clone recipe will yield enough for eight generous portions, but if you cut slightly smaller slices, it can satisfy twelve lasagna-craving appetites.

 Dissecting sandwiches and burgers is easy, but foods like this lasagna can be tricky, especially if you deconstruct them after they have been refrigerated. When the cheese chills, it hardens and becomes like glue, making a clean dissection difficult. However, if you heat the food until warm (not hot) in your microwave, the cheese will soften, and the layers will separate much more easily for a clean analysis.

FOR MEAT SAUCE:

3 tablespoons extra-virgin olive oil
2 cups peeled and diced white onion (1 medium onion)
1 tablespoon minced garlic
12 ounces 80/20 ground beef
8 ounces Italian sausage with no casing
2 (28-ounce) cans crushed tomatoes
1 tablespoon minced fresh parsley
1¼ teaspoons salt
1¼ teaspoons dried oregano
1 teaspoon dried basil
½ teaspoon ground black pepper

FOR CHEESE FILLING:

4 cups whole milk ricotta cheese
2 cups shredded mozzarella cheese
1 cup grated Romano cheese
2 tablespoons minced fresh parsley
1 teaspoon salt
¾ teaspoon dried oregano
½ teaspoon dried basil
¼ teaspoon ground black pepper
2 large eggs, beaten

TO COMPLETE LASAGNA:

1 (16-ounce) box uncooked lasagna noodles
1½ cups shredded mild Cheddar cheese
2 cups shredded mozzarella cheese
2 teaspoons minced fresh parsley

RECIPE STEPS:

1. To make meat sauce: Heat olive oil in a 3-quart or larger saucepan over medium-low heat. Add onion and garlic and cook at a low simmer until onions are translucent, about 5 minutes.

2. Add beef and sausage to pan and cook meats until no pink remains, about 10 minutes. Use a large spoon to break apart beef and sausage while cooking.

3. Stir in crushed tomatoes, parsley, salt, oregano, basil, and pepper, then simmer sauce uncovered for 30 minutes. Remove from heat and cover until ready to use.

4. To make cheese filling: Combine ricotta, mozzarella, Romano, parsley, salt, oregano, basil, and pepper in a large bowl. Stir in beaten eggs.

5. Preheat oven to 350°F.

6. Cook noodles in a large pot of boiling water for 10 minutes. Strain noodles and rinse them with cold water to make them easier to handle.

7. Spoon about 2 cups of meat sauce onto bottom of a 9" × 13" baking pan and spread sauce evenly over bottom of pan. Place 4 noodles on top of sauce, right up to edge of pan, overlapping them as needed. Cut small pieces from an additional noodle to cover any exposed sauce in pan.

8. Spread approximately one-third of cheese filling (about 1¾ cups) on sauce. Use a large spoon or spatula to distribute cheese filling evenly over pasta.

9. Spoon another 2 cups of meat sauce over cheese filling and spread it out evenly. Sprinkle Cheddar cheese over meat sauce.

10. Add another layer of noodles. Spoon another one-third of cheese filling over noodles and spread it evenly.

11. Add another layer of noodles on top of cheese filling. Spoon another 2 cups of sauce over noodles and spread it out evenly.

12. Use remaining cheese filling by adding small dollops of it on top of meat sauce and spreading it out without mixing it into sauce.

13. Add final layer of noodles. Spoon rest of meat sauce over top of lasagna and spread it to edges. At this stage, pan should be filled to brim.

14. Set pan on a large baking sheet to catch any overflow and bake lasagna for 50 minutes.

15. Sprinkle shredded mozzarella over top of lasagna and turn oven to high broil. When cheese is lightly browned, in 2 to 3 minutes, take it out of oven and let it sit for 20 minutes.

16. Slice lasagna lengthwise down middle, then slice across lasagna three times to create eight servings. Before serving, sprinkle a little parsley on each slice. Leftovers will keep chilled for up to 4 days.

FIELD NOTES

Like a thick steak, lasagna must be allowed to sit for at least 20 minutes before slicing. This resting time will allow the layers to settle and will give you cleaner slices that look better on the plates.

ON THE BORDER

Chicken Tortilla Soup

 PREP TIME:
Active: 20 minutes
Inactive: 40 minutes

 DIFFICULTY:
Medium

 **MAKES:**
10 servings

Ingredients you don't find in other tortilla soups are probably the reason this offering from On The Border is such a hit. You'll notice some standout ingredients, including zucchini, fresh corn kernels, diced Roma tomato, rice, and a garnish of Monterey jack cheese and avocado, but the ingredient that brings this soup together is the generous portion of perfectly seasoned chicken tinga. The shredded chicken tenderizes nicely in the soup and adds flavor and color to the pot.

To create the best chicken tinga recipe for this copycat version of the soup, I started with uncooked white and dark chicken fillets, but soon found that a supermarket rotisserie chicken worked even better and saved lots of time. I made a tinga sauce with chipotle, tomato, onion, garlic, and spices and mixed it with the shredded chicken; then I constructed the rest of the soup around the tinga.

When your soup is done, you'll have enough for ten bowls, each garnished with jack cheese, tortilla strips or chips, cilantro, and a fresh wedge of avocado. The tasty chicken tinga recipe here also makes an excellent filling for tacos, burritos, and enchiladas.

 Roma tomatoes are a great choice for recipes like this one. Their high pectin content helps thicken sauces, and their firm flesh makes Roma tomatoes great for soups—they don't break down and become mushy like other tomato varieties.

FOR RICE:

1 cup water
½ cup uncooked jasmine rice
¼ teaspoon salt

FOR CHICKEN TINGA:

1 tablespoon extra-virgin olive oil
1 cup peeled and chopped white or yellow onion
2 teaspoons minced garlic
1 cup chicken broth
½ cup chopped Roma tomato

FOR CHICKEN TINGA (continued):

1 tablespoon canned chipotles in adobo sauce, diced
¾ teaspoon dried Mexican oregano
½ teaspoon ground cumin
½ teaspoon salt
¼ teaspoon course ground black pepper
1½ teaspoons lime juice
1 cooked rotisserie chicken, skin removed

FOR SOUP:

1 tablespoon extra-virgin olive oil
¾ cup peeled and diced white or yellow onion
⅓ cup diced poblano pepper
2 teaspoons minced garlic
10 cups chicken broth
1½ cups zucchini sliced into half wheels
¾ cup yellow corn kernels, fresh or frozen
1 teaspoon salt
¾ cup diced Roma tomato
2 tablespoons lime juice

FOR GARNISH:

1¼ cups shredded Monterey jack cheese
1¼ cups fried tortilla chips or strips
2 tablespoons minced fresh cilantro
1 large avocado, sliced into wedges

RECIPE STEPS:

1. To make rice: Bring water to a boil in a small saucepan. Stir in rice and salt, then cover, reduce heat, and simmer rice for 20–25 minutes until all water is absorbed and rice is tender. Set aside until needed.

2. To make chicken tinga: Heat olive oil in a medium saucepan over medium-low heat. Add onion and cook for 4 minutes until soft, then add garlic and sauté for 1 more minute.

3. Add chicken broth to pan, followed by tomato, chipotle, oregano, cumin, salt, and pepper. Raise heat to medium until sauce bubbles, then reduce heat and simmer for 5 minutes.

4. Turn off heat and add lime juice to pan. Cover and let it cool for 5 minutes.

5. Pour sauce into a blender and blend on medium speed for 10 seconds, just enough so that a few small bits of tomato, pepper, and herbs are still visible.

6. Shred chicken using two forks. Combine chicken with sauce in a large sauté pan and heat it over medium until most liquid is gone. Stir often to shred chicken a bit more. Cover chicken tinga and set it aside until needed.

7. To make soup: Heat olive oil in a saucepan or pot that holds at least 4½ quarts over medium-low heat. Add onion and poblano pepper and cook for 4 minutes until vegetables are tender but not browned. Add garlic and cook for 1 more minute.

8. Add chicken broth to pan, followed by zucchini, corn, and salt, plus all chicken tinga and cooked rice, and raise heat to medium-high. When soup bubbles, reduce heat so soup simmers, and cook it for 5 minutes.

9. Add Roma tomato and lime juice, and when soup bubbles again, simmer it for 5 more minutes, then turn off heat and cover it.

10. To serve, ladle 1½ cups of soup each into ten serving bowls. Garnish each bowl with approximately 2 tablespoons of Monterey jack cheese, some crumbled tortilla chips or fried tortilla strips, a few pinches of minced cilantro, and a wedge of avocado.

🔍 FIELD NOTES

Mesquite, which is abundant along the border of Texas and Mexico, has been used for generations to cook food similar to what is served at On The Border. That's why the chain burns real mesquite wood in the open-flame grills used to cook many of the restaurant's popular dishes.

ON THE BORDER

Enchiladas

 PREP TIME:
Active: 25 minutes (Cheese)/
30 minutes (Chicken)
Inactive: 2 hours (Cheese)/
30 minutes (Chicken)

 DIFFICULTY:
Medium

MAKES:
10 enchiladas

Of the four different enchilada dishes served at this popular national Mexican chain, the cheese enchilada and chicken tinga enchilada stand out. They are filled with delicious ingredients, and the sauces on top make them special. The cheese enchilada is covered with slow-cooked chili con carne sauce, while the tender chicken tinga enchilada is topped with a flavorful sour cream sauce and jack cheese. Can't decide which enchilada is your favorite? Using this hack, you can make them both!

For the cheese enchiladas copycat recipe, you'll learn how to make a great con carne sauce and stuff the enchiladas with a blend of perfectly melted cheese. And for the chicken tinga enchiladas hack, you'll discover how to make moist and flavorful chicken tinga with a grocery store rotisserie chicken and how to copy the restaurant's sour cream sauce with just four ingredients.

Each secret recipe makes ten enchiladas in one 9" × 13" baking pan, so there should be enough to go around.

 Identify parts of a recipe that can be used to create other recipes from that chain. Restaurants often use components from one recipe in others to streamline kitchen operations. For instance, at On The Border, they incorporate their chicken tinga into the enchiladas and the tortilla soup. You can develop multiple hacks with minimal extra effort by recognizing recipes that share ingredients. Once I had re-created the chicken tinga for the On the Border Chicken Tortilla Soup, all I needed to figure out was a clone of the chain's sour cream sauce, and I had an all-new hack for the chain's chicken tinga enchilada.

Cheese Enchiladas

FOR CHILI CON CARNE:

½ pound 80/20 ground beef
⅓ cup peeled and finely minced white or yellow onion
2 teaspoons minced garlic
⅓ cup chili powder (I used Mexene)
2 teaspoons beef bouillon powder or 1 large beef bouillon cube
3 cups boiling water
2 tablespoons plus 2 teaspoons all-purpose flour
1 cup room-temperature water
1 tablespoon tomato paste
1½ teaspoons lime juice
1 teaspoon ground coriander
¼ teaspoon plus ⅛ teaspoon salt

FOR ENCHILADAS:

3 cups shredded Monterey jack cheese (hand-shredded is best)
3 cups shredded sharp Cheddar cheese (hand-shredded is best)
Extra-virgin olive oil
10 (6") corn tortillas
10 fresh jalapeño slices (coins)

RECIPE STEPS:

1. To make chili con carne: Brown ground beef in a large skillet over medium heat. Crumble beef as much as you can while it cooks. You don't want any big chunks in your chili. When no pink is visible, in about 5 minutes, push all meat to one side of pan, then tilt it to spoon out fat and reserve it. Turn off heat and set beef aside for now.

2. Measure 1 tablespoon of reserved beef fat into a medium saucepan over medium-low heat and toss out any remaining fat. When fat is hot, add onion and cook for 2 minutes, then add garlic and cook for 1 more minute.

3. Add cooked ground beef to saucepan and turn heat to medium.

4. Sprinkle chili powder on beef and stir it in. Cook for 3 minutes.

5. Dissolve bouillon in boiling water and add it to saucepan. Whisk flour into room-temperature water and add it to pan.

6. Add tomato paste, lime juice, coriander, and salt, then cook chili until it bubbles. Reduce heat and simmer chili uncovered for 1½ hours until sauce thickens and reduces by about half. Stir occasionally to prevent sauce from sticking to bottom of pan. Cover sauce and keep it warm over low heat.

7. To make enchiladas: Preheat oven to 350°F. Preheat a medium skillet over medium-low heat.

8. Combine jack cheese and Cheddar cheese in a medium bowl.

9. Add about ½ teaspoon of olive oil to hot pan and swirl it around. Warm a tortilla in hot pan for 10–15 seconds on each side. Tortilla should absorb most of oil, ensuring it is thoroughly coated and pliable.

10. Place heated tortilla on a flat surface and press about ½ cup of cheese blend into its center. Use your fingers to compress cheese into a cigar shape so that it stays in tortilla, then tightly roll tortilla around cheese.

11. Repeat process for each enchilada and arrange them in two rows in a 9" × 13" baking pan. Bake for 7 minutes.

12. Take enchiladas out of oven and spoon chili con carne over each one. Sprinkle a few pinches of remaining cheese blend on top of each.

13. Bake enchiladas for 4 more minutes until cheese on top is melted.

14. Top each enchilada with a jalapeño slice and serve.

Enchiladas

Chicken Tinga Enchiladas

FOR CHICKEN TINGA:

1 tablespoon extra-virgin olive oil
1 cup peeled and chopped white or yellow onion
2 teaspoons minced garlic
1 cup chicken broth
½ cup chopped Roma tomato
1 tablespoon canned chipotles in adobo sauce, diced
¾ teaspoon dried Mexican oregano
½ teaspoon ground cumin
½ teaspoon salt
¼ teaspoon ground black pepper
1½ teaspoons lime juice
1 rotisserie chicken, skin removed

FOR SOUR CREAM SAUCE:

⅔ cup sour cream
⅔ cup heavy cream
1½ teaspoons chicken bouillon powder (or crushed cubes)
1 teaspoon lime juice

FOR ENCHILADAS:

Extra-virgin olive oil
10 (6") corn tortillas
½ cup shredded Monterey jack cheese
¼ teaspoon paprika
10 fresh jalapeño slices (coins)

RECIPE STEPS:

1. Preheat oven to 350°F.
2. To make chicken tinga: Heat olive oil in a medium saucepan over medium-low heat. Add onion and cook for 4 minutes until soft, then stir in garlic and cook for 1 more minute.
3. Add chicken broth to pan, followed by tomato, chipotle, oregano, cumin, salt, and pepper. Increase heat to medium until sauce bubbles, then lower heat and let it simmer for 5 minutes.
4. Turn off heat and add lime juice to pan. Cover and let it cool for 5 minutes.
5. Pour sauce into a blender and blend on medium speed for 10 seconds, just enough so that a few small bits of tomato, pepper, and herbs are still visible.
6. Shred chicken using two forks. Combine with sauce in a large saucepan and heat over medium until most liquid has evaporated, about 10 minutes. Stir frequently to shred chicken a bit more. Cover chicken tinga and set it over low heat to keep it warm.
7. Make the sour cream sauce by whisking ingredients in a small bowl until smooth. Set aside.
8. To make enchiladas: Preheat a medium skillet over medium-low heat.
9. Add about 1 teaspoon of olive oil to hot pan and swirl it around. Warm a tortilla in pan for 10–15 seconds on each side. Tortilla should absorb most of oil so it's thoroughly coated.
10. Place warm tortilla on a flat surface and roll about ⅓ cup of chicken tinga into each tortilla. Repeat process for remaining enchiladas and arrange them in two rows in a 9" × 13" baking pan.
11. Bake for 7 minutes. Remove enchiladas from oven and spoon sour cream sauce over each one. Sprinkle each with Monterey jack cheese and paprika, and bake for 4 more minutes until cheese is melted.
12. Remove from oven, top each one with a jalapeño slice, and serve.

 **FIELD NOTES**

The word "tinga" comes from the Central American Nahuatl word "tingatl," meaning "to tear," or "shred."

THE ORIGINAL PANCAKE HOUSE

49er Flap Jacks

 PREP TIME:
Active: 20 minutes
Inactive: 20 minutes

 DIFFICULTY:
Easy

 SERVES:
4

These flat, crepe-like flapjacks are reminiscent of the hotcakes enjoyed by miners during the California Gold Rush of 1849, and they are also a signature dish at The Original Pancake House. The chain's 49er Flap Jacks are thin, slightly chewy, lightly sweetened, and so large that they cover your entire plate. And this home version is one of the easiest meals you'll ever prepare; after all, breakfast shouldn't be complicated.

This copycat recipe is as simple as mixing up a thin pancake batter and cooking it in a pan coated with clarified butter. According to my food spy intel, The Original Pancake House uses clarified butter, and you'll discover how to make it in step 1.

Stack the warm flapjacks on a plate and serve them with soft butter and maple syrup on the side, just like the real thing.

 Many breakfast chains use a commercial butter-flavored oil blend to grease the grill for pancakes, eggs, and omelets. This oil has a higher smoke point than butter and is cheaper. However, clarified butter tastes better and is less likely to burn than butter is, because the milk solids have been removed, making it an excellent fat to use here. The Original Pancake House is one of the few breakfast chains that use clarified butter.

FOR CLARIFIED BUTTER:

½ cup unsalted butter

FOR FLAPJACKS:

3 large eggs
6 tablespoons granulated sugar
1 teaspoon salt
2¼ cups whole or 2% milk
1½ cups (7½ ounces) all-purpose flour
2 teaspoons baking powder
2 tablespoons unsalted butter, melted
1 tablespoon peanut oil (or vegetable oil)

RECIPE STEPS:

1. To make clarified butter: Melt butter in a small saucepan over medium-low heat. Once butter has melted, skim off white foam from surface using a spoon. When foam is removed, carefully pour butter into a small bowl. Stop pouring just before reaching water at bottom of pan. Set bowl of clarified butter aside until ready to make flapjacks.

2. Preheat a 10" skillet over medium heat.

3. To make flapjacks: Combine eggs, sugar, and salt in a large bowl with an electric mixer on high speed for 30 seconds. Mix in milk.

4. In a medium bowl, combine flour and baking powder, then mix this into wet ingredients in large bowl. Continue mixing for 30 seconds until no lumps of flour remain visible.

5. Add butter and oil and mix until combined.

6. Spoon 2 teaspoons of clarified butter into hot pan, then pour $1/2$ cup of batter into pan and spread it to edges. Cook for $1 1/2$–2 minutes until edges of batter are dry and bubbles form on most of pancake's surface. Use a large spatula to flip flapjack and cook it for another $1 1/2$–2 minutes until it's browned. Stack flapjacks onto four serving plates.

FIELD NOTES

When regular butter reaches its smoke point of 350°F, the milk solids burn, resulting in a bitter and undesirable taste. On the other hand, clarified butter has a smoke point of 485°F, so it stays flavorful and is ideal for high-heat cooking methods, such as sautéing and frying. Also, clarified butter has a significantly longer shelf life than regular butter.

THE ORIGINAL PANCAKE HOUSE

Buttermilk Pancakes

 PREP TIME:
Active: 40 minutes
Inactive: 20 minutes

 DIFFICULTY:
Easy

 **MAKES:**
16 pancakes

If a restaurant's pancake skills are best judged by how well they craft a stack of old-fashioned buttermilks, then this chain deserves a ribbon. Breakfast fans can't seem to get enough.

The first step in creating the perfect clone is to use clarified butter on your skillet or flat grill to prevent the pancakes from sticking. This method enhances the flavor of your pancakes more than oil, and it's the technique used by The Original Pancake House.

When you've got your clarified butter ready, the rest is a cinch. Mix the batter, and measure ⅓-cup portions onto a hot pan or griddle greased with the butter. Cook the pancakes until golden brown on both sides, then serve up a stack with whipped butter and warm maple syrup on the side.

 Don't overmix! The best pancake batter for the fluffiest pancakes should have tiny lumps of flour in it. Those lumps are air pockets that will give your pancakes more lift when they cook. Overmixing will also tighten the gluten in the flour, leading to a tough texture, which is not a good thing for pancakes.

FOR CLARIFIED BUTTER:

½ cup unsalted butter

FOR PANCAKES:

2 large eggs
¼ cup granulated sugar
¾ teaspoon salt
2 cups buttermilk
¾ cup plus 2 tablespoons whole or 2% milk
2½ cups (12½ ounces) all-purpose flour
2½ teaspoons baking soda
2 tablespoons unsalted butter, melted
1 tablespoon peanut oil

RECIPE STEPS:

1. To make clarified butter: Melt butter in a small saucepan over medium-low heat. Once butter has melted, skim off white foam from surface using a spoon. When foam is removed, carefully pour butter into a small bowl. Stop pouring just before reaching water at bottom of pan. Set aside.

2. To make pancakes: Preheat a large skillet or flat griddle pan to medium heat.

3. Combine eggs, sugar, and salt in a large bowl with an electric mixer on high speed. Mix for 30 seconds. Mix in buttermilk and milk.

4. Whisk together flour and baking soda in a medium bowl. Then, pour flour into wet mixture and mix it with an electric mixer on high speed for 30 seconds, until only tiny lumps of flour remain visible.

5. Add butter and oil and mix until combined.

6. Grease cooking surface with clarified butter and pour $1/3$-cup portions of batter into pan. Cook for 1–2 minutes, until first side is browned, then flip pancakes and cook for another 1–2 minutes until browned. Repeat with remaining batter. Serve pancakes stacked on large plates.

FIELD NOTES

Traditional buttermilk is the liquid byproduct of churning cream into butter and is typically not sold in grocery stores. The buttermilk bought today in the dairy section is cultured by adding bacteria to milk until it ferments. This process thickens the milk and gives it an acidic, sour quality that makes it great for baking, marinades, and salad dressings.

OUTBACK STEAKHOUSE

Seared Peppered Ahi

 PREP TIME:
Active: 15 minutes
Inactive: 2 hours to chill

 DIFFICULTY:
Medium

 SERVES:
1–2

Outback's seared ahi appetizer, featuring an herb crust and a secret ginger soy dipping sauce, is a top choice at the nationwide steakhouse chain. I was surprised during my sleuthing when the dish arrived at the table less than a minute after I ordered it, making it clear that the fish had been seared and chilled earlier in the day.

To make this copycat version of the dish, you'll want to pick the thickest frozen ahi tuna fillet. Ahi is one of the safest fish to eat raw, but nearly all sushi restaurants in the US freeze their fish first for at least 7 days to minimize the risk of contaminants and bacteria, so make sure your fish is frozen.

As in the restaurant, sear your fish ahead of time, then chill the fillet. When you're ready to eat, the dish can then be prepped in the short time it takes to slice the chilled ahi and plate it with some wasabi and mixed greens on the side.

 It can be easier to cut the fish to the right size before it's fully defrosted, while it remains somewhat firm. When slicing tuna, ensure that the grain of the fish runs lengthwise so that when you cut the ahi after it's cooked, you're slicing against the grain. Alternatively, you can use a whole fillet, without trimming it to 2" × 3", but it will yield slices of varying sizes, unlike the restaurant version, where slices are uniform in size.

FOR SEASONED AHI:

- ½ teaspoon ground black pepper (freshly ground is best)
- ½ teaspoon garlic powder
- ½ teaspoon dried thyme
- ½ teaspoon dried parsley
- ¼ teaspoon dried marjoram
- ¼ teaspoon onion powder
- ⅛ teaspoon salt
- ⅛ teaspoon ground coriander
- ⅛ teaspoon crushed red pepper
- 1 (4- to 5-ounce) ahi tuna fillet, trimmed to 2" × 3"
- 2 tablespoons plus 1 teaspoon vegetable oil, divided

FOR CREAMY GINGER SOY SAUCE:

- ½ cup mayonnaise
- 1 tablespoon soy sauce
- 1¾ teaspoons granulated sugar
- 1½ teaspoons rice vinegar
- 1 teaspoon ginger paste
- ¼ teaspoon garlic powder
- ¼ teaspoon paprika
- ⅛ teaspoon ground cayenne pepper

FOR SERVING:

- 2 cups mixed greens
- 1 tablespoon wasabi paste
- 1 green onion (green part only), chopped

Seared Peppered Ahi

RECIPE STEPS:

1. To make ahi seasoning: Mix all dry ingredients in a small bowl. Use back of a spoon to crush mixture to reduce size of dry herb pieces.

2. Rub 1 teaspoon of vegetable oil over fish, then press fish into seasoning blend on a plate so that four sides of fish are coated with seasoning. You don't need to coat two ends of fish fillet, since those will be sliced off before serving.

3. Heat 2 tablespoons of oil in a small or medium skillet over medium heat.

4. When pan is hot, sear four seasoned sides of fillet for 15–20 seconds, just until outside of fish is cooked. Only exterior of fish gets cooked, while center remains raw. After searing, chill fish for at least 2 hours up to overnight in your refrigerator.

5. To make creamy ginger soy sauce: Combine ingredients in a small bowl, then cover and chill until needed.

6. When ready to serve fish, use a very sharp knife to slice about $1/8$" off ends of ahi. Then cut remaining fillet into nine slices, each about $1/4$" thick.

7. Arrange a bed of mixed greens on each plate and drizzle with creamy ginger soy sauce. Fan out ahi portions over greens, top with chopped green onion, then serve dish with a small cup of creamy ginger soy sauce and a portion of wasabi on side.

FIELD NOTES

Did you know the wasabi you're eating is probably fake? Ninety-five percent of all wasabi, or Japanese horseradish, sold in North America is imitation, made with European horseradish, mustard flour, and green food coloring. Real wasabi is difficult to grow and loses its flavor shortly after grating, so the imitation product is more practical and cheaper to make.

OUTBACK STEAKHOUSE

Tasmanian Chili

 PREP TIME:
Active: 15 minutes
Inactive: 2 hours

 DIFFICULTY:
Easy

 MAKES:
6 cups

Good chili con carne is hard to find at casual restaurant chains, so this delicious bowl of red from Outback Steakhouse is a real treat. It's a straightforward recipe made with peppers, onions, tomatoes, and garlic, but it's the chunks of tender filet mignon that elevate this secret formula above the rest. For this Outback Tasmanian Chili copycat recipe, I also included a small can of El Pato hot tomato sauce, which is my secret ingredient for great flavor and the perfect level of spiciness.

After 2 hours of simmering, you'll have a fantastic pot of chili—enough for six big servings, each topped with a blend of shredded cheese and chopped green onion, just like in the restaurant.

 Try to design your copycat recipe to use the entire contents of packaged ingredients. In this chili hack, I call for one large carton of chicken broth (32 ounces), 1 can of diced tomatoes, and 1 can of El Pato tomato sauce. Using everything in the container makes the recipe more convenient, economical, and less wasteful.

FOR CHILI:

- 2 tablespoons extra-virgin olive oil, divided
- 1 pound beef tenderloin fillet, diced to a variety of sizes
- 1½ cups peeled and diced yellow onion
- 1 cup diced Anaheim green chilies
- 1 cup diced red bell pepper
- 1 tablespoon minced garlic
- ¼ cup chili powder
- 1 tablespoon dark brown sugar, packed
- 1½ teaspoons salt
- 1½ teaspoons coarse ground black pepper
- 1 teaspoon ground cumin

FOR CHILI (continued):

- 2 tablespoons all-purpose flour
- 4 cups chicken broth
- 1 (14.5-ounce) can diced tomatoes
- 1 (7¾-ounce) can El Pato hot tomato sauce
- 2 tablespoons apple cider vinegar

FOR GARNISH:

- 6 tablespoons shredded Cheddar cheese
- 6 tablespoons shredded Monterey jack cheese
- 2 tablespoons chopped green onion

RECIPE STEPS:

1. Heat 1 tablespoon olive oil in a large saucepan or Dutch oven over medium-high heat. Add diced fillet and sear 5 minutes, stirring occasionally. Remove from pan and set aside.

2. Pour remaining tablespoon of oil into uncleaned pan, heat 1 minute, then add onion, green chilies, and red bell pepper. Sauté 2 minutes, stirring frequently, then add garlic and cook 1 minute.

3. Add beef back to pan, along with chili powder, brown sugar, salt, pepper, and cumin. Cook 2 minutes.

4. Stir flour into chicken broth, then add broth to pan with tomatoes, tomato sauce, and vinegar. Cook uncovered 2 hours until it thickens.

5. Serve chili in bowls, garnished with shredded Cheddar and Monterey jack cheese and chopped green onions.

FIELD NOTES

Don't wait long before examining your take-away. The sample of the food you took home to study changes with every passing hour. Even when refrigerated, the flavors and textures are in a constant state of flux, so the quicker you work on your copycat recipe, the better. When my hack is done, I often return to the restaurant to grab a fresh sample of the target product for a final taste test.

OUTBACK STEAKHOUSE

Aussie Twisted Ribs

 PREP TIME:
Active: 1 hour
Inactive: Overnight plus 7 hours

 DIFFICULTY:
Medium

 SERVES:
2 as an appetizer

Creative chefs at Outback Steakhouse have transformed the chain's fall-off-the-bone baby back ribs into a fantastic appetizer by adding crispy Bloomin' Onion breading, sweet barbecue sauce, and a drizzle of Bloomin' Onion creamy dipping sauce. I reverse-engineered the Outback Aussie Twisted Ribs recipe thanks to a kind server who let me take some home with sauces on the side, and now you can copy every twisted bit of it yourself with this exclusive hack.

Outback's ribs are smoked, but this recipe replicates the taste without a smoker by using a liquid smoke brine. This marinade will not only enhance the flavor of the ribs but also help keep the meat moist and juicy when cooked twice. Updated hacks for Bloomin' Onion breading and creamy dipping sauce (which I originally copied in 1997) are here to complete your twisted appetizer, and you'll also get a new, easy way to knock off the chain's tasty house-made spicy pickles that come on the side. Plan to make the spicy pickles, sauce, and marinated ribs 1 day in advance of cooking for the best flavor.

 For better pickles, add ⅛ teaspoon of calcium chloride (Pickle Crisp) to the jar. Calcium chloride keeps the cell walls of the cucumber firm so that you end up with crunchy—not mushy—pickle slices.

FOR SPICY PICKLES:

1 medium Kirby cucumber
2 teaspoons peeled and minced red onion
¾ teaspoon crushed red pepper
⅛ teaspoon ground black pepper
⅔ cup water
⅔ cup white wine vinegar
¼ cup granulated sugar
1 teaspoon salt

FOR CREAMY SAUCE:

½ cup mayonnaise
1 tablespoon prepared horseradish
1 tablespoon whole or 2% milk
1½ teaspoons paprika
1 teaspoon cayenne pepper sauce (such as Frank's RedHot or Louisiana)
⅛ teaspoon garlic powder
⅛ teaspoon onion powder
⅛ teaspoon salt
⅛ teaspoon dried oregano
2 pinches ground black pepper
2 pinches ground cayenne pepper

Aussie Twisted Ribs

FOR MARINADE:

2 cups chicken broth, divided
2 tablespoons hickory liquid smoke
2 tablespoons kosher salt
½ rack pork loin back ribs
Vegetable oil, for frying

FOR BREADING:

¾ cup all-purpose flour
1¼ teaspoons salt
1 tablespoon plus 1 teaspoon paprika
½ teaspoon baking powder
½ teaspoon ground cayenne pepper
¼ teaspoon onion powder
¼ teaspoon garlic powder
⅛ teaspoon ground cumin
⅛ teaspoon ground white pepper
1 cup whole or 2% milk
1 large egg, beaten
1 cup Sweet Baby Ray's Original Barbecue Sauce

FOR GARNISH:

1 teaspoon minced fresh parsley

RECIPE STEPS:

1. To make spicy pickles: Slice cucumber into ⅛"-thick pieces. If you have a mandoline, this is a good time to use it. Fill a 16-ounce canning jar with sliced cucumbers, arranging them to allow liquid to flow between slices. Spoon onion over cucumbers, then add crushed pepper and black pepper. Set jar aside.

2. Combine water, vinegar, sugar, and salt in a small saucepan over medium heat, stirring occasionally until liquid is hot but never boiling and sugar is dissolved. Cool mixture for 20 minutes until it is just warm, then pour it into jar, filling it to top. Secure lid and refrigerate overnight.

3. To make creamy sauce: Whisk all ingredients in a medium bowl, then cover and refrigerate overnight.

4. To make marinade: Whisk 1 cup broth, liquid smoke, and salt in a medium bowl until salt has dissolved. Add ribs to a large resealable plastic bag along with marinade. Seal bag and place it in a large bowl in refrigerator for 3 hours.

5. Preheat oven to 275°F.

6. After 3 hours, rinse ribs and add them to a baking pan with 1 cup of chicken broth. Cover pan with foil and place in oven for 2 hours to braise until ribs become fork-tender. After 2 hours, remove pan from oven, but keep it covered for 15–20 minutes to allow ribs to cool a bit.

7. When you can handle ribs, transfer rack into a clean resealable plastic bag and chill it for at least 2 hours, up to overnight.

8. When your ribs have chilled, fill a large saucepan, Dutch oven, or deep fryer with at least 3" of oil and heat it to 350°F.

9. To make breading: Mix dry ingredients (flour through white pepper) in a large bowl. In another large bowl, combine milk and egg.

10. When oil is hot, slice ribs between bones. To bread ribs, first toss in flour mixture. Tap off excess flour, then submerge rib in milk and egg and return it to flour. To achieve a nice crust on rib, repeat breading process by dunking it into milk and egg, then again coating it with flour. Apply breading steps to each rib and let them sit for a few minutes so that breading will stick better.

11. Carefully lower ribs into hot oil and fry for 4 minutes until breading turns golden brown. Transfer ribs to a rack or paper towels to drain for 1 minute, and then brush ribs with barbecue sauce until fully coated.

12. Stack ribs on a serving plate, then fill a squirt bottle with creamy sauce and drizzle it over ribs. Sprinkle minced parsley over plate and serve with a small bowl of spicy pickles on side.

FIELD NOTES

While many chains bowed to the pressure campaign of the late 1980s to switch frying oils from beef fat to vegetable oil, Outback quietly refused to alter its recipe for the iconic Bloomin' Onion. During my time in the kitchens at Outback headquarters in Tampa in 2011 to shoot an episode of *Top Secret Recipe*, I saw tubs of fat next to the fryer that were clearly labeled "Beef Tallow."

P.F. CHANG'S
Kung Pao Brussels Sprouts

 PREP TIME:
Active: 15 minutes
Inactive: 3 minutes

 DIFFICULTY:
Medium

 SERVES:
4

Use this copycat hack of the great P.F. Chang's kung pao sauce, toss it with fried Brussels sprouts, peanuts, and Thai chilies, and you'll have re-created one of the Chinese bistro's most popular sides. This recipe makes ½ cup of the secret sauce, which will be enough for 1 pound of Brussels sprouts in two batches.

Baking the Brussels sprouts in the oven, as recommended by some food hackers, will not duplicate the crispy texture of the original. To create a perfect clone of this easy dish, deep-frying is essential. You'll be frying 8 ounces of Brussels sprouts at a time, so it's best to use a wide-mouthed pan, such as a large saucepot, Dutch oven, or deep fryer, to avoid crowding the sprouts. Once the oil is hot and the sauce is made, it takes just 5 minutes to get this tasty dupe on the table.

 To make Brussels sprouts like those served in restaurants, with crispy leaves and tender centers, the secret is to deep-fry them. But be careful! Brussels sprouts contain a lot of water and will pop ferociously in the oil, so wear an apron and use a lid or splatter guard. After frying, flavor the crispy sprouts by tossing them with seasoning, sauce, and other ingredients. Because Brussels sprouts are bitter, a sweet-and-salty, lightly acidic flavor profile is recommended.

1 tablespoon vegetable oil or peanut oil, plus more for frying
3 tablespoons hot water
¼ cup dark brown sugar, packed
1 tablespoon soy sauce
1 tablespoon oyster sauce
1 tablespoon rice wine vinegar
2 teaspoons chili oil
1 teaspoon cornstarch
1 teaspoon crushed garlic
1 pound Brussels sprouts
½ cup peanuts
10–12 Thai chilies

RECIPE STEPS:

1. Preheat at least 1" of oil in a deep pot, Dutch oven, or deep fryer to 350°F.

2. Combine hot water and brown sugar in a small bowl, then whisk in soy sauce, oyster sauce, vinegar, and chili oil until sugar has dissolved. Whisk in cornstarch until no lumps remain. Stir in garlic and set aside.

3. Gently lower half of Brussels sprouts into oil. Fry Brussels sprouts for 3 minutes until crispy and browned, then transfer them to an ungreased baking sheet or plate.

4. When Brussels sprouts are done, add a tablespoon of oil to a wok or heavy sauté pan over high heat. Add ¼ cup of peanuts and 5 or 6 chilies to hot oil, stirring for 20–30 seconds until peanuts begin to bubble. Then add crispy Brussels sprouts to pan, and cook while tossing occasionally for 1 minute.

5. Pour ¼ cup of sauce (about half) into pan and cook for 20–30 seconds until sauce thickens. Stir or toss contents of pan so that Brussels sprouts are well coated with sauce, then pour everything into a serving bowl. Repeat process for second serving.

FIELD NOTES

Brussels sprouts were not often found on restaurant menus until the 2010s, when cooking shows, food media, and rising chefs discovered and promoted delicious new ways to prepare the bitter cruciferous vegetable.

PANDA EXPRESS

Blazing Bourbon Chicken

PREP TIME: Active: 45 minutes Inactive: None	**DIFFICULTY:** Medium	**SERVES:** 4

In collaboration with the *YouTube* talk show "Hot Ones," Panda Express launched its spiciest dish yet, featuring a new sauce made with the treacherous Apollo chili pepper. The Apollo pepper was developed by renowned chili breeder Ed Currie, who also cultivated the Carolina Reaper, once rated the world's hottest chili pepper. With a heat level of approximately 3 million Scoville units, the Apollo pepper is 1.4 times hotter than the Carolina Reaper.

Hot Ones The Last Dab Apollo Hot Sauce costs around $30 a bottle, and it's so hot that you would only need one drop for this hack of Panda Express Blazing Bourbon Chicken. So, for this copycat recipe, I found a cheaper, less fiery substitute: ghost pepper sauce. At 1 million Scoville units, the ghost pepper is one-third as hot as the Apollo pepper. When ghost pepper puree is blended with other ingredients in a sauce like Melinda's Ghost Pepper Sauce (which I used for this clone), it becomes diluted, flavorful, and milder. The ghost pepper sauce, combined with garlic, ginger, soy sauce, brown sugar, and a hint of bourbon, will create the perfect blend to mix with onion, bell pepper, and crispy chicken for a delicious, fiery, yet not overly spicy home hack of this tasty, limited-time entrée.

Hacking Blazing Bourbon Chicken (and other spicy menu items) can be a slow process when your taste buds are on fire. It's hard to distinguish flavors with numb taste buds, so you'll want to cool down your mouth between bites to accurately judge the taste. The best way is to drink whole milk. Casein, the main protein in milk, will wash away the capsaicin in the peppers, which is responsible for the sting. You can also try eating peanut butter or drinking an acidic beverage like lemonade, orange juice, or tomato juice until your mouth cools down.

FOR SAUCE:

- 2 teaspoons vegetable oil
- 1/2 teaspoon sesame oil
- 2 teaspoons minced garlic
- 1/2 teaspoon minced ginger
- 1 tablespoon plus 1 teaspoon bourbon
- 2 tablespoons plus 1 1/2 teaspoons soy sauce
- 2 tablespoons rice vinegar

FOR SAUCE (continued):

- 1 teaspoon ghost pepper hot sauce (I used Melinda's)
- 2 teaspoons cornstarch
- 2/3 cup water
- 1/3 cup plus 1 tablespoon dark brown sugar, packed

FOR CHICKEN:

2 tablespoons vegetable oil, plus more for frying
1 pound chicken breast fillets or chicken breast tenders
2 cups all-purpose flour
3 tablespoons cornstarch
2 teaspoons baking powder
1½ teaspoons salt
2 large eggs, beaten
1 cup whole milk
1½ cups chopped green bell pepper
1½ cups chopped white onion
16 small dried Chinese chili peppers, stemless

FOR GARNISH:

2 teaspoons white sesame seeds

RECIPE STEPS:

1. To make sauce: Combine oils in a small saucepan over medium heat. Add garlic and ginger and cook for 2 minutes.
2. Add bourbon and cook it off for about 30 seconds, then add soy sauce, rice vinegar, and pepper sauce.
3. Stir cornstarch into water and add it to pan along with brown sugar. Heat sauce until it bubbles, then reduce heat and simmer it for 5 minutes. Cover and remove from heat.
4. To make chicken: Fill a Dutch oven, large saucepan, or deep fryer with at least 2" of oil and preheat it to 350°F. Preheat oven to 225°F.
5. Cut chicken into small, bite-sized pieces roughly size of table grapes. Chicken pieces will double in size when battered and cooked, so small pieces work best.
6. Combine flour with cornstarch, baking powder, and salt in a medium bowl.
7. Combine eggs with milk in another medium bowl.
8. When oil is hot, bread several pieces of chicken at once by dropping them into flour and tossing to coat. Transfer chicken pieces to milk and egg mixture, submerging them to coat thoroughly. Use a slotted spoon to remove chicken pieces and transfer them to flour blend. Toss well, let chicken sit for about a minute, and repeat breading process by transferring chicken back to milk and egg mixture. Use a slotted spoon to remove chicken from milk and egg, then transfer it back to flour. Toss well, let chicken sit for 1–2 minutes, and then place chicken pieces on a baking sheet to rest while you bread remaining chicken.
9. Fry chicken in hot oil in batches for 3–4 minutes until golden brown, then transfer to a rack or tray lined with paper towels.
10. Keep chicken warm on a baking sheet in preheated oven.
11. To complete dish, heat 2 tablespoons of oil in a large sauté pan or wok over medium-high heat. (If you don't have a large pan that can accommodate everything, you can divide ingredients and prepare two servings at a time.) Add bell pepper and onion and cook for 2 minutes while tossing or stirring. Then add dry peppers and continue cooking for 1 more minute.
12. Add chicken to pan and cook for 2 minutes. Toss or stir a few times as it cooks.
13. Pour sauce over chicken and vegetables in pan. Cook for 1–2 minutes, stirring until coated and sauce is bubbling. Transfer dish to serving plates and sprinkle each serving with sesame seeds.

🔍 FIELD NOTES

In 1987, Andy Kao, a chef at Panda Express, invented orange chicken, which became the chain's signature entrée. That iconic recipe also serves as the inspiration for many spin-off dishes at Panda Express, including this one.

Chow Mein

PANDA EXPRESS

Chow Mein

 PREP TIME:
Active: 10 minutes
Inactive: 5 minutes

 DIFFICULTY:
Easy

 SERVES:
2

It can be frustrating when you're standing in line at a buffet and they run out of the dish you wanted before it's your turn. But that scenario is how this recipe was hacked. From the line, I watched a cook whip up a new batch of Chow Mein in the clearly visible kitchen and took plenty of mental notes. The dish was done in just a few minutes, and before I knew it I was out the door with a hot serving of fresh Chow Mein and great intel to hack a perfect clone.

As with the authentic dish, the beauty of this re-creation lies in its simplicity. There are only seven ingredients, and the prep work is low-impact. I used dry chow mein noodles (also known as Chinese stir fry noodles), which are easy to find and inexpensive, along with dark soy sauce for its deep caramel color. If you don't have a wok to prepare your Panda Express dupe, a large skillet with sloped sides for tossing will work nicely.

 When you're watching cooks prepare food in an open kitchen from a distance, it's hard to determine exact measurements for the ingredients they are using. It's much easier to note the ratios of the ingredients they add, comparatively. You can pinpoint the measurements later, when you make the recipe, by using the approximate ratios you observed the cook using.

8 ounces dry chow mein noodles
2½ tablespoons vegetable oil or peanut oil
1½ cups peeled and sliced white onion
½ cup chopped celery
2 cups sliced green cabbage
2 tablespoons dark soy sauce
1 tablespoon oyster sauce

RECIPE STEPS:

1. Cook noodles in boiling water for 3–4 minutes until tender. Then rinse them with cold water to stop cooking process, and set aside.

2. Heat oil in a wok or large skillet over high heat.

3. When oil begins to shimmer, add onions and celery. Cook, stirring or tossing occasionally, for 1 minute until edges of onions start to brown.

4. Add cabbage and noodles and cook for 1 minute, tossing pan to coat noodles.

5. Add soy sauce and oyster sauce and cook for 2 more minutes, tossing well until noodles are coated with sauces. Serve.

FIELD NOTES

"Chow mein" means "fried noodles" and is made with noodles that are fried. "Lo mein," which means "dredged noodles," is made with noodles that are boiled. So, the chow mein made in this recipe is actually lo mein.

PEI WEI

Chicken Pad Thai

 PREP TIME:
Active: 20 minutes
Inactive: 3½ hours

 DIFFICULTY:
Easy

 SERVES:
2

Pei Wei's tasty take on the dish is perfectly balanced with sweetness, sourness, saltiness, and a hint of spice, while the chicken is moist, tender, and packed with great flavor.

For this copycat hack recipe, you'll start by brining the chicken to prevent it from drying out, as white meat tends to do. The secret marinade includes fish sauce, which functions like MSG in Thai dishes. Soaking the chicken in this salty sauce allows the natural aminos to contribute fantastic umami goodness, and cooking it with moist heat, as detailed in the following steps, will result in fork-tender, juicy chicken.

The noodles at Pei Wei are thin, so select the thinnest rice noodles available on the shelf.

This hack will make two large meal-sized entrées, just like what you get at the restaurant, which can easily be divided into four more modest servings.

 Ingredients that add high levels of glutamate to a dish are crucial for umami savoriness in the flavor profile and cannot be overlooked when creating your clone. Look for glutamic acid in its many forms to add to your recipes to enhance flavor, including MSG, soy sauce, yeast extract, broths, Parmesan cheese, mushrooms, tomatoes, and fish sauce (as in this recipe).

FOR BRINE:

2 cups water
1 tablespoon plus 1 teaspoon kosher salt
2 tablespoons fish sauce
1 skinless chicken breast fillet

FOR NOODLES:

1 cup chicken broth
8 ounces uncooked rice noodles
⅓ cup sweet chili sauce
2 tablespoons fish sauce
2 tablespoons rice wine vinegar
2 tablespoons lime juice
2 tablespoons ketchup

FOR NOODLES (continued):

2 tablespoons dark brown sugar, packed
1½ teaspoons soy sauce
1 tablespoon peanut oil
2 teaspoons minced garlic
1 egg, beaten
⅓ cup chopped peanuts, divided
2 cups bean sprouts
2 green onions, cut into 2" lengths (green part only)
6–8 sprigs fresh cilantro
2 lime wedges

RECIPE STEPS:

1. To make brine: Add water, salt, and fish sauce to a medium bowl or storage container. Whisk until salt dissolves, then add chicken and refrigerate for 3 hours.

2. To make noodles: Bring 1 cup of chicken broth to a low boil in a medium saucepan with a steamer basket over medium heat. Add chicken and cover. Steam for 10 minutes, then turn off heat and let chicken sit covered for an additional 6 minutes. Remove chicken from pan and let it cool until you can handle it. Slice it into $1/8$"-thick bite-sized pieces and set aside.

3. Soak noodles in hot water for 10 minutes until tender. Drain and rinse them under cold water, then set aside.

4. To make sauce, in a small bowl, mix sweet chili sauce, fish sauce, rice wine vinegar, lime juice, ketchup, brown sugar, and soy sauce. Whisk until brown sugar is dissolved, then set it aside.

5. Heat up a wok or large sauté pan over medium-high heat.

6. Add oil to pan, and when it's hot add garlic and chicken. Cook for 1 minute.

7. Move chicken to one side of pan and pour beaten egg into cleared area. As egg cooks, break it into roughly pea-sized pieces.

8. Once egg is cooked and crumbled, increase heat to high and add sauce. Cook for 1 minute.

9. Add noodles and toss them to coat with sauce. Cook for 2 minutes until noodles are heated through.

10. Add peanuts (reserving 1 tablespoon for later), bean sprouts, and green onions.

11. Toss to mix all ingredients, then divide onto two serving plates. Garnish with reserved peanuts and add three to four cilantro sprigs on top of each serving. Place a lime wedge on each plate and serve.

FIELD NOTES

Rice noodles were invented more than 2,000 years ago in southern China as a staple for invaders from the north. People from the country's northern region customarily ate noodles made with wheat flour, but wheat didn't grow well in the south, so they improvised with rice.

PIZZA HUT

Creamy Italian Dressing

 PREP TIME:
Active: 5 minutes
Inactive: 30 minutes

 DIFFICULTY:
Easy

 MAKES:
1 cup

As Pizza Hut has shifted away from salads in recent years, it has become more difficult to find its popular Italian dressing. As a food hacker, I have received an increasing number of requests to replicate the chain's endangered salad sauce before it disappears completely. When my search for the dressing in Las Vegas reached a dead end, I was grateful to a *Top Secret Recipes* fan in Pennsylvania who managed to send me a massive 1-gallon bottle that should last me through the next decade.

With this bottle, I was able to hack a dupe with basic ingredients and some MSG. You can find MSG in stores under the brand name Ac'cent or in bulk online.

 To reverse-engineer recipes like this dressing, learn which major ingredients can be identified by their components in the ingredient list. For example, if a food contains soybean oil, egg yolk, and vinegar, you know it's made with mayonnaise. If the food contains sugar and molasses, you know it's made with brown sugar. If a food contains molasses, anchovies, and tamarind, you know it's made with Worcestershire sauce. If a food contains tomato purée, corn syrup, and vinegar, you know the food is made with ketchup. If the ingredients include mustard powder, vinegar, and turmeric, you know the food is made with yellow mustard.

1 cup mayonnaise
⅓ cup white vinegar
1 tablespoon plus 1 teaspoon granulated sugar
½ teaspoon salt
¼ teaspoon MSG (monosodium glutamate)
¼ teaspoon garlic powder
¼ teaspoon onion powder
¼ teaspoon Italian seasoning blend (oregano, marjoram, rosemary, basil, etc.)
¼ teaspoon dried parsley
¼ teaspoon crushed red pepper

Whisk together all ingredients in a small bowl until smooth and creamy. Cover and chill dressing for at least 30 minutes before using. Will keep for up to 3 weeks.

 FIELD NOTES

The restaurant dressing contains propylene glycol alginate and xanthan gum, which thicken, emulsify, and stabilize the commercial dressing to prevent separation and maintain a consistent appearance. You won't need heavy emulsifiers like those in your home clone, since you can shake the dressing before using it.

Ghost Pepper Wings

 PREP TIME:
Active: 1 hour
Inactive: 4½ hours

 DIFFICULTY:
Medium

 SERVES:
4–6 (20 wings)

The Scoville heat rating of bhut jolokia, commonly known as ghost pepper, exceeds 1 million units, making it 200 times hotter than a jalapeño! But that didn't stop Popeyes from creating an eye-watering breading with the pepper for their scorching crispy wings. Yes, these wings are seriously spicy, but they're not so extreme that they become inedible, and the fantastic flavor is sure to tempt you back for more.

This Popeyes Ghost Pepper Wings recipe hack starts with brining the wing segments in a marinade of buttermilk and pepper sauce. Salt, MSG, and cayenne pepper sauce infuse the wings with flavor, while the breading, which contains a decent amount of ground ghost pepper, adds a spicy kick. Ghost pepper has rapidly gained popularity in recent years, and you should have no trouble finding ground ghost pepper online. Even brick-and-mortar grocery stores are beginning to stock it.

Serve up this dupe with blue cheese or ranch dressing on the side for dipping.

 Ghost pepper is very hot, so be careful with it. You might even want to wear gloves when breading these wings, especially if you need clean fingers later for inserting a contact lens—or any other activity that doesn't go well with ferociously fiery digits.

FOR BRINE:

- 2 cups water
- 1 cup cayenne pepper sauce (such as Louisiana or Frank's RedHot)
- 1 cup buttermilk
- 2 tablespoons plus 2 teaspoons salt
- 2 tablespoons granulated sugar
- 1 tablespoon plus 1 teaspoon MSG (monosodium glutamate)
- 1 tablespoon paprika
- 20 chicken wings (drumettes and flats)

FOR BREADING:

- 2 cups all-purpose flour
- 1½ teaspoons ground ghost pepper (bhut jolokia)
- 1¼ teaspoons salt
- 1¼ teaspoons MSG
- 1½ teaspoons baking powder
- ½ teaspoon ground white pepper
- ½ teaspoon onion powder
- ¼ teaspoon garlic powder
- 2 cups buttermilk
- Vegetable oil, for frying

RECIPE STEPS:

1. To make brine: In a medium bowl, combine brine ingredients and whisk until salt and sugar dissolve. Add wings and chill for 4–5 hours. Once wings have finished brining, rinse them and blot them dry.

2. To make breading: Whisk together dry ingredients in a large bowl.

3. Pour buttermilk into a medium bowl.

4. Working with a couple of wings at a time, coat wings in flour blend, then gently lower each one into buttermilk until they are completely moistened. Remove wings from buttermilk and toss them in flour until a nice coating forms on each. Set wings aside on a tray until all are breaded. A short rest will ensure that flour sticks to wings.

5. In a deep fryer or a large saucepan with a thermometer attached, preheat enough oil for frying wings to 300°F.

6. Fry wings in batches of four or five for 4 minutes, then remove them from oil and let them rest for 5 minutes. Lower them back into oil for another 7–9 minutes until browned. Keep finished wings warm on a sheet pan in an oven set to 250°F until all are done frying. Serve warm.

FIELD NOTES

A buttermilk brine offers a range of benefits. The lactic acid in buttermilk tenderizes meat by breaking down proteins, which helps other flavors penetrate more effectively. The flavor is enhanced with a sweet tanginess, and the meat becomes juicier as it retains more moisture. Also, the final color is improved when the sugars in buttermilk caramelize on the surface.

Famous Chocolate Cake

 PREP TIME:
Active: 40 minutes
Inactive: 1 hour 35 minutes

 DIFFICULTY:
Medium

 SERVES:
12

Portillo's Famous Chocolate Cake is an incredibly moist mayonnaise cake topped with chocolate frosting. It includes ingredients commonly found in grocery store cake mixes: diglycerides, dicalcium phosphate, and propylene glycol. After baking over a dozen cakes, I developed this copycat recipe from scratch, using more wholesome ingredients for the cake and the icing. The cake still tastes like Portillo's Famous Chocolate Cake, but it doesn't include the hard-to-spell additives found in the original.

If mayonnaise seems like an unusual ingredient for a cake, fear not. Almost everything in it benefits your cake batter. The combination of eggs and fat helps keep the cake fluffy and moist, while salt and sugar enhance the flavor. Additionally, vinegar and lemon juice aid in the leavening process to create a tall cake with a light crumb. You could say mayonnaise is the perfect ingredient for this recipe.

 By ordering this chocolate cake for delivery from Portillo's, I confirmed that the ingredients are identical to those in a box of Betty Crocker chocolate cake mix. If you want to save time and ingredients, you can replicate Portillo's cake by using boxed cake mix and store-bought chocolate frosting in place of the homemade cake and frosting recipes provided here. Just add 1 cup of mayonnaise, 1 cup of water, and 3 eggs to the boxed mix and bake as instructed. Once cool, top with two tubs of chocolate frosting.

FOR CHOCOLATE CAKE:

- ¼ cup Dutch-process cocoa (dark cocoa)
- 1½ cups boiling water
- 4 ounces semi-sweet chocolate (bar or chips)
- ¾ cup plus 1 tablespoon mayonnaise
- ½ cup unsalted butter, softened
- 1¾ cups plus 1 tablespoon granulated sugar
- 3 large eggs
- 1¾ teaspoons vanilla extract
- 2 cups (10 ounces) all-purpose flour
- 1¼ teaspoons baking soda
- 1 teaspoon salt

FOR CHOCOLATE FROSTING:

- ½ cup heavy cream
- ⅓ cup granulated sugar
- 12 ounces semi-sweet chocolate (bar or chips)
- 3 tablespoons Dutch-process cocoa
- 10 tablespoons unsalted butter
- ½ cup plus 2 tablespoons light corn syrup
- 1 teaspoon vanilla extract
- ¾ cup (3 ounces) powdered sugar
- ½ teaspoon salt

RECIPE STEPS:

1. Preheat oven to 350°F.
2. To make chocolate cake: Whisk cocoa powder into boiling water until smooth, then stir in semi-sweet chocolate with a spoon. Set this chocolate syrup aside to cool during next steps.
3. Use a stand mixer with paddle attachment or a handheld mixer to cream together mayonnaise, butter, and sugar. Mix on high speed for 3 minutes until it's fluffy and pearlescent.
4. Add eggs, one at a time, mixing just until blended after each addition. Add vanilla and mix it in.
5. Add chocolate syrup, a little at a time, mixing on medium speed after each addition until it's fully blended in.
6. In a medium bowl, whisk together flour, baking soda, and salt. Incorporate this flour mixture into batter in two batches, mixing thoroughly after each addition to prevent lumps. Once all flour is added, mix batter for an additional 30 seconds.
7. Split batter into two (9") cake pans that have been well-greased, bottoms lined with parchment paper.
8. Bake 28–35 minutes until a toothpick stuck into center of cake comes out clean. Cool for at least 1 hour before frosting.
9. To make chocolate frosting: Heat a large pan filled about halfway with hot water over medium-low heat. Add cream to a large glass or metal bowl and set it over pan so that warm water gently heats cream. When cream is hot, add sugar and stir until it is dissolved. Add semi-sweet chocolate and stir frequently until sauce becomes smooth. Remove bowl from heat and mix in cocoa and butter until butter is melted.
10. Add corn syrup, vanilla, powdered sugar, and salt and mix with an electric mixer on medium speed until smooth. If frosting is too thin, place it in your refrigerator until it cools and thickens.
11. Frost cake by flipping one layer, bottom side up, onto a serving platter. Spoon half of frosting onto center of cake and spread it over edges using a spatula. This extra overhang of frosting will help you frost sides of cake. Turn other layer, bottom side up, onto first layer, and spoon remaining frosting onto center of cake. As before, spread frosting just beyond edge of cake so that extra frosting can be used to cover sides. Once top is complete, smooth out frosting on sides until cake is fully covered. Cut it into twelve slices to serve.

FIELD NOTES

Pay attention to the cocoa you're using. Dutch-process cocoa, as used in this recipe, has been alkalized to reduce its acidity. This process makes the cocoa darker and gives it a stronger dark chocolate flavor, making it the perfect choice for this chocolate cake and frosting. Natural cocoa powder retains its acidity and is chemically effective when baking soda is used in a recipe. It is also a good choice when a lighter chocolate color and flavor are preferred.

Famous Chocolate Cake

QDOBA

3-Cheese Queso

 PREP TIME:
Active: 15 minutes
Inactive: 40 minutes

 DIFFICULTY:
Easy

 MAKES:
3 cups (12 servings)

There are many ways to formulate good queso, but to make queso the Qdoba way, you must start with the correct ingredients, and most copycat recipes miss the mark. A few recipes get one of the peppers and two of the cheeses right, but nearly every recipe I've seen veers away from the restaurant flavor.

Queso can be made with various cheeses, including queso fresco, asadero, and Muenster, but this particular queso includes a cheese you probably didn't expect: Swiss. That cheese is slow to melt, so you'll first shred it, along with the jack, and add white American cheese in the mix. Next, red bell peppers are roasted, peeled, and seeded, along with the poblano and jalapeños, before being diced and added to the cheese sauce. The sauce cooks on low heat, without bubbling, ensuring it remains smooth and creamy.

When it's done, your queso may appear thin in the pan, but it will thicken as it cools to a perfect consistency for dipping tortilla chips or as a topping for tacos and burrito bowls.

 For smooth cheese sauces, there's no need to make a roux using fat and flour. Instead, you can use sliced American cheese to introduce sodium citrate or sodium phosphate into the mix. These emulsifiers prevent the cheese sauce from becoming grainy and ensure a smooth, creamy texture. American cheese and most sliced, individually wrapped cheeses contain one of these ingredients.

1 medium poblano pepper
1 medium red bell pepper
2–3 medium jalapeños
1½ cups whole milk
8 ounces diced white American cheese
4 ounces shredded Monterey jack cheese

1½ ounces shredded Swiss cheese
½ teaspoon minced garlic
½ teaspoon salt
¼ teaspoon plus ⅛ teaspoon ground cayenne pepper

RECIPE STEPS:

1. Roast poblano, red bell pepper, and jalapeños on a greased baking sheet in your oven preheated to 450°F. Bake for 20–30 minutes, turning twice during baking, until skins are wrinkled and charred. If you have a gas stove, you can roast peppers more quickly by placing them directly over a high flame, turning often until they are completely blackened. Pierce each jalapeño with a skewer to hold it over flame without burning your fingers. After charring, drop blackened peppers into a covered container or paper bag for a couple of minutes, and skins should easily wash off in cold water. Remove stems and seeds, then dice peppers.

2. Combine milk and white American cheese in a medium saucepan over medium-low heat. Heat, stirring often, until cheese melts and sauce becomes smooth, about 10 minutes.

3. Add all shredded cheese to pan and continue heating, stirring frequently with a whisk until cheese melts and sauce becomes smooth, about 5 minutes.

4. Add 6 tablespoons of diced poblano, 3 tablespoons of diced red bell pepper, 3 tablespoons of diced jalapeño, garlic, salt, and cayenne pepper to sauce. Continue cooking on medium-low heat, stirring often, but lower heat if sauce bubbles. Cook for 20 more minutes until sauce thickens slightly and peppers become soft, then turn off heat and cover it for 10 minutes before serving.

FIELD NOTES

Melted cheese dips were popular in Texas homes and restaurants in the early 1900s, but the popularity of queso soared throughout America in the 1980s when Kraft advertised the simple, now-famous recipe of 1 can of Ro-Tel diced tomatoes mixed with 1 pound of melted Velveeta cheese.

RED LOSTER

Crab Your Way

 PREP TIME:
Active: 5 minutes
Inactive: 5 minutes (Cajun)/
20 minutes (Garlic)

 DIFFICULTY:
Easy

 **MAKES:**
1 pound

With Crab Your Way, patrons can customize their steamed crab meal at Red Lobster by choosing between snow crab or bairdi crab (a sweeter-tasting snow crab) and pairing it with one of two flavorful butter sauces: Cajun (currently the most popular, according to servers) or roasted garlic. This dish offers a flavorful way to serve crab, and here you'll find all the tips you'll need to replicate it at home in just minutes.

Preparing the crab is simple. Steam the legs for 5–10 minutes until hot, then brush them with the sauce and serve additional sauce on the side for dipping. Each sauce recipe yields enough for 1 pound of crab, so if you plan to make more, you'll just need to adjust the sauce accordingly.

 Don't rely on your memory; find a good way to document the details of a recipe. At Red Lobster, I asked the waitress for the ingredients for the Cajun butter, which she retrieved from the chef and repeated to me. Immediately after she left, I pulled out my phone to make notes before I forgot what she said. If I had been prepared, I would have discreetly tapped "record" on my phone to save the entire conversation and later take notes from the recording.

FOR CAJUN BUTTER:

- ½ cup unsalted butter
- ½ teaspoon pressed garlic
- 1½ teaspoons cayenne pepper sauce (such as Louisiana or Frank's RedHot)
- 1½ teaspoons ground black pepper
- ½ teaspoon lemon juice
- ½ teaspoon white wine vinegar
- ¼ teaspoon plus ⅛ teaspoon celery salt
- ¼ teaspoon prepared horseradish
- ¼ teaspoon granulated sugar
- ⅛ teaspoon paprika
- ⅛ teaspoon onion powder
- ⅛ teaspoon ground cayenne pepper

FOR ROASTED GARLIC BUTTER:

- 1 large head garlic
- 1 tablespoon extra-virgin olive oil
- ½ cup unsalted butter
- ¾ teaspoon dried parsley
- ½ teaspoon lemon juice
- ¼ teaspoon salt

FOR FINISHING THE RECIPE:

- 1 pound chilled cooked crab legs (snow crab, Dungeness crab, or king crab)

RECIPE STEPS:

1. To make Cajun butter: Melt butter in a small saucepan over medium-low heat. Add pressed garlic and cook for 3 minutes. Stir in remaining ingredients, then cover pan and remove from heat.

2. To make roasted garlic butter: Preheat oven to 375°F.

3. Remove all garlic cloves from head without peeling skin off cloves. Place unpeeled cloves in a small oven-safe bowl and toss with olive oil until coated. Cover bowl with foil and bake 15 minutes.

4. Remove garlic from oven to cool for 15 minutes, peel skin off cloves, and mince. You should have around ¼ cup of garlic.

5. Melt butter in a small saucepan over medium-low heat. Add garlic, parsley, lemon juice, and salt, then cover pan and remove it from heat.

6. Steam crab in a steamer basket over boiling water 5–10 minutes until hot.

7. Brush crab with butter sauce and serve remaining sauce on side for dipping.

FIELD NOTES

Which crab should you choose for this recipe? You have a few options:

Snow crab: long, thin legs that may be difficult to crack, but the flavorful meat is worth the effort.

Dungeness crab: thick legs filled with sweet, flaky meat. Similar to king crab, but less expensive.

King crab: long, thick legs, filled with tubes of sweet meat, similar to but less rich than lobster. It is the most expensive of the three, and it's a real treat if you can find it.

Walt's Favorite Shrimp

RED LOBSTER

Walt's Favorite Shrimp

 PREP TIME:
Active: 1 hour
Inactive: 1½ hours

 DIFFICULTY:
Medium

 SERVES:
4–6

Many recognize Red Lobster as the restaurant that popularized popcorn shrimp. Introduced in 1974, Walt's Favorite Shrimp is butterflied, breaded, and lightly fried, making a simple-to-eat finger food. However, there's more than just breading and frying: You must start with a brine. Serve alongside cocktail sauce for dipping and lemon slices to squeeze over each bite.

 Instead of a classic salt brine, I used a 1-hour chicken bouillon brine for a delicious flavor. Bouillon brines also work great for flavoring fried vegetables, such as zucchini, green beans, and asparagus. Marinate your vegetables for 1–2 hours in the brine made with this recipe, then dry, batter, and fry.

- 2 large chicken bouillon cubes
- 2 cups boiling water
- 2 teaspoons kosher salt
- 1 pound large shrimp (31–40), peeled and butterflied, tails on
- Vegetable oil, for frying
- 2 large eggs, beaten
- 1 cup whole or 2% milk
- ¾ cup all-purpose flour
- 1 cup plain breadcrumbs
- ¾ teaspoon ground white pepper
- ¼ teaspoon salt
- ¼ teaspoon garlic powder

RECIPE STEPS:

1. Dissolve bouillon cubes in boiling water with salt. Once cooled, add shrimp and marinate in refrigerator for 1 hour, then rinse and dry shrimp.
2. Preheat at least 2" of oil in a Dutch oven, large saucepan, or deep fryer to 350°F.
3. In a bowl, combine egg and milk. In another bowl, measure flour.
4. In a third bowl, mix breadcrumbs with white pepper, salt, and garlic powder.
5. To avoid breading tails of shrimp, hold each by the tail as you dip it into flour and then into egg and milk mixture. Repeat breading process two more times for three coats of flour. Finally, dunk shrimp once more into egg and milk, then coat with seasoned breadcrumbs. Arrange on a tray or baking sheet until all are coated, then let sit 10 minutes.
6. Fry shrimp in batches for 1–1½ minutes until golden brown, then drain on a rack or a plate lined with paper towels.

FIELD NOTES

Properly breading shrimp for frying is a multi-step process. You'll first add a coating of flour. Next, the food is dipped into an egg wash, milk, or a mixture of the two. After some liquid drips off, it goes back into the flour for a thicker coating. For a crispier breading, these steps may be repeated and you can also add a layer of breadcrumbs for extra crunch.

Mojo Potatoes

 PREP TIME:
Active: 30 minutes
Inactive: 1 hour 20 minutes

 DIFFICULTY:
Medium

 SERVES:
4–6

Sherwood Johnson survived a case of malaria while serving in World War II, which left him with some residual nerve damage and earned him a new nickname: Shakey. Despite his affliction, Shakey Johnson could play toe-tapping Dixieland jazz on the piano night after night in the pizza parlor he opened in Sacramento in 1954, where the live jazz accompanied thin-crust pizza and cold pitchers of beer.

Shakey's became the first franchised pizza restaurant in the US, and by 1974, the chain had 500 stores nationwide. The top dish is the made-to-order pizza, but the chain's trademarked crispy battered potato slices are also a favorite—and a great recipe to hack.

Copycat recipes claiming that pancake mix is the secret seasoning ingredient in Mojo Potatoes fail to recognize that pancake mix contains sugar, yet there is no noticeable sweetness in the breading. I also concluded that dry breading wouldn't work, as my tests showed that the paprika failed to bloom and contribute the same color as it does when the mixture is wet.

For this Shakey's Mojo Potatoes recipe, I eventually created a wet batter made with seasoned salt, flour, cornstarch, and paprika to match the flavor, crispiness, and red/orange tint of the real thing from America's first pizza chain.

 If the surface of the sliced potatoes is wet when battered, steam will form and push the batter away from the potatoes. When the water has cooked off and the steam stops, a vacuum will be created, causing the food to absorb oil and become overly greasy. For the best results, be sure to thoroughly dry any food you are frying before you batter it.

4 medium russet potatoes
½ cup plus 1 tablespoon all-purpose flour
½ cup cornstarch
2 tablespoons Lawry's seasoned salt
2 teaspoons paprika
¾ teaspoon ground black pepper
¾ cup water
Peanut oil or vegetable oil, for frying

RECIPE STEPS:

1. Slice unpeeled potatoes with a large, sharp knife or a mandoline into ¼"-thick slices. Cut potatoes lengthwise for longer slices. Rinse potato slices in a bowl of cold water to remove excess starch, then drain and cover potatoes with fresh cold water. Potatoes should soak for 30 minutes up to 1 hour.

2. Make batter by whisking together flour, cornstarch, seasoned salt, paprika, and pepper. Whisk in water and continue whisking until batter is smooth with no lumps.

3. Before battering potato slices, dry them with towels and let them sit for at least 10 minutes.

4. Dip each slice into batter, allowing excess to drip off. Arrange all slices on a rack over a baking sheet to let more batter drain off.

5. Heat at least 2" oil in a large saucepan, Dutch oven, or deep fryer to 350°F while battered potatoes rest.

6. When oil is hot, par-fry battered potatoes in small batches for 1 minute by gently lowering each slice into oil. Drain par-fried slices on a rack over a baking sheet or on a paper towel–lined plate. When all potato slices have been fried, let them cool for 15–20 minutes until they are no longer warm.

7. Fry potato slices a second time in hot oil in batches for 4–5 minutes until they are browned and crispy. Drain crispy potatoes on a rack over a baking sheet or on a paper towel–lined plate and serve warm.

FIELD NOTES

Cornstarch is gluten-free and primarily made of starch. When fried, the starch absorbs moisture and expands, forming a light, crispy crust. Flour contains starch, but it also has a significant amount of gluten, resulting in a thicker and less crunchy texture. If you want a crispier fried coating for battered fried food, add cornstarch to the batter along with the flour.

SmashFries, Smash Tots, and Smash Sauce

 PREP TIME:
Active: 20 minutes
Inactive: 35 minutes

 DIFFICULTY:
Medium

 SERVES:
2–4

When Smashburger opened its first restaurant in Denver, Colorado, in 2007, the concept of creating a flavorful crust by smashing a hamburger patty onto a flat grill was not new. However, this chain, which has expanded to over 240 locations across seven countries and thirty-four states, significantly popularized this burger patty cooking style.

What sets Smashburger's hamburgers apart from other smashed patty burgers is the addition of a top secret sauce slathered on the face of the top bun. The Smashburger Smash Sauce copycat recipe included here is a simple combination of mayonnaise, mustard, lemon juice, plus a few other crucial ingredients, and it will take you less than 5 minutes to make.

You can use the sauce on your home burgers or for dipping clones of the chain's signature SmashFries and Smash Tots, which are tossed with olive oil, garlic, and fresh herbs, and are hacked for you here. I noticed that the herbs on the real fries were tender, indicating they have been cooked. After testing several methods to soften the herbs for this SmashFries and Smash Tots copycat recipe, I finally settled on blanching the freshly minced herbs in simmering water and then straining them. I rehydrated garlic granules and simmered them in olive oil with the herbs just long enough for the all the water to evaporate. You'll know that the garlic and herbs still contain water if they clump together in the oil. When they separate, the water has cooked off.

 Become familiar with herbs to help you identify them in recipes such as this one by growing them in a kitchen window or other sunlit area. The rosemary and thyme will thrive in a space with bright sunlight most of the day. The parsley, on the other hand, does best in partial sunlight. To grow any of these herbs, use small pots with a drainage hole filled with good potting soil, and harvest regularly to encourage new growth.

SmashFries, Smash Tots, and Smash Sauce

FOR SMASHFRIES OR SMASH TOTS:

1½ cups plus 1 teaspoon water, divided
1 teaspoon minced fresh rosemary
1 teaspoon fresh thyme, leaves only
1 teaspoon minced fresh parsley
¼ teaspoon salt
½ teaspoon garlic granules
2 tablespoons extra-virgin olive oil
16 ounces frozen unpeeled French fries or potato tots

FOR SMASH SAUCE:

½ cup mayonnaise
2 tablespoons plus 1 teaspoon yellow prepared mustard
1½ teaspoons finely minced dill pickles
1½ teaspoons peeled and finely minced white onion
1 teaspoon granulated sugar
¼ teaspoon lemon juice

RECIPE STEPS:

1. To make fries or tots: Soften herbs by adding them to 1½ cups of water in a small saucepan over medium heat. When water bubbles, turn heat to medium-low and simmer for 25 minutes. Strain herbs and set aside.

2. While herbs are simmering, rehydrate garlic by combining it with remaining teaspoon of water in a small bowl. Let it sit for 2 minutes to absorb water.

3. Combine softened herbs and rehydrated garlic with oil in a small saucepan over medium-low heat. When oil starts to bubble, reduce heat to low and cook for 2–3 minutes until all water has evaporated, then remove saucepan from heat.

4. Prepare fries or tots as directed on package. Frying yields best results, although you can also use baking method.

5. When fries or tots are cooked, transfer them to a large bowl and add herbed oil.

6. Toss fries or tots until coated.

7. To make smash sauce: Combine all ingredients in a small bowl. Chill until ready to use. Sauce will keep in your refrigerator for up to 2 weeks.

FIELD NOTES

I tried my best to get the server at the counter to tell me which herbs were in the fresh blend tossed with these fries, but they kept the secret. Once home with a sample, I used my phone to take a photo of the herbs on the fries and then zoomed in on the image to identify them.

SOUTHERN COMFORT

Traditional Egg Nog

 PREP TIME:
Active: 30 minutes
Inactive: 3 hours to chill

 DIFFICULTY:
Easy

 MAKES:
36 ounces

Southern Comfort often ranks high with its delicious "traditional" egg nog (which contains no alcohol). But the first egg nog, invented in medieval Britain, was quite intoxicating. It was a warm drink made with milk and sherry, thickened with egg yolks. The cartons of nog available today are typically made with corn syrup, and much of the egg yolk has been replaced with cheaper, longer-lasting natural gums like carrageenan and guar gum. For this recipe, I've turned back the clock to make classic egg nog with lots of real egg yolks to thicken the batch.

 You can use the nutrition facts on packaged products to check on how close your hack is to the real thing. I calculated the calories for the ingredients in my version for a total of 1,765 calories, and when I divide that by the total number of servings (nine), I get 196 calories. That number is very close to the 190 calories per serving of Southern Comfort Traditional Egg Nog.

6 egg yolks
2/3 cup granulated sugar
3 cups whole milk
1 1/4 cups heavy cream
1/4 teaspoon salt
1/8 teaspoon ground cloves
1 pinch ground nutmeg
1 pinch ground cinnamon
1 teaspoon vanilla extract
16 drops yellow food coloring
3 drops red food coloring

RECIPE STEPS:

1. Whisk egg yolks with sugar until mixture is creamy and pale yellow.

2. Combine milk, cream, salt, cloves, nutmeg, and cinnamon in a medium saucepan over medium-low heat. Cook mixture, stirring often, until it simmers, about 12–15 minutes, then turn off heat.

3. Warm eggs gradually to prevent cooking by stirring 1/4-cup portions of hot milk mixture into yolks until you've incorporated one-quarter of hot liquid. Pour warm egg yolk mixture into hot milk in saucepan while stirring, then return heat to medium-low. Cook 5 minutes, stirring frequently until very hot but not simmering.

4. Cool egg nog for 5 minutes, then strain out any solids by pouring it through a fine mesh strainer. Stir in vanilla and colors, then chill for 3 hours until cold. Shake well before serving.

 FIELD NOTES

Guar gum and carrageenan are thickening agents known as hydrocolloids, which are often used together. Guar gum is a starch that thickens when it absorbs water. Carrageenan thickens food by forming a gel.

Almond Croissants

 PREP TIME:
Active: 1 hour
Inactive: 7½ hours to 3 days

 DIFFICULTY:
Hard

 MAKES:
9–10 croissants

The plain butter croissant at Starbucks is perfectly golden brown, flaky, buttery, and delicious. If you add almond filling and top it off with a pile of sliced almonds, you have one of the chain's most popular pastries.

Making croissants takes time and patience, since the dough must be rested, rolled, and folded multiple times to create the dozens of buttery layers found in good croissants. The dough performs best when the process is spread over 3 days, including 2 overnight rests in the refrigerator to relax and ferment. Your patience will pay off, as the long rests develop better flavor and make the dough easier to work with. (If you'd rather skip the longer prep, you can create a copycat batch of Starbucks Almond Croissants in the same day in about 7½ hours without resting the dough overnight.)

The laminated dough for traditional croissants is created by enclosing a flat block of butter within the dough, rolling it out, and folding it over several times. This process produces paper-thin, chewy layers inside and a golden-brown flakiness on the outside, and you will find all the steps included in this recipe.

As for the filling and topping, I discovered that they could be easily hacked with pudding mix and ground almonds. A small amount of cornstarch thickens the filling, preventing it from melting into the croissant dough or squirting out as the croissant bakes.

 Don't be fooled by "croissant" dough in a tube, such as Pillsbury Crescents. Authentic croissants are traditionally made with yeast dough, but yeast dough trapped in a paper tube will eventually produce so much gas that it splits the tube open in a delivery truck or on a store shelf. This is why tube dough manufacturers use sodium bicarbonate (baking soda) instead. Baking soda can be contained, and it leavens, but it produces a less desirable finished product, without the yeasty flavor. For legitimate almond croissants, it's best to start from scratch and use yeast.

FOR CROISSANT DOUGH:

3½ cups (17½ ounces) all-purpose flour
1 tablespoon plus ½ teaspoon instant yeast
⅓ cup granulated sugar
2 teaspoons salt
1½ cups whole milk, cold
3 tablespoons unsalted butter, cold, diced (higher-fat European-style is best)

FOR BUTTER BLOCK:

1 cup plus 2 tablespoons unsalted butter, softened

FOR ALMOND FILLING AND TOPPING:

1 (3.4-ounce) box Jell-O vanilla pudding mix
¾ cup plus 2 tablespoons water
1 heaping cup slivered almonds
½ teaspoon almond extract
⅛ teaspoon salt
1 tablespoon cornstarch

FOR EGG WASH:

1 large egg, beaten
1 tablespoon water

FOR GARNISH:

¾ cup sliced almonds

RECIPE STEPS:

1. To make croissant dough: Whisk together flour, yeast, sugar, and salt in a large bowl.

2. Add milk to a bowl of a stand mixer equipped with a dough hook.

3. Add flour into milk, set mixer to low speed, and mix for 5 minutes. Dough should form a loose ball.

4. Add butter and continue mixing on low speed for 5 more minutes until butter is fully incorporated into dough and dough is smooth. Spray a medium bowl with oil cooking spray, place dough in bowl, cover it with plastic wrap, and set it in a warm place for 2 hours. After 2 hours, punch down dough, remove it from bowl, wrap it in plastic, and chill it 1–2 hours, or overnight.

5. To make butter block: While dough chills, shape butter into a flat 8" square on parchment paper or plastic wrap, then cover it with another piece of parchment or plastic wrap. Refrigerate butter block for 1–2 hours, or overnight.

6. When ready to form croissants, take butter block out of refrigerator and let it sit on counter for 10 minutes to soften while you roll out dough. Just be sure not to let butter get too soft, or it will be difficult to work with. Butter and dough should be about same temperature.

7. Roll out dough on a lightly floured surface until it forms a 12" square. Peel paper from one side of butter and position it on dough so that corners of butter block touch middle of each flat edge of dough—it should resemble a diamond on top of a square. Fold corners of dough over butter and pinch them together wherever necessary to seal seam, ensuring that butter is completely enclosed in dough. Roll dough, seam-side up, until it forms a 16" square. Fold dough like a letter into thirds, then fold long ends over into thirds, creating a square. Place dough onto a lightly floured sheet pan and cover it with plastic wrap. Refrigerate for 1 hour.

continued on next page

Almond Croissants

RECIPE STEPS (continued):

8. Roll dough out again on a lightly floured surface until it forms a 16" square, and fold it into thirds, then again into thirds the other way to create a small square. Cover and chill for 1 hour or overnight.

9. Roll out dough into a 10" square that will fit on sheet pan. Lightly flour sheet pan, then transfer dough to it, cover it with plastic wrap, and let it rest in refrigerator 1 hour.

10. To make almond filling and topping: Whisk together water and pudding mix in a medium bowl. Use a food processor or blender on high speed to grind almonds into coarse almond flour, which should yield about ¾ cup plus 2 tablespoons of ground almonds. Combine ground almonds, almond extract, and salt with pudding. Remove ¾ cup of pudding mixture and mix it with cornstarch in a small microwave-safe bowl. Microwave this mixture on high for 1 minute to activate cornstarch; then stir, cover, and chill until needed. This thicker pudding blend will serve as filling, while remaining pudding mixture will be used as topping.

11. When ready to fill croissants, roll dough into a rectangle on a lightly floured surface, approximately 20" long and 12" wide. Use a pizza slicer or a sharp knife to trim any rough edges. You may want to use a ruler or another straight edge to guide your hand.

12. Slice dough to make 12"-long triangles that are 4" across on wide end. You should get nine or ten triangles.

13. Position a triangle of dough on counter in front of you, with wide edge nearest to you. Spoon a generous tablespoon of thicker filling onto widest end of dough, then fold sides over it and roll up dough to seal in filling. Continue rolling while stretching dough to make a tight roll.

14. Place croissant on a sheet pan lined with a silicone baking mat or parchment paper, ensuring that tip of rolled dough is underneath croissant to prevent it from lifting during baking. You will likely need two sheet pans for all croissants, since six will fill a half sheet pan after proofing. They will expand quite a bit. If you keep it covered and chilled, you can divide dough in half and make second batch later or next day.

15. To make egg wash: Combine egg and water in a small bowl. Brush entire surface of each croissant with mixture.

16. Place croissants in unheated oven along with a large saucepan of boiling water. Allow croissants to rest 1½–2 hours until they have doubled in size. Remove from oven, along with pan of water.

17. Preheat oven to 400°F. Place each baking sheet in oven and lower temperature to 350°F. Bake 22 minutes.

18. Use a butter knife to spread a thin layer of topping over top of each croissant. Sprinkle each one with sliced almonds, then place croissants back into oven 4–6 minutes to set topping. Cool croissants for 20 minutes on baking sheets before serving.

🔍 FIELD NOTES

There is a secret code for croissants. According to French pastry chef tradition, if the croissants are made with 100% pure butter, as these are, they are left straight after rolling. If the croissants are made with margarine or other fats, they are formed with a slight curve before baking. Curved croissants in French supermarkets are perceived as less authentic and of lower quality than traditional straight croissants.

STARBUCKS

Dark Toffee Bundt

 PREP TIME:
Active: 25 minutes
Inactive: 1 hour

 DIFFICULTY:
Easy

 MAKES:
10 mini cakes

This seasonal pastry is Starbucks's take on sticky toffee pudding, presented in a portable, single-serving size. Like the traditional recipe, this mini Bundt cake is partially sweetened with date paste and coated with a sticky, sweet glaze. However, this version deviates from tradition with a dusting of a sugar-salt blend and is decorated with Christmas sprinkles.

I turned to the chain's online ingredients list to create this Starbucks Dark Toffee Bundt copycat recipe. Using that information, I estimated ingredient ratios based on the initial weight of the date paste. I determined measurements for the flour, butter, sugar, eggs, brown sugar, and more, knowing that the list is organized by weight. Getting the leavening right took some trial and error, but with the help of a mini Bundt cake pan, I re-created the cakes in both appearance and taste. Starbucks uses little trees for the sprinkles, but feel free to top your cakes with whatever you like.

 If you don't have a mini Bundt cake pan, no problem. You can bake these cakes in a large (Texas-size) muffin pan or even a standard muffin pan. Cooking time for the large muffins will be the same as in the Bundt pan, but cut the baking time by 8 minutes for the smaller muffins. Coat muffin cups with nonstick oil spray before adding batter.

FOR CAKES:

- 6 ounces pitted Medjool dates, roughly chopped
- 1 cup boiling water
- ¾ cup plus 3 tablespoons unsalted butter, softened
- ½ cup plus 1 tablespoon granulated sugar
- ½ cup dark brown sugar, packed
- ½ teaspoon salt
- 2 large eggs
- 2 teaspoons vanilla extract
- 1 teaspoon butterscotch or caramel flavoring
- 1½ cups (7½ ounces) all-purpose flour
- ½ teaspoon baking powder
- ¼ teaspoon baking soda

FOR GLAZE:

- ¼ cup water
- ¾ cup granulated sugar
- ½ teaspoon lemon juice

FOR SUGAR/SALT BLEND:

- 1 tablespoon granulated sugar
- ⅛ teaspoon salt
- 3 tablespoons Christmas sprinkles

RECIPE STEPS:

1. Preheat oven to 350°F.

2. Add dates to a medium bowl and pour boiling water over top, ensuring all pieces are submerged. Soak for 20 minutes to soften dates, then purée them with the soaking water in a food processor or blender on high speed for 1–2 minutes until only small pieces are visible.

3. In a large bowl, use an electric mixer to beat butter, sugars, and salt at high speed for 1 minute. Add eggs, vanilla, and flavoring, and mix for 1 minute.

4. Whisk flour, baking powder, and baking soda in a separate medium bowl.

5. Add flour to wet blend and mix on medium speed until combined. Add date purée and mix on medium speed for 30 seconds. Scrape sides of bowl so all ingredients are combined.

6. Spray cups of mini Bundt cake pan with oil spray, then fill each cup with ½ cup batter, or just over halfway. If mini Bundt pan has fewer than ten cups, make cakes in two batches. For a six-cup pan, bake in two batches of five each. Bake 25–28 minutes until tops are evenly browned. Let cakes cool for 15 minutes before turning them out of pan.

7. To make glaze: Combine water and sugar in a small saucepan over medium heat. Whisk often until sugar dissolves, then remove from heat and stir in lemon juice.

8. Let glaze cool 5 minutes, then use a brush to coat entire surface of each Bundt cake.

9. To make sugar/salt blend: Mix ingredients in a small bowl. Sprinkle a few pinches of blend on top of each cake.

10. Finish cakes by topping each with approximately 2 teaspoons of sprinkles. Eat immediately or store Bundt cakes in a covered container for up to 4 days. They can also be frozen in a sealed container or individually wrapped in plastic for several weeks.

FIELD NOTES

Bundt cakes are named after the pan in which they are baked. In the 1950s, the Minnesota-based company Nordic Ware invented the special donut-shaped pan with fluted sides and called it Bundt, based on the German word "bundkuchen," which translates to "a cake for gatherings."

STARBUCKS

Pink Drink

 PREP TIME:
Active: 5 minutes
Inactive: None

 DIFFICULTY:
Easy

 MAKES:
1 (16-ounce) drink

Many new food product ideas emerge from corporate test kitchens, but Starbucks's Pink Drink was born on social media in 2016. That's where customers learned to request coconut milk in their orders of the chain's Strawberry Acai Refresher. When they gave that combo a good shake, it turned pink. When high demand persisted for the "secret menu" item, Starbucks added the Pink Drink to its permanent menu in 2017.

You'll have no trouble creating this Starbucks Pink Drink copycat recipe at home with a bottle of the strawberry and acai–flavored Dr. Smoothie Refreshers. This lightly caffeinated, concentrated drink mix can be found online in 46-ounce bottles and will be enough to make eleven (16-ounce) Pink Drink clones. You'll also need coconut milk that isn't too thick or chunky (Goya brand is good) and freeze-dried strawberries.

Finish the drink by shaking everything together in a shaker with ice, then pour the pink goodness into a 16-ounce glass and enjoy.

 To simplify your hack, look for products that blend several ingredients you need. Starbucks uses a special strawberry-acai caffeinated beverage as the main ingredient in this popular drink. It would be hard to clone that special drink from scratch, but fortunately, I found a similar blend online that made this one of the easiest hacks to create. Dr. Smoothie Refreshers had all the right flavors and ingredients needed in a concentrated mix. Once adjusted for the concentrated formula in this recipe, the knockoff tastes like the real thing and is cheaper.

- ½ cup strawberry acai Dr. Smoothie Refreshers
- ½ cup unsweetened coconut milk (shake well before measuring)
- 4–6 slices freeze-dried strawberries
- 1 heaping cup ice cubes

Combine all ingredients in a shaker and shake well until foamy and pink. Pour drink into a 16-ounce cup or glass and serve.

 FIELD NOTES

The Refreshers drink contains caffeine from coffee bean extract, but only a small amount. You get about 45 milligrams of caffeine in a 16-ounce drink, just a fraction of the 300 milligrams of caffeine in a typical 16-ounce cup of coffee.

Pink Drink

Raspberry Cheesecake Cookies

 PREP TIME:
Active: 40 minutes
Inactive: 6 hours

 DIFFICULTY:
Medium

 MAKES:
22 cookies

Subway's most popular freshly baked cookie will remind you of biting into a scrumptious slice of berry cheesecake. The cookies have cream cheese baked into them, and they are studded with creamy white chocolate chips and flavorful real raspberry baking bits.

The challenge of making a good clone is re-creating the raspberry bits found in the real cookie through easy steps. I experimented with raspberry candy bits similar to Turkish delight, as well as gummies and fruit rolls, but each technique took too long. Eventually, I mixed concentrated raspberry purée with white chocolate chips and created meltable raspberry baking bits that were easy to make and delicious.

Combine the bits with white chocolate chips and other ingredients to create a batch of twenty-two cookies that will come out of your oven crispy on the edges and chewy in the middle, just like the real ones at the world's biggest sandwich shop.

 This technique for making raspberry baking chips can be used to make chips with other fruit flavors to put your personal spin on these cookies, or to use in a variety of other baked recipes. Replace the raspberries in this recipe with 1 cup of thawed frozen fruit of your choice and follow steps 1 through 6 to make the bits in any flavor you like.

FOR RASPBERRY BAKING BITS:

⅓ cup water
1 cup frozen raspberries, thawed
2 tablespoons granulated sugar
1/16 teaspoon salt
1 teaspoon all-purpose flour
¾ cup white chocolate chips

FOR COOKIES:

½ cup plus 2 tablespoons unsalted butter, softened
⅓ cup vegetable oil
⅔ cup dark brown sugar, packed
⅔ cup granulated sugar
1 large egg
2 tablespoons cream cheese, softened
1 tablespoon whole or 2% milk
2 teaspoons vanilla extract
1 teaspoon salt
2½ cups (12½ ounces) all-purpose flour
1¼ teaspoons baking soda
¾ teaspoon baking powder
¾ cup white chocolate chips

RECIPE STEPS:

1. To make raspberry baking bits: Combine water with raspberries and their juice in a blender, and blend on high speed for 15 seconds until raspberries are puréed. Strain raspberry purée through a fine mesh strainer to remove seeds. You should end up with about 1/2 cup of seedless raspberry purée after straining.

2. Combine raspberry purée with sugar and salt in a small saucepan over medium-low heat. When mixture bubbles, reduce heat so that purée steams but barely bubbles. Continue cooking for 40–45 minutes, stirring occasionally, until purée thickens and reduces by half to 1/4 cup.

3. Whisk in flour and continue to cook purée, whisking often for 5 minutes until mixture thickens and becomes slightly gummy. Remove purée from heat and pour it into a small bowl over white chocolate chips. Fold raspberry purée into white chocolate chips until they are completely melted and mixture is homogenous. If any white chocolate does not melt, microwave mixture on high for 15 seconds and stir gently until all white chocolate is incorporated.

4. Place bowl in refrigerator to chill for 20–30 minutes until mixture is no longer tacky and can be shaped.

5. Roll raspberry baking chips mixture into 4–5 long ropes, each 1/4"–3/8" thick. Place ropes on a baking sheet lined with wax paper or a baking mat, then chill for 2 hours or overnight until ropes are firm enough to slice.

6. Slice each rope lengthwise down middle, then place two halves side by side and slice into 1/8"-thick bits. Separate any raspberry bits that are stuck together, then let them sit out while you make cookie dough. Raspberry bits will be easier to work with if they dry out.

7. To make cookie dough: Combine butter, oil, and sugars in a large bowl with a mixer on medium speed for 1 minute. Add egg and mix for 30 seconds, then add cream cheese, milk, vanilla, and salt, and mix for another 30 seconds on medium speed.

8. In a separate medium bowl, combine flour with baking soda and baking powder, then add this mixture to wet blend and mix on medium speed, or by hand, just until all ingredients are combined.

9. Add white chocolate chips and stir them into dough by hand.

10. Measure 1 3/4-ounce portions of dough, press 10–12 raspberry baking chips into top of each portion, and shape them into pucks that are 1 3/4" across. Arrange dough pucks on wax paper and freeze for at least 2 hours until completely frozen.

11. When ready to bake cookies, preheat a conventional oven to 325°F, or a convection oven to 300°F.

12. Arrange frozen cookie dough pucks 2 1/2" apart on parchment paper or a baking mat–lined baking sheet and bake 18–20 minutes, until cookies are lightly browned around edges. Store in a covered container at room temperature for up to 5 days.

🔍 FIELD NOTES

Otis Spunkmeyer manufactures the cookie dough for Subway, so when you clone a Subway cookie, you're essentially cloning an Otis Spunkmeyer cookie. The company also produces Subway's bread. In fact, Otis Spunkmeyer manufactures products behind the scenes for several chains, including McDonald's, Costco, and Panera Bread.

TACO BELL

Avocado Verde Salsa

 PREP TIME:
Active: 10 minutes
Inactive: None

 DIFFICULTY:
Easy

 MAKES:
3½ cups

In March 2024, Taco Bell introduced the Cantina Chicken menu, featuring two types of tacos, a burrito, a quesadilla, and a chicken bowl, all showcasing the chain's new slow-roasted chicken. As a companion to the new items, the Mexican chain also unveiled a surprising new avocado salsa made with peppers, tomatillos, and avocado. Unlike all the other hot sauces at the chain, this one isn't free with your order. Luckily, you can now whip up a large helping of copycat salsa. The amount of salsa made with this recipe is equivalent to sixty-seven Taco Bell sauce packs. Use it on homemade tacos, taco salads, burritos, and burrito bowls.

 **TOP SECRET HACK**
The first ingredient in Taco Bell's version of this salsa is a lot of oil to extend its shelf life, and the same is true for this hack recipe. But feel free to reduce the amount of oil in your clone if you plan to consume it quickly and want to limit added fat.

¾ cup mashed avocado (1 large avocado)
½ cup water
2 teaspoons lime juice
¼ teaspoon citric acid
8 ounces canned tomatillos, drained
⅔ cup canned diced jalapeños
⅓ cup canned diced green chilies
1 tablespoon plus 2 teaspoons granulated sugar
1½ tablespoons minced fresh cilantro
1¼ teaspoons salt
½ teaspoon dried minced onion
½ teaspoon onion powder
½ teaspoon garlic powder
¼ teaspoon ground mustard
½ cup vegetable oil

RECIPE STEPS:

1. Add mashed avocado, water, lime juice, and citric acid to a blender.

2. Blend on high speed until avocado is smooth. If you don't have citric acid, add an extra teaspoon of lime juice. Use a spatula to scrape down sides of blender.

3. Add remaining ingredients, excluding oil, and pulse repeatedly on high speed until only very small bits remain, with visible tomatillo seeds. Be careful not to purée mixture by overblending it.

4. Pour salsa into a medium bowl and whisk in oil. Cover and chill until ready to use. Salsa will keep for up to 1 week.

 FIELD NOTES

Canned tomatillos and peppers are are already cooked and softened, which saves you from having to take that step yourself.

TACO BELL

Cantina Chicken

PREP TIME:
Active: 10 minutes
Inactive: 20 minutes

DIFFICULTY:
Easy

MAKES:
4 cups

In March of 2024, Taco Bell introduced Cantina Chicken, a versatile menu item that can be ordered on tacos, burritos, quesadillas, and bowls. The slow-roasted chicken is seasoned with chilies, onion, and garlic and is often paired with the chain's Avocado Verde Salsa, which is also hacked in this book. For this clone, I've made the process quick and easy by using a cooked rotisserie chicken, which can be found in most supermarkets and big box stores. Once you've chopped the chicken into bite-sized pieces, just combine it with chicken broth and the secret combination of spices here in a large sauté pan over medium heat. When the liquid has cooked off, you'll have 4 cups of chicken, which you can use in your homemade tacos, burritos, bowls, or whatever you're craving.

TOP SECRET HACK

When you sense that a dish needs acidity to enhance its flavor, consider the type of cuisine you're preparing when deciding which acid to incorporate. For a Mexican dish like this one, use lime and occasionally lemon. For French cuisine, opt for white wine and/or lemon. For Italian dishes, use red or white wine, lemon, or balsamic vinegar. For Asian recipes, use rice vinegar. When incorporating an acid, it's usually best to add it near or at the end of cooking: the sour taste of an acid tends to become more muted the longer it cooks.

4 cups rotisserie chicken (1 3-pound chicken)
1 tablespoon extra-virgin olive oil
1 cup chicken broth
2 tablespoons lime juice
1 tablespoon plus 1 teaspoon chili powder (I used Mexene)
½ teaspoon onion powder
¼ teaspoon garlic powder
¼ teaspoon MSG (monosodium glutamate)

RECIPE STEPS:

1. Chop rotisserie chicken into pieces roughly size of grapes.
2. Add olive oil to a medium saucepan over medium heat.
3. When oil is hot, transfer chicken to pan. Gently stir chicken to coat pieces with oil and cook for 5 minutes.
4. Add remaining ingredients to pan. When liquid bubbles, reduce heat and simmer for 20–25 minutes until no liquid remains.

FIELD NOTES

Supermarket rotisserie chickens are a convenient, time-saving ingredient to consider for many recipes that call for shredded or chopped chicken. After removing the skin and bones, you will get around 4 cups of shredded or diced chicken.

Cinnamon Twists

 PREP TIME:
Active: 15 minutes
Inactive: 10 minutes

 DIFFICULTY:
Easy

 SERVES:
8

Taco Bell's popular Cinnamon Twists are inspired by a traditional Mexican treat made by frying duros de harina until puffy, then sprinkling the crunchy spirals with cinnamon and sugar. You can find duros in various shapes at Latin markets or online; for this hack, you will want spirals that resemble rotini. Most duros you find will likely be saltier and denser than those used by Taco Bell, since the chain developed a custom recipe for American tastes. It takes just 10–15 seconds for the pasta to puff up in the oil, causing the duros crisps to float to the top. When they do, gently poke at them and stir them in the hot oil until they are evenly cooked. Frying each batch takes only about a minute. Once you've sprinkled your crispy twists with the cinnamon/sugar blend, they're ready to eat.

 Don't just rely on your thermometer. Test the hot oil with one duro. If it puffs up in 10–15 seconds, the oil is hot enough. If the duro doesn't fully puff and begins to darken in color, your oil isn't hot enough. You can often use a test like this, frying a sample of the food to double-check the temperature of the oil before you drop in a big batch.

Vegetable oil, for frying
¼ cup granulated sugar
1 teaspoon ground cinnamon
4 ounces duros or duritos pasta

RECIPE STEPS:

1. Preheat at least 2" of oil in a deep fryer, saucepan, or Dutch oven to 350°F.
2. Combine sugar and cinnamon in a bowl.
3. Fry pasta in hot oil in batches for 1 minute each. Use a large spoon or tongs to move pasta around as it fries so that it cooks evenly.
4. Remove fried pasta from oil and let it cool on a paper towel–covered plate or on a cooling rack for 10 minutes.
5. When all pasta is cooked, transfer it to a large bowl and sprinkle some cinnamon/sugar over it. Toss pasta, then sprinkle it again, and continue sprinkling and tossing until all cinnamon/sugar is used. Eat immediately, or save in a sealed container for up to 2 weeks.

🔍 FIELD NOTES

Duros is a Mexican dry wheat pasta containing sodium bicarbonate (baking soda), which puffs up when flash-fried. The snack has been compared to pork rinds and is traditionally seasoned with chili powder and lime juice but can also be coated with other savory toppings, including fajita seasoning, garlic salt, lemon pepper, and cayenne pepper.

TACO BELL

Meximelts

 PREP TIME:
Active: 30 minutes
Inactive: None

 DIFFICULTY:
Medium

 MAKES:
12

In 2024, Taco Bell brought back five iconic menu items as part of the chain's new "Decades" menu: the Tostada from the 1960s, the Green Sauce Burrito from the 1970s, the Meximelt from the 1980s, the Gordita Supreme from the 1990s, and the Caramel Apple Empanada from the 2000s. The Meximelt in particular generated a lot of excitement. It's a small flour tortilla filled with the chain's seasoned beef, a melted combination of three cheeses, and fresh pico de gallo. I tackled this copycat recipe by first duping the mild pico de gallo with a simple combination of tomatoes, onion, cilantro, lime juice, and salt. And I made sure to dice the tomato and onion super small to match the real thing. Next, I copied the seasoned beef using my previously hacked recipe for the chain's Chalupa Supreme and determined the ratios for a three-cheese blend of shredded Cheddar, jack, and mozzarella. Pile everything on a warm 6" flour tortilla, take a big bite, and enjoy a tasty trip back in time.

 If you don't have a tortilla warmer, you can heat your tortillas by placing a moist paper towel in between each of the tortillas in a stack. Microwave the stack on high for 30 seconds, then in 15-second increments until warm through the middle.

FOR PICO DE GALLO:

2 cups petite diced, seeded Roma tomatoes
½ cup peeled and petite diced yellow onion
¼ cups minced fresh cilantro
1 teaspoon lime juice
⅛ teaspoon salt

FOR BEEF:

1 pound 80/20 ground beef
3 tablespoons all-purpose flour
1 tablespoon plus 2 teaspoons chili powder (I used Gebhardt)
2½ teaspoons Knorr tomato bouillon with chicken flavor powder
½ teaspoon onion powder
½ teaspoon granulated sugar
⅛ teaspoon salt
½ cup water

Meximelts

FOR MEXIMELTS:

1 cup shredded Cheddar cheese
½ cup shredded Monterey jack cheese
½ cup shredded mozzarella cheese
12 (6") flour tortillas

RECIPE STEPS:

1. To make pico de gallo: Combine all ingredients in a medium bowl. Set aside.

2. To make beef: Combine all ingredients except water in a medium bowl. Use your hands to work all dry ingredients into ground beef, then transfer it to a large sauté pan over medium heat.

3. Cook seasoned beef for 3 minutes until it is partially browned. Stir meat as it cooks and break it apart with a firm spatula or wooden spoon.

4. Add water and cook ground beef for 4 minutes until water has evaporated. Then turn heat to low to keep it warm. Stir meat often as it cooks so that large chunks are broken up and it cooks thoroughly.

5. Combine shredded cheeses in a medium bowl.

6. Steam flour tortillas by microwaving them in moist towels or by using a tortilla warmer.

7. Build each Meximelt clone by spooning ¼ cup of warm, seasoned beef onto a tortilla, slightly off-center so that tortilla will fold evenly.

8. Sprinkle 2–3 tablespoons of cheese over beef. For extra-melty cheese, microwave on high for 10–15 seconds.

9. Spoon 2 tablespoons of pico de gallo over cheese, then fold tortilla over fillings. Repeat for remaining ingredients. Serve.

FIELD NOTES

In 2011, Taco Bell responded to the rumors and a subsequent lawsuit that claimed the chain's seasoned ground beef was just 36% beef. According to the chain's official statement, Taco Bell's seasoned beef is 88% ground beef, and the other 12% is water, seasonings, and ingredients added for texture. The lawsuit was eventually dropped.

TOOTSIE ROLL INDUSTRIES

Sugar Daddy Pops

 PREP TIME:
Active: 30 minutes
Inactive: 55 minutes

 DIFFICULTY:
Medium

 MAKES:
20 pops

The milk caramel lollipop that has been sticking to teeth for over 100 years is an iconic American candy treat. Robert Welch invented the pop in 1925 and originally called it Papa Sucker, a name that lasted until 1932, when it was replaced by a popular expression of the time, Sugar Daddy. A chocolate-covered version of the pop called Sugar Mama was discontinued in the 1980s, but the caramel jellybeans called Sugar Babies are still found on candy shelves today.

Making a home version of a Sugar Daddy involves cooking caramel from a simple mixture of condensed milk, sugar, corn syrup, butter, and vanilla, then heating it to a specific temperature that creates the desired firmness when the candy cools. If the temperature is too low, your caramel will be too soft. If the caramel gets too hot, it will scorch, darken, and become overly brittle. You need to achieve a target temperature of exactly 250°F, and to do that a candy thermometer is essential. You will also need lollipop sticks.

Unlike the real Sugar Daddy, this clone doesn't contain artificial flavoring, so you will experience richer, purer flavors from ingredients likely similar to those used in the original pop before the recipe was adjusted for greater shelf stability.

 If you need a mold that is a specific size for a hack, you may have to create one from found objects or discarded packaging. For this candy hack, I used an empty spaghetti box to make a cheap and disposable mold that is the ideal size for replicating this classic hard caramel lollipop.

3 tablespoons unsalted butter, divided
1 cup granulated sugar
½ cup light corn syrup
½ cup sweetened condensed milk
¼ teaspoon plus ⅛ teaspoon salt
1½ teaspoons vanilla extract

RECIPE STEPS:

1. To create a mold for caramel pops, start by opening spaghetti box from both ends and removing pasta. Cut box in half lengthwise with scissors, creating 2 shallow trays. Fold in corner flaps and tape them securely on both outside and inside of each half. Trim long flaps so they are even with rest of box. You should have 2 shallow rimmed trays.

2. Use a ruler and a pen to prepare trays for ten pops each. Measure $1/2"$ from one end of tray and make a dot halfway up side. Next, make a dot every 1" horizontally from there until you have ten dots along the side of tray. Depending on size of your box, there may be some extra space at end of tray, and that's okay. You can trim off any excess candy later. Repeat process for other tray, then use a single-hole punch to create a hole at each dot.

3. Now we'll line the trays with foil to hold the hot caramel. Cut four (4"-long) pieces of heavy-duty foil to same width as trays, then fold them over both ends of each tray and tape them in place. Tear off two more pieces of foil, each about 8" long, and trim width of foil to match length of trays. Tape foil in place on each tray, then melt 1 tablespoon of butter and brush foil inside trays with melted butter.

4. Use a toothpick or skewer to poke a hole through foil where each hole was punched out. Push all lollipop sticks through holes from inside. Make two stick rests out of foil by tearing off two 4" long strips of foil. Fold each piece of foil in half multiple times until you create a long strip that can be placed under lollipop sticks to keep them level while candy sets. Now, it's time to make some great caramel.

5. Make candy by combining sugar and corn syrup in a medium saucepan over medium-low heat. When sugar has melted, stir in condensed milk and salt, add a candy thermometer, and bring it to 250°F, stirring often to prevent caramel from burning on bottom of pan.

6. When temperature reaches 250°F, remove it from heat and gently stir in remaining 2 tablespoons butter. When butter has been fully incorporated, stir in vanilla.

7. Pour caramel into molds, then straighten all sticks. After about 25 minutes, check candy to see if it's firming up. Caramel should be fairly firm for a clean cut, so check on it every 5 minutes until it seems like candy will hold its shape. It may take as long as 45 minutes before you can cut it cleanly.

8. When candy is ready, use scissors to cut a slit in box mold above every lollipop stick, then fold down that side of mold. Cut a slit down side of mold at each corner then fold all sides down flat. Use a sharp knife that's been lightly coated with vegetable oil to slice between sticks to make 1"-wide pops, then peel foil off of each pop. One pop at end of each mold may be extra wide, but you can just trim off excess. Wrap each pop individually in wax paper, and they will keep for at least 2 weeks.

FIELD NOTES

You may notice the temperature of your caramel will stall around 212°F. That's because there is still water in the mixture that hasn't cooked off (in the butter, corn syrup, and condensed milk). When more than 80% of the water has evaporated, the temperature will continue rising and your caramel will start to darken.

Pizza Rolls

 PREP TIME:
Active: 1 hour 50 minutes
Inactive: 3 hours

 DIFFICULTY:
Hard

 **MAKES:**
50 pizza rolls

Luigino "Jeno" Paulucci had been manufacturing prepared Chinese food products for a couple of decades when he realized that egg rolls could be filled with pretty much anything. Jeno tested dozens of fillings, but it was the egg rolls filled with pizza toppings that got the most raves, so that became Jeno's new product. The pizza rolls were so successful that Jeno sold his Chinese food company and dedicated himself to producing the world's best frozen pizza and original pizza rolls. His vision paid off. Twenty years later, in 1985, Jeno scored a $135 million payday when he sold his company to Pillsbury, the manufacturer of Totino's—a competing pizza rolls brand inspired by Jeno's invention. Pillsbury combined the two brands in the early 1990s, and today all pizza rolls are produced under the Totino's name.

As I studied the ingredients to replicate Totino's Pizza Rolls, I was surprised to discover that they do not contain real cheese. I'm not sure why that is, but for this clone, you'll be using all real ingredients.

For the dough, I initially tried using pre-made egg roll wrappers, but they didn't bake well and were not a suitable match for Totino's dough. So I made a simple egg roll wrapper dough from scratch.

Once your dough is rolled thin, you'll just fill it and fold it. After a quick par-fry, the rolls are frozen and, just like the famous original product, can be baked anytime you feel a pizza roll craving coming on.

 You can save time by using a pasta maker to make the thin dough. Roll out small batches of dough on the thickest setting, gradually working down to the thinner settings until you reach the second-thinnest. Be sure to flour the sheets of dough lightly and set them aside for a few minutes to dry so they are easier to work with.

Pizza Rolls

FOR SAUCE:

⅔ cup water
1 tablespoon cornstarch
⅓ cup tomato paste
1 tablespoon heavy cream
¾ teaspoon granulated sugar
¼ teaspoon plus ⅛ teaspoon salt
¼ teaspoon dried oregano
⅛ teaspoon dried basil
⅛ teaspoon ground black pepper
⅛ teaspoon onion powder
⅛ teaspoon garlic powder

FOR FILLING:

½ cup petite diced mozzarella cheese
¼ cup petite diced pepperoni

FOR DOUGH:

2 cups (10 ounces) bread flour
¾ teaspoon salt
½ cup plus 1 tablespoon water
1 large egg

FOR SEALING AND FRYING:

¼ cup water
1 tablespoon cornstarch
Vegetable oil, for frying

RECIPE STEPS:

1. To make sauce: Mix cornstarch into water and combine it with all sauce ingredients in a small saucepan over medium heat. Once mixture begins to bubble, reduce heat and simmer for 5 minutes, stirring frequently. Cover pan and let it cool for 30 minutes.

2. To make filling: When sauce has cooled, stir in petite diced mozzarella and pepperoni. Cover sauce and refrigerate it until needed.

3. To make dough: Combine flour and salt in a mixing bowl. Then add water and egg, mixing by hand or with a stand mixer equipped with a dough hook until dough forms. Continue kneading for 5 minutes until it is smooth, then wrap dough in plastic and refrigerate 30–45 minutes, or until surface is cold.

4. Roll dough out on a generously floured surface until very thin—just until you can see through it. Frequently lift dough to prevent sticking and to add more flour. Be sure to rotate dough as you roll it out for an even thickness.

5. Combine water and cornstarch in a small bowl.

6. On a lightly floured surface, trim one sheet of dough to 3" wide and 9"–12" long. A pizza wheel is ideal for trimming thin dough like this.

7. Dip a brush in cornstarch slurry, wipe off brush on side of bowl so that it's just moist, then brush whole top surface of dough with slurry. Be sure not to make dough too wet, or it'll be tough to work with. A light coating of slurry is all you need.

8. Measure 5–6 teaspoon-sized portions of filling onto center of slurry-brushed dough, spacing them about ½" apart. Fold top of dough down over filling, then fold bottom flap of dough over top flap. Use your finger to press down on dough between spoonfuls of filling, then slice dough there. Press down with your fingers on both sides of each pizza roll to seal, and slice off any excess dough. Use a sharp knife to help lift each pizza roll, being careful not to cut or tear them, then place them on wax paper–lined baking sheets and freeze for 1 hour until frozen solid.

9. Preheat oil to 350°F.

10. Fry frozen pizza rolls in small batches for 1½ minutes until they begin to turn light brown around edges. You're frying them too long if filling starts to seep out. Transfer pizza rolls to a rack or a paper towel–lined plate to drain and cool for 20 minutes. Once cool, freeze at least 1 hour until they're solidly frozen. You can keep pizza rolls frozen in a covered container for several weeks until you're ready to bake them.

11. To serve pizza rolls, preheat oven to 425°F. Bake pizza rolls on a baking sheet for 11–13 minutes until crispy around edges.

FIELD NOTES

Hacking a pizza roll recipe? Defrost several rolls and slice them open with a sharp knife to empty the contents. Examine the construction of the dough so you'll know how to fold yours. Rinse the filling through a strainer to see what solid bits are left behind so you know what to include in your sauce. Make batches of rolls, modifying the dough and filling until the recipe works.

Shortbread

PREP TIME: Active: 30 minutes Inactive: 1 hour 40 minutes	**DIFFICULTY:** Easy	 **MAKES:** 2 dozen cookies

Joseph Walker used only the finest ingredients to create his famous pure butter shortbread recipe, crafted in 1898 at his bakery in Speyside, Scotland. More than a century later, Walker's remains one of the bestselling shortbreads in the world, still made with the same four high-quality ingredients: flour, butter, sugar, and salt.

The secret ingredient for a perfect Walker's Shortbread cookies knockoff is pastry flour. It contains less gluten than all-purpose flour, resulting in a tender bite that mirrors the original cookies while providing a stable structure that won't spread during baking. I used Bob's Red Mill brand.

These cookies contain no leavening (hence their name, shortbread), so the sugar and salt are whipped into the butter until fluffy, creating air bubbles that help the shortbread rise moderately when baked. This recipe uses superfine sugar (baker's sugar) and superfine salt (popcorn salt) to make shortbread with a clean bite, free of any detectable sugar or salt granules.

 Different flours have different amounts of gluten, so choose wisely. Bread flour is highest in gluten; use it when you want a tough and chewy finished product, such as for bread or pizza dough. Cake flour contains very little gluten and is used for baked goods that are tender and crumbly, like cakes and some pastries. All-purpose flour is in the middle of the range, with enough gluten for bite but not enough to make the finished product chewy. This is the best flour for cookies and for general use in breading and batters. Other flours with gluten levels that fall between these should also be considered, such as pastry flour. Pastry flour contains more gluten than cake flour but less than all-purpose flour, so it works great for tender unleavened pastries like this shortbread.

11 tablespoons unsalted butter, softened

6 tablespoons (3 ounces) baker's sugar (fine granulated sugar)

¾ teaspoon superfine salt (popcorn salt)

2⅓ cups (10 ounces) pastry flour

RECIPE STEPS:

1. Combine butter, sugar, and salt in a medium bowl. Blend on high speed with an electric handheld mixer for 2 minutes until butter becomes white and fluffy.

2. In a large bowl, mix butter mixture with flour using a big spoon. Once dough is manageable, shape it into a ball, cover or wrap it, and allow it to sit for 1–2 hours at room temperature.

3. Preheat oven to 325°F for convection bake or 350°F for conventional bake.

4. After dough has rested, roll it out onto a hard, flat surface to a thickness of $1/2$", then slice it into fingers measuring $2 1/2$" long and $3/4$" wide. Dough will be fragile, so carefully arrange shortbread fingers on a nonstick surface, such as parchment paper or a baking mat, on a sheet pan.

5. Use blunt end of a wooden skewer to create two rows of six indentations (not holes) on top of each shortbread. Add one more indentation in center of each shortbread, positioned slightly closer to one end.

6. Bake 18–22 minutes until light brown, and cool for 20 minutes before eating. Shortbread can last up to several weeks if stored in a dry place.

FIELD NOTES

These sweet Scottish biscuits, created in the sixteenth century, were called shortcakes to avoid taxes imposed by the government on biscuits. In the eighteenth century, "shortcakes" were renamed "shortbread" when the government levied taxes on all cakes.

Chili Roasted Pistachios

PREP TIME: Active: 5 minutes Inactive: 1 hour 15 minutes	**DIFFICULTY:** Easy	**MAKES:** 1–4 cups

Wonderful shelled pistachios come in a variety of flavors, including BBQ, sea salt and vinegar, and honey roasted. However, the clear favorite—and the one often sold out in stores—is the version that packs the most heat, featuring a seasoning blend that includes garlic, vinegar, and ground red chili peppers.

The seasoning blend is the secret to the great taste of these addictive snacking nuts, and to make a hot and sour flavor you'll need a few special ingredients. The real thing contains dry tabasco peppers, but the ground tabasco peppers I found were not hot enough for a good clone, so I've enhanced this formula with ground cayenne pepper. Also, I found that ground tabasco pepper was not as fine as ground cayenne pepper, so this recipe grinds it further in a coffee grinder and sifts out the fine powder.

For this Wonderful Chili Roasted Pistachios copycat recipe, you'll also want to grind the nutritional yeast, which adds an umami flavor similar to MSG. Nutritional yeast typically comes in small flakes, and you'll want to transform it into a fine powder, just like the other ingredients. For a sour flavor that hits all the right notes, you'll need citric acid (very sour), malic acid (less sour), and powdered vinegar (even less sour). If you can't find malic acid, substitute ¼ teaspoon more of citric acid.

After combining the ingredients for the magical seasoning, sprinkle 1¾ teaspoons of the blend over each cup of moistened unsalted pistachios and lightly roast until dry.

Certain foods can't be hacked without a few special ingredients. Fortunately, you can usually find those key ingredients either in stores or online. To re-create a fine, dry texture, it's best to use baker's sugar (an extra-fine sugar) and popcorn salt (an extra-fine salt), as I did here. For the sour flavors, find citric acid, malic acid, and vinegar powder online. For the heat, you'll find ground tabasco peppers online and ground cayenne pepper in most grocery stores. Nutritional yeast is now stocked in major grocery stores. Paprika and turmeric aren't essential ingredients for flavor in this hack, but paprika adds a red color, and turmeric adds yellow.

FOR CHILI SEASONING:

- 1 tablespoon tabasco pepper flakes
- 1 tablespoon nutritional yeast
- 2 teaspoons superfine salt (popcorn salt)
- 1 1/2 teaspoons ground cayenne pepper
- 1/2 teaspoon citric acid
- 1/4 teaspoon malic acid
- 1/2 teaspoon fine granulated sugar (baker's sugar)
- 1/2 teaspoon fine garlic powder
- 1/2 teaspoon vinegar powder

FOR CHILI ROASTED PISTACHIOS:

- 1–4 cups unsalted roasted shelled pistachios
- 1/2 teaspoon to 2 teaspoons water

RECIPE STEPS:

1. Preheat oven to 300°F.
2. Grind about 1 tablespoon dry tabasco pepper flakes until fine, then sift through a fine mesh strainer to remove larger pieces and measure sifted pepper, ending up with 1 1/4 teaspoons very fine pepper. Repeat process with nutritional yeast: Grind, sift, and then measure, resulting in 1/2 teaspoon of fine yeast.
3. Combine all chili seasoning ingredients in a small bowl.
4. To coat nuts, use 1/2 teaspoon of water for every cup of pistachios, up to 4 cups. If using 4 cups of nuts, use 2 teaspoons water. Stir water into nuts until they're well coated.
5. Measure 1 3/4 teaspoons of seasoning blend for each cup of pistachios and sprinkle it over nuts while stirring. If using 4 cups of pistachios, use all seasoning and mix well until all pistachios are coated.
6. Spread seasoned nuts onto a baking sheet and bake in preheated oven for 12–15 minutes until nuts are dry. Cool for at least 1 hour before eating. Store at room temperature in a sealed container for several weeks.

FIELD NOTES

A coffee grinder works fine for pulverizing the relatively soft ingredients in this recipe, but if you plan to grind hard spices for other recipes, a spice grinder is a better choice. The blades and motors in spice grinders are designed to make a uniform grind for cooking, and they can handle even the toughest spices, like peppercorns, cloves, and cinnamon sticks.

STANDARD US/METRIC MEASUREMENT CONVERSIONS

VOLUME CONVERSIONS

US Volume Measure	Metric Equivalent
⅛ teaspoon	0.5 milliliter
¼ teaspoon	1 milliliter
½ teaspoon	2 milliliters
1 teaspoon	5 milliliters
½ tablespoon	7 milliliters
1 tablespoon (3 teaspoons)	15 milliliters
2 tablespoons (1 fluid ounce)	30 milliliters
¼ cup (4 tablespoons)	60 milliliters
⅓ cup	90 milliliters
½ cup (4 fluid ounces)	125 milliliters
⅔ cup	160 milliliters
¾ cup (6 fluid ounces)	180 milliliters
1 cup (16 tablespoons)	250 milliliters
1 pint (2 cups)	500 milliliters
1 quart (4 cups)	1 liter (about)

WEIGHT CONVERSIONS

US Weight Measure	Metric Equivalent
½ ounce	15 grams
1 ounce	30 grams
2 ounces	60 grams
3 ounces	85 grams
¼ pound (4 ounces)	115 grams
½ pound (8 ounces)	225 grams
¾ pound (12 ounces)	340 grams
1 pound (16 ounces)	454 grams

OVEN TEMPERATURE CONVERSIONS

Degrees Fahrenheit	Degrees Celsius
200 degrees F	95 degrees C
250 degrees F	120 degrees C
275 degrees F	135 degrees C
300 degrees F	150 degrees C
325 degrees F	160 degrees C
350 degrees F	180 degrees C
375 degrees F	190 degrees C
400 degrees F	205 degrees C
425 degrees F	220 degrees C
450 degrees F	230 degrees C

BAKING PAN SIZES

American	Metric
8 × 1½ inch round baking pan	20 × 4 cm cake tin
9 × 1½ inch round baking pan	23 × 3.5 cm cake tin
11 × 7 × 1½ inch baking pan	28 × 18 × 4 cm baking tin
13 × 9 × 2 inch baking pan	30 × 20 × 5 cm baking tin
2 quart rectangular baking dish	30 × 20 × 3 cm baking tin
15 × 10 × 2 inch baking pan	30 × 25 × 2 cm baking tin (Swiss roll tin)
9 inch pie plate	22 × 4 or 23 × 4 cm pie plate
7 or 8 inch springform pan	18 or 20 cm springform or loose bottom cake tin
9 × 5 × 3 inch loaf pan	23 × 13 × 7 cm or 2 lb narrow loaf or pate tin
1½ quart casserole	1.5 liter casserole
2 quart casserole	2 liter casserole

Index

Applebee's
    Chicken Wonton Tacos, 13–15
    Riblets, 16–17
    Spinach & Artichoke Dip, 18–19
Artichokes, in Spinach & Artichoke Dip, 18–19
Asparagus, in Mushroom and Asparagus
    Risotto, 39–41
Aussie Twisted Ribs, 194–97
Avocados, in Guacamole, 76
Avocado Verde Salsa, 234

Bacon
    Bacon Candy, 141–42
    Bacon, Egg & Cheese McGriddles, 162–65
    Bacon Jam Wings, 20–21
    Loaded Tots (Cheddar Bacon), 112–14
Banana Pudding Milkshake, 62
Beef
    Aussie Twisted Ribs, 194–97
    Carne Asada, 71–73
    Carne Asada Pizza, 32–33
    Country Fried Steak, 93–94
    Italian Meatballs, 151–52
    Lasagna Classico, 177–78
    Loaded Tots (Philly Cheese Steak), 112–14
    Meatloaf, 95–96
    Meximelts, 237–39
    Original Beef Jerky, 134–35
    Original Sloppy Joe Sauce, 156–57
    Shredded Beef Birria, 115–17
    Smoked Brisket, 77–79
    Steak Diane, 60–61
    Tasmanian Chili, 192–93
Berries
    Fresh Strawberry Pie, 160–61
    Fruit Roll, 139–40
    Pink Drink, 230–31
    Raspberry Cheesecake Cookies, 232–33
    Strawberry & Crème Pie, 168–69
BJ's Restaurant & Brewhouse, Bacon Jam
    Wings, 20–21
Blazing Bourbon Chicken, 200–201
Blow Pops, 50–52
Bonchon, Chicken Wings, 23–24
Bonefish Grill, Imperial Dip, 25–26
On The Border
    Chicken Tortilla Soup, 179–80
    Enchiladas (Cheese, and Chicken Tinga),
        181–84
Brach's, Candy Corn, 27–28
Breads and such. *See also* Pizza
    Almond Croissants, 224–27
    Almond Poppy Muffins, 88–89
    Pizza Rolls, 242–45
Brussels sprouts, P.F. Chang's Kung Pao
    Brussels Sprouts, 198–99
Butter Cake, 29–31
Butterfinger, 118–19
Buttermilk Pancakes, 187–88
Buttermilk Pie, 90–91

Cajun Fries, 120–21
California Pizza Kitchen
    Butter Cake, 29–31
    Carne Asada Pizza, 32–33
    Roasted Garlic Chicken Pizza, 35–37
Candy. *See* Desserts and candies
Cannoli and cannoli cake, 45–49
Cantina Chicken, 235
Capital City, Sweet Hot Mambo Sauce, 38
Capital Grille, Mushroom and Asparagus
    Risotto, 39–41

Carl's Jr/Hardee's, Hand-Breaded Chicken & Waffle Sandwich, 42–43
Carne. *See* Beef
Carrabba's Italian Grill
    Cannoli Cake for Two, 45–47
    Traditional Cannoli, 48–49
Charms Candy Company, Blow Pops, 50–52
Cheese. *See also* Eggs; Pasta/noodles; Pizza; Potatoes
    Cannoli Cake for Two, and Traditional Cannoli, 45–49
    Enchiladas (Cheese, and Chicken Tinga), 181–84
    Mozzarella Marinara, 153–54
    Raspberry Cheesecake Cookies, 232–33
    Strawberry & Crème Pie, 168–69
    3-Cheese Queso, 212–13
The Cheesecake Factory
    Chicken Piccata, 53–55
    Shrimp Scampi, 56–57
    Spicy Cashew Chicken, 58–59
    Steak Diane, 60–61
Chicken
    Bacon Jam Wings, 20–21
    Blazing Bourbon Chicken, 200–201
    Cantina Chicken, 235
    Chicken al Pastor, 74–75
    Chicken Marsala Fettuccine, 171–73
    Chicken Pad Thai, 204–5
    Chicken Piccata, 53–55
    Chicken Taco Pizza, 107
    Chicken Tortilla Soup, 179–80
    Chicken Wings, 23–24
    Chicken Wonton Tacos, 13–15
    Enchiladas (Cheese, and Chicken Tinga), 181–84
    Famous Rigatoni "D," 148–50
    Fried Chicken, 83–84
    Ghost Pepper Wings, 207–8
    Hand-Breaded Chicken & Waffle Sandwich, 42–43
    Spicy Cashew Chicken, 58–59
    Spicy Deluxe Chicken Sandwich, 65–66
    Spicy Southwest Salad, 67–69
Chick-fil-A
    Banana Pudding Milkshake, 62
    Spicy Deluxe Chicken Sandwich, 65–66
    Spicy Southwest Salad, 67–69
    Zesty Apple Cider Vinaigrette Dressing, 70
Chili Roasted Pistachios, 248–49
Chipotle
    Carne Asada, 71–73
    Chicken al Pastor, 74–75
    Guacamole, 76
    Smoked Brisket, 77–79
    Tomatillo-Red Chili Salsa, 80–81
Chocolate
    Chocolate Lava Crunch Cake, 109–11
    Chocolate Satin Pie, 158–59
    Famous Chocolate Cake, 209–11
    Semi-Sweet Chocolate Chunk Cookies, 97–99
Chow Mein, 203
Church's Texas Chicken, Fried Chicken, 83–84
Cinnamon Twists, 236
The Coffee Bean & Tea Leaf, Vanilla Ice Blended Drink, 85–87
Costco (Kirkland), Almond Poppy Muffins, 88–89
Country Fried Steak, 93–94
Cracker Barrel
    Buttermilk Pie, 90–91
    Country Fried Steak, 93–94
    Meatloaf, 95–96
Crazy Puffs, 146–47
Creamy Italian Dressing, 206
Crepes, Swedish, 132–33
Crumbl, Semi-Sweet Chocolate Chunk Cookies, 97–99

Daelmans, Stroopwafels, 100–101
Dark Toffee Bundt, 228–29
Deep Dish Pizza, 122–24
Del Taco, Tamales, 102–4
Desserts and candies. *See also* Chocolate
    Almond Croissants, 224–27

Bacon Candy, 141–42
Blow Pops, 50–52
Butter Cake, 29–31
Butterfinger, 118–19
Buttermilk Pie, 90–91
Candy Corn, 27–28
Cannoli Cake for Two, 45–47
Cinnamon Twists, 236
Dark Toffee Bundt, 228–29
Dole Whip, 105–6
Fruit Roll, 139–40
Raspberry Cheesecake Cookies, 232–33
Shortbread, 246–47
Stroopwafels, 100–101
Sugar Daddy Pops, 240–41
Vanilla Ice Cream, 125–26
Deviled eggs, crispy, 143–45
Dole Food Company, Dole Whip, 105–6
Dole Whip, 105–6
Domino's
    Chicken Taco Pizza, 107
    Chocolate Lava Crunch Cake, 109–11
    Loaded Tots, 112–14
Drinks
    Banana Pudding Milkshake, 62
    Pink Drink, 230–31
    Traditional Egg Nog, 223
    Vanilla Ice Blended Drink, 85–87

Eggs. *See also* Pancakes and crepes
    Bacon, Egg & Cheese McGriddles, 162–65
    Classic Eggs Benedict, 127–29
    Crispy Deviled Eggs, 143–45
    Traditional Egg Nog, 223
El Pollo Loco, Shredded Beef Birria, 115–17
Enchiladas (Cheese, and Chicken Tinga), 181–84

Ferrara Candy Company, Butterfinger, 118–19
Fish and seafood
    Crab Your Way, 214–15
    Imperial Dip, 25–26
    Seared Peppered Ahi, 189–91
    Shrimp Scampi, 56–57
Five Cheese Ziti al Forno, 174–75
Five Guys, Cajun Fries, 120–21
49er Flap Jacks, 185–86
Fried Chicken. *See* Chicken
Fruit Roll, 139–40

Garlic
    Garlic Spread, 108
    Roasted Garlic Butter, 214–15
    Roasted Garlic Chicken Pizza, 35–37
    Soy Garlic Sauce, 24
Ghost Pepper Wings, 207–8
Gino's East, Deep Dish Pizza, 122–24
Guacamole, 76

Häagen-Dazs, Vanilla Ice Cream, 125–26
Hacking recipes
    about: this book and, 8, 9
    finalizing recipe, 11–12
    ingredients list, 11
    making first batch, 11
    research (away from and at home), 10–11
    step-by-step process, 10–23
    taste tests, 11
    Top Secret Recipe and, 7–8
Hand-Breaded Chicken & Waffle Sandwich, 42–43
Hotcakes, 166–67. *See also* Pancakes

IHOP
    Classic Eggs Benedict, 127–29
    Protein Power Pancakes, 130–31
    Swedish Crepes, 132–33
Imperial Dip, 25–26
Irish Potato Soup, 136–38
Italian Meatballs, 151–52

Jack Link's, Original Beef Jerky, 134–35
Jason's Deli, Irish Potato Soup, 136–38
Jovy Candy, Fruit Roll, 139–40

Kung Pao Brussels Sprouts, 198–99

Lasagna Classico, 177–78
Lazy Dog
    Bacon Candy, 141–42
    Crispy Deviled Eggs, 143–45
Little Caesars, Crazy Puffs, 146–47

Maggiano's Little Italy
    Famous Rigatoni "D," 148–50
    Italian Meatballs, 151–52
    Mozzarella Marinara, 153–54
Manwich, Original Sloppy Joe Sauce, 156–57
Marie Callender's
    Chocolate Satin Pie, 158–59
    Fresh Strawberry Pie, 160–61
McDonald's
    Bacon, Egg & Cheese McGriddles, 162–65
    Hotcakes, 166–67
    Strawberry & Crème Pie, 168–69
Meatballs, Italian, 151–52
Meatloaf, 95–96
Meximelts, 237–39
Mojo Potatoes, 218–19
Mozzarella Marinara, 153–54
Mushroom and Asparagus Risotto, 39–41

Nuts and seeds
    Almond Croissants, 224–27
    Almond Poppy Muffins, 88–89
    Butterfinger, 118–19
    Chili Roasted Pistachios, 248–49
    Spicy Cashew Chicken, 58–59

Old El Paso, Taco Seasoning Mix, 170
Olive Garden
    Chicken Marsala Fettuccine, 171–73
    Five Cheese Ziti al Forno, 174–75
    Lasagna Classico, 177–78
The Original Pancake House
    Buttermilk Pancakes, 187–88
    49er Flap Jacks, 185–86
Outback Steakhouse
    Aussie Twisted Ribs, 194–97
    Seared Peppered Ahi, 189–91
    Tasmanian Chili, 192–93

Pad Thai, chicken, 204–5
Pancakes and crepes
    Buttermilk Pancakes, 187–88
    49er Flap Jacks, 185–86
    Hotcakes, 166–67
    Protein Power Pancakes, 130–31
    Swedish Crepes, 132–33
Panda Express
    Blazing Bourbon Chicken, 200–201
    Chow Mein, 203
Pasta/noodles
    Chicken Marsala Fettuccine, 171–73
    Chicken Pad Thai, 204–5
    Chow Mein, 203
    Cinnamon Twists, 236
    Famous Rigatoni "D," 148–50
    Five Cheese Ziti al Forno, 174–75
    Lasagna Classico, 177–78
Pei Wei, Chicken Pad Thai, 204–5
P.F. Chang's, Kung Pao Brussels Sprouts, 198–99
Pineapple, Dole Whip, 105–6
Pink Drink, 230–31
Pizza
    Carne Asada Pizza, 32–33
    Chicken Taco Pizza, 107
    Crazy Puffs, 146–47
    Deep Dish Pizza, 122–24
    Roasted Garlic Chicken Pizza, 35–37
Pizza Hut, Creamy Italian Dressing, 206
Pizza Rolls, 242–45
Popeyes, Ghost Pepper Wings, 207–8
Pork. *See also* Bacon
    Aussie Twisted Ribs, 194–97
    Riblets, 16–17
    Tamales, 102–4
Portillo's, Famous Chocolate Cake, 209–11
Potatoes
    Cajun Fries, 120–21

Irish Potato Soup, 136–38
Loaded Tots, 112–14
Mojo Potatoes, 218–19
SmashFries, Smash Tots, and Smash Sauce, 220–22
Protein Power Pancakes, 130–31

Qdoba, 3-Cheese Queso, 212–13

Red Lobster
Crab Your Way, 214–15
Walt's Favorite Shrimp, 217
Riblets, 16–17
Rice, in Mushroom and Asparagus Risotto, 39–41
Roasted Garlic Chicken Pizza, 35–37

Salad, spicy Southwest, 67–69
Sandwiches and wraps. *See also* Tacos
Bacon, Egg & Cheese McGriddles, 162–65
Hand-Breaded Chicken & Waffle Sandwich, 42–43
Meximelts, 237–39
Spicy Deluxe Chicken Sandwich, 65–66
Tamales, 102–4
Sauces and dips. *See also* Pizza
al Pastor Sauce, 75
Avocado Verde Salsa, 234
Bacon Jam, 20–21
Barbecue Sauce and Mop Sauce, 78
Cajun Butter, and Roasted Garlic Butter, 214–15
Cilantro Pesto, 33
Creamy Ginger Soy Sauce, 189–91
Creamy Italian Dressing, 206
Creamy Salsa Dressing, 68–69
Creamy Scampi Sauce, 56–57
Dumpling Sauce, 13–14
Garlic Spread, 108
Guacamole, 76
Honey Barbecue Sauce, 16–17
Imperial Dip, 25–26
Lemon Sauce, 53–55
Mandarin Sauce, 58–59
Maple Butter Sauce, 42–43
Marinara Sauce, 151–52, 153–54
Marsala Cream Sauce, 148–50
Marsala Sauce, 171–72
Original Sloppy Joe Sauce, 156–57
Picco de Gallo, 237–39
Salsa Verde, 33
Sawmill Gravy, 94
SmashFries, Smash Tots, and Smash Sauce, 220–22
Soy Garlic Sauce, 24
Spinach & Artichoke Dip, 18–19
Sweet Hot Mambo Sauce, 38
3-Cheese Queso, 212–13
Tomatillo-Red Chili Salsa, 80–81
Zesty Apple Cider Vinaigrette Dressing, 70
Seared Peppered Ahi, 189–91
Semi-Sweet Chocolate Chunk Cookies, 97–99
Shakey's, Mojo Potatoes, 218–19
Shortbread, 246–47
Shredded Beef Birria, 115–17
Shrimp. *See* Fish and seafood
Sloppy Joe sauce, original, 156–57
Smashburger, SmashFries, Smash Tots, and Smash Sauce, 220–22
Soups and stews
Chicken Tortilla Soup, 179–80
Irish Potato Soup, 136–38
Tasmanian Chili, 192–93
Southern Comfort, Traditional Egg Nog, 223
Spicy Cashew Chicken, 58–59
Spicy Deluxe Chicken Sandwich, 65–66
Spicy Southwest Salad, 67–69
Spinach & Artichoke Dip, 18–19
Starbucks
Almond Croissants, 224–27
Dark Toffee Bundt, 228–29
Pink Drink, 230–31
Steak. *See* Beef
Strawberries. *See* Berries
Stroopwafels, 100–101

Subway, Raspberry Cheesecake Cookies, 232–33
Sugar Daddy Pops, 240–41
Swedish Crepes, 132–33
Sweet Hot Mambo Sauce, 38

Taco Bell
    Avocado Verde Salsa, 234
    Cantina Chicken, 235
    Cinnamon Twists, 236
    Meximelts, 237–39
Tacos. *See also* Tamales
    Chicken Taco Pizza, 107
    Chicken Wonton Tacos, 13–15
    Taco Seasoning Mix, 170
Tamales, 102–4
Tasmanian Chili, 192–93
3-Cheese Queso, 212–13

Tomatillo-Red Chili Salsa, 80–81
Tootsie Roll Industries, Sugar Daddy Pops, 240–41
Totino's, Pizza Rolls, 242–45

Vanilla Ice Blended Drink, 85–87
Vanilla Ice Cream, Häagen-Dazs, 125–26

Walker's, Shortbread, 246–47
Walt's Favorite Shrimp, 217
Whipped Cream Topping, 161
Wonderful, Chili Roasted Pistachios, 248–49

Zesty Apple Cider Vinaigrette Dressing, 70